THE CANADIAN ECONOMY
IN THE GREAT DEPRESSION

CARLETON LIBRARY SERIES

The Carleton Library Series, funded by Carleton University under the general editorship of the dean of the School of Graduate Studies and Research, publishes books about Canadian economics, geography, history, politics, society, and related subjects. It includes important new works as well as reprints of classics in the fields. The editorial committee welcomes manuscripts and suggestions, which should be sent to the dean of the School of Graduate Studies and Research, Carleton University.

A. E. Safarian

The Canadian Economy
in the Great Depression

THIRD EDITION

The Carleton Library No. 217

McGill-Queen's University Press
Montreal & Kingston • London • Ithaca

© McGill-Queen's University Press 2009
ISBN 978-0-7735-3702-6 (cloth)
ISBN 978-0-7735-3713-2 (pbk)

Legal deposit fourth quarter 2009
Bibliothèque nationale du Québec

Printed in Canada on acid-free paper that is 100% ancient forest free
(100% post-consumer recycled), processed chlorine free

First published in 1959 by the University of Toronto Press. First CLS edition
published in 1970 by McClelland and Stewart Limited.

McGill-Queen's University Press acknowledges the support of the Canada
Council for the Arts for our publishing program. We also acknowledge the
financial support of the Government of Canada through the Book Publishing
Industry Development Program (BPIDP) for our publishing activities.

Library and Archives Canada Cataloguing in Publication

Safarian, A. E., 1924–
   The Canadian economy in the Great Depression / A.E. Safarian.

(The Carleton library; no. 217)
Includes bibliographical references and index.
ISBN 978-0-7735-3702-6 (bnd)
ISBN 978-0-7735-3713-2 (pbk)

   1. Depressions – 1929 – Canada.   2. Canada – Economic conditions –
1918–1945.   I. Title.   II. Series: Carleton library; no. 217

HC115.S24 2009   330.971'062   C2009-905542-2

Contents

Tables

Preface to the 2009 Carleton Library Edition

This book examines why the economic decline in Canada in the early 1930s was so severe and the recovery to 1937 so incomplete, both absolutely and relative to our main trading partners. There are several reasons why its re-issue at this time is appropriate.

First, there is an intrinsic and growing interest in the Great Depression of the 1930s. In the two-hundred-year recorded history of business fluctuations, no other depression, with the possible exception of one in the late nineteenth century, was as severe or had so many lasting consequences. There has been a surge of publications on the thirties, both popular and academic, in recent decades. In part this interest reflects increasing recognition of the links between business cycles and many developments in macroeconomics and economic growth. There are competing schools of thought in this literature that reflect very different views on the reasons for fluctuations in output and employment. This edition includes an addition to the 1959 bibliography that lists some of the more recent literature for Canada and internationally. From my perspective, particularly significant additions include Bernanke (2000), Betts et. al. (1996), Friedman and Schwartz (1963), Kindleberger (1986), and Temin (1988). Gordon (1990) is an excellent example of the many contributions by the National Bureau of Economic Research. There is also a short summary of work on business cycles generally in Romer (2008).

Second, despite all this publication, no other broad study of the Canadian experience, with a focus also on developments in key sectors, has appeared in all these years. Fifty years after its original publication, professors of history and economic history as well as specialists in business cycles, among others, continue to cite it in their research and refer their students to it. Since 1987 the federal Public Lending Right Commission has surveyed annually a number of public and, until recently, university libraries as a basis for compensating Canadian writers for the use of their books in Canada's libraries. This book has always been in all of the libraries surveyed.

Third, the underlying theoretical, historical, and quantitative approach of this study seems to have some lasting merit as shown in the conclusions of a very careful theoretical and empirical test of various explanations of the onset, depth and duration of output collapse in Canada and the United States in the 1930s (Betts et. al., 1996). The authors report that "results are consistent with hypotheses such as those of Fisher (1933), Bernstein (1987) and Safarian (1959), that emphasize secular factors in explaining the Depression" (p. 35).

The crisis in the financial sector and the business cycle decline beginning in late 2007 have led to renewed interest in the Great Depression. The recent credit crisis, which struck first in the United States, centered on a host of problems that had developed initially in the sub-prime mortgage market, accompanied by weaknesses in the "shadow banking system" of largely unregulated investment banks, private equity, and hedge funds. The unwinding of the large amounts of leverage involved as loans were called, the accompanying forced merger or bankruptcy of some major financial institutions, and instability in financial markets all continued through 2008 and early in 2009. As the crisis spread, major investment banks in the United States and the EU became bankrupt, were merged or rescued by government, or took on commercial banking business to create a broader creditor base. Falling stock prices and profits and difficulties in borrowing put huge pressures on firms that had effected mergers and acquisitions at extremely high prices and now had to manage the large debts involved during a period of falling sales and profit. Canada could not escape all of this, but prompt expansionary and rescue actions in the United States and parts of the EU, plus the remarkable stability provided by its own banks and in its social security system, helped cushion the shocks.

It is too early for conclusive analysis of the recent developments, including the important monetary, fiscal, and regulatory changes that are under way. The penultimate paragraph of the 1970 preface to this book noted there were special circumstances in the 1930s but also some continuing lessons. It is easy to draw up a list of similarities to and differences from the recent crisis. For example, there was a financial collapse in both cases, although the reasons and the timing relative to the business cycle decline were different. A major difference was the much larger role of agriculture in the thirties, an industry that suffered a decade of drought. However, the point to be emphasized here is the ways in which decisions, both private and public, made well before each crisis greatly influenced the nature and severity of the declines.

In the case of the 1930s, this study emphasizes several points. One is the Canadian government's decision, at the end of the nineteenth century, to disregard the advice of its surveyors not to go north of the early frost line or south of the drought line in settling the prairie west, with devastating results for the agricultural sector in the 1930s. The other is the consequences of the decision to resolve the problems of railway finance by merging railways (except for the CPR) in 1923 into the CNR. The government decided to guarantee all the debt of the new entity, although it was liable for only part of it. The debt was payable in sterling, US, or Canadian dollars at the option of the lenders, who were largely located abroad. By 1935 well over $1 billion of the $2.8 billion net federal debt of Canada was due to railway investments. This debt limited fiscal and exchange rate policy, in the latter case because of the effect of any depreciation on the cost of railway debt. (Running a fiscal deficit was considered heresy at the time and there was no central bank in Canada until 1937.)

Correspondingly, it is not difficult to point to earlier policy decisions, or the lack thereof, that greatly influenced the crash of 2007-08. The repeal of the Glass-Steagall act, which separated commercial and investment banking, and the failure to regulate the huge expansion in the largely unregulated shadow-banking system are just two of a number of earlier policy failures.

As for the private sector, the considerable long-term overexpansion of investment in a number of major new industries in the 1920s is documented in this study. With regard to 2007-08, there has been much comment and some analysis on the insufficient attention paid to risk in some recent financial innovations that played a major role in the recent collapse, as well as some serious ethical problems in accounting and related areas and large bonuses unrelated to performance. Also in the background to the recent collapse lie the huge imbalances that developed in the international accounts. One imbalance was the result of a combination of a loose fiscal and monetary policy in the United States with large budget and current account deficits. The other, related, imbalance was due to excessive savings in the Middle East and East Asia, leading to large current account surpluses invested in U.S. Treasuries, as well as attempts in China and other countries to help keep the exchange rate from appreciating.

One pertinent question is what can be done to minimize such mistakes in the future. In terms of decisions by governments, one can always argue that they are free to disregard any long-term advice and are subject to many pressures which can limit optimum decisions. If, however, there is significant publicity or formal public examination of those decisions, governments may have to at least listen more closely to such advice. One approach would be to require that major policy changes be reviewed or reconsidered at given intervals, as is done with the Canadian banks and in some other cases. This could create increased uncertainty and costs for business but the potential gains from corrected policy might well swamp such costs. Another possibility is to not only examine policy carefully and openly to start with but also to initiate it on a small scale regionally or in groups in order to sort out potential problems before such policies are adopted for entire populations.

I would like to express my appreciation to the McGill-Queen's University Press for its decision to re-issue this study and to Philip Cercone and Joan McGilvray for their help throughout.

A.E. Safarian

August, 2009
University of Toronto

Additional Publications on Economic Fluctuations in the Thirties

BARBER, CLARENCE L. *Inventories and Business Cycles with Special Reference to Canada.* Toronto: University of Toronto Press, 1958.

BERNANKE, BEN. *Essays on the Great Depression.* Princeton: Princeton University Press, 2000.

BERNSTEIN, MICHAEL A. *The Great Depression: Delayed Recovery and Economic Change in America, 1929-1939.* Cambridge: Cambridge University Press, 1987.

BETTS, CAROLINE M., BORDO, MICHAEL D., and REDISH, ANGELA "A Small Open Economy in Depression: Lessons from Canada in the 1930s." *Canadian Journal of Economics* 29, 1 (February 1996): 1-36.

BRECHER, I. *Monetary and Fiscal Thought and Policy in Canada, 1919-1939.* Toronto: University of Toronto Press, 1957.

BRECHER, I., and REISMAN, S. S. *Canada-United States Economic Relations.* Ottawa: Royal Commission on Canada's Economic Prospects, 1957.

BROWN, T. M. *Canadian Economic Growth.* Ottawa: Staff Study for the Royal Commission on Health Services. 1965.

CHAMBERS, EDWARD J. "Canadian Business Cycles since 1919." *Canadian Journal of Economics and Political Science* 24 (May 1958).

– "Canadian Business Cycles and Merchandise Exports." *Canadian Journal of Economics and Political Science* 24 (August, 1958).

CHANDLER, LESTER V. *America's Greatest Depression, 1929-1941.* New York: Harper and Row, 1970.

COURCHENE, THOMAS J. "An Analysis of the Canadian Money Supply: 1925-1934." *Journal of Political Economy* 77 (June, 1969).

DIEBOLD, FRANCIS X., and RUDEBUSH, GLENN D. *Business Cycles: Durations, Dynamics and Forecasting.* Princeton: Princeton University Press, 1999.

EGGERTSSON, GAUTI B. "Great Expectations and the End of the Depression." *American Economic Review* 98, 4 (2008): 1476-516.

FISHER, IRVING. "The Debt-Deflation Theory of Great Depressions." *Econometrica* 1 (1933): 337-57.

FRIEDMAN, MILTON, and SCHWARTZ, ANNA J. *A Monetary History of the United States*. Princeton: Princeton University Press, 1963.

GORDON, ROBERT A., and KLEIN, LAWRENCE R. (eds.). *Readings in Business Cycles*. Burr Ridge, IL: Richard D. Irwin, 1965. Prepared for the American Economic Association.

GORDON, ROBERT J. (ed.) *The American Business Cycle*. NBER Studies in Business Cycles, Vol. 5. Chicago: University of Chicago Press, 1990.

HAY, K. A. J. "Early Twentieth Century Business Cycles in Canada." *Canadian Journal of Economics and Political Science* 32 (August, 1965).

HAY, K. A. J. "Money and Business Cycles in Post-Confederation Canada." *Journal of Political Economy* 75 (June 1967).

KINDLEBERGER, C. P. *The World in Depression, 1929-1939*. Berkeley: University of California Press, 1986.

LAMONTAGNE, Maurice *Business Cycles in Canada*. Canadian Institute for Economic Policy. Toronto: James Lorimer, 1984.

MACESICH, GEORGE. "The Quantity Theory and the Income Expenditure Theory in an Open Economy: Canada, 1926-1958." Comment by Clarence L. Barber and Reply by George Macesich. *Canadian Journal of Economics and Political Science* 30, 32 (August 1964).

NATIONAL BUREAU OF ECONOMIC RESEARCH, Book Series Studies in Business Cycles. Various years.

ROMER, CHRISTINA D. "Changes in Business cycles: Evidence and Explanations." *Journal of Economic Perspectives* 13 (1999) 23-44.

– (2008) *Business Cycles*. In David R. Henderson (ed.) The Concise Encyclopedia of Economics, 47-51. Indianpolis: Liberty Fund, 2008.

ROSENBLUTH, G. "Changes in Canadian Sensitivity to United States Business Fluctuations." *Canadian Journal of Economics and Political Science* 23 (Nov. 1957). Feb. 1958, XXIV.

– "Changing Structural Factors in Canada's Cyclical Sensitivity, 1903-54." *Canadian Journal of Economics and Political Science* 24 (Feb. 1958).

TEMIN, PETER *Lessons from the Great Depression*. Boston: MIT Press, 1989.

– "Real Business Cycle Views of the Great Depression and Recent Events: A Review of Timothy J. Kehoe and Edward C. Prescott's *Great Depressions of the Twentieth Century*. *Journal of Economic Literature* 46, 3 (2008): 669–84.

THOMPSON, R. W. *International Trade and Domestic Prosperity: Canada 1926–38*. Toronto: University of Toronto Press, 1970.

URQUHART, M. C., and BUCKLEY, K. A. H. (eds.). *Historical Statistics of Canada*. Toronto: Macmillan Company of Canada Ltd., 1965.

WHITE, DEREK A. *Business Cycles in Canada*. Ottawa: Economic Council of Canada. Staff Study 17, 1967.

Preface to the 1970
Carleton Library Edition

Just over forty years ago Canada plunged into a depression of unusual severity. No other economic decline in this century has had such a wide and prolonged impact. The failure to reach anything like full employment for a decade imposed tragic social, political and economic costs. It also forced some major changes in attitudes towards the responsibilities of the state.

When it was originally written, this study reflected my dissatisfaction with the existing explanations of the depression of the 'thirties, especially the failure of the economy to return to full employment until World War II. In particular, it seemed to me that the period required a broad frame of reference, along the lines outlined in the original preface to the book. It also required that the theories one used be subjected to the available statistical evidence, and that the entire study be placed firmly in its historical context.

Since the book was written, there has been a renewed interest in the history of the period, and some refinements in the theory and measurement of economic fluctuations. A selection from these later studies is listed at the end of the bibliography. They improve on the timing of the turning points in my analysis, further clarify the interrelation of domestic and external variables, and contribute a number of other refinements on monetary variables in particular. No comprehensive economic study concentrating on the depression of the 'thirties has appeared since this book was originally published, however. The re-issue of this work should help, therefore, to fill a gap in the literature of an important period. It is reprinted without alteration.

I have emphasized that the economic collapse of the 'thirties was unique in many respects, and I would hope that it is now largely of historic significance. At the very least, governments now have the knowledge and the means of responding more positively and strenuously to a decline of similar magnitude. Yet the depression of the 'thirties continues to command attention. In part, of course, this is because of the major impact it had on events and attitudes both then and for many years afterwards. In part, also, it is because of the painful realization that we are still far from having learned how to ensure full employment while achieving other objectives of economic and social policy. In spite of the special circumstances of the 'thirties, the insights drawn from a study of that period may not be without interest in the understanding of more recent times. The failure in aggregate demand was at the root of the problem, for example, but the effects were complicated by severe built-in rigidities and structural problems extending over many years. External influences were important then, as now. Nevertheless, it is clear that the failure of the recovery was due in good part to the lack of adequate government institutions and policies even after a decade of depression. No doubt much has changed in the Canada of today. Some of our problems and not a few of our attitudes to their solution will find familiar counterparts in the Canada of the 'thirties.

I would like to express my appreciation to the Carleton Library for making possible the re-issuing of this volume, and to James Marsh for his editorial assistance.

A. E. Safarian

October, 1970
University of Toronto

Preface

The Canadian experience with economic fluctuations in the thirties was exceptionally severe. No other period of decline in this century had quite the same prolonged impact on Canada. The experience of this country in the thirties appears to have been more extreme than that of many other countries.

In this study I have attempted to explain the reasons for the severity of the decline in economic activity in Canada, and, more particularly, for the very incomplete nature of the recovery up to 1937. Only by the use of a broad frame of reference can one hope to find satisfactory explanations for such problems. It has been necessary, for example, to examine certain developments long before the thirties, since these had considerable effects in that decade. In addition, while giving due weight to the important external determinants of Canadian activity, I have also emphasized the nature of the reaction of the domestic economy to external forces, and the place of largely domestic determinants. Finally, the aggregate analysis has been supplemented by an examination of the experience of some significant industries, particularly to help explain the behaviour of domestic investment.

An earlier draft of this study was completed in 1955 under the supervision of Professor R. A. Gordon, and accepted by the University of California, Berkeley, as a doctoral dissertation. I owe a considerable debt to Professor Gordon for his many excellent suggestions on the approach and the content of this study.

Even a cursory glance at the bibliography will indicate the extent to which I have drawn on the work of those who have contributed to the analysis of the thirties. I would like particularly to express my appreciation to the many friends and former colleagues at the Dominion Bureau of Statistics who supplied me with statistical material and contributed to my understanding of that material. Professor V. W. Bladen facilitated in several ways the completion of the dissertation, and both he and Miss Elizabeth Chalmers of the University of Toronto Press gave invaluable editorial assistance with this study. I am grateful also to the Canadian Social Science Research Council for a grant-in-aid of research in 1951 and for the publication of this volume, to the Economists' Summer Study Group at Queen's University for the opportunity to develop some of the material on investment, and to the University of Saskatchewan for typing assistance. My wife has contributed to this study in a very real way by her aid and encouragement throughout.

This book is dedicated to my mother and father.

A. E. S.

December, 1957
University of Saskatchewan

THE CANADIAN ECONOMY
IN THE GREAT DEPRESSION

CHAPTER ONE

Introduction

The downswings in economic activity which have affected Canada in the last sixty years have often been mild and brief. Renewed economic expansion and, in 1914, war intervened before the downswings could become serious. The sharp decline in prices after 1920 was an exception, but even in this case another great surge of investment was under way within a few years.

The thirties were quite unlike any other period in the past sixty years. For almost every year of the decade the number of workers unemployed exceeded 10 per cent of the total labour force, and in 1933 amounted to 20 per cent. The decline in activity to 1933 was severe, prolonged, and uneven. The recovery after 1933 was also uneven, and it was far from complete when World War II began.

The extent of the over-all downswing in Canada can be seen most simply in the decline of gross national expenditure – 42 per cent from 1929 to 1933.[1] Consumer and government expenditures each fell by less than this, but exports of goods and services declined by one-half and investment in durable assets by 82 per cent. As late as 1937, GNE was still 13 per cent below the 1929 level. Although government expenditure and export of goods and services had virtually recovered to their 1929 levels, consumer expenditure was still 14 per cent below the 1929 level, and investment in durable assets was less than half the 1929 level.

These developments in the thirties were paralleled by, and reflected to an important degree, economic fluctuations in other countries. An economy so closely linked by trade, finance, and business ties to other countries can hardly hope to escape many of the effects of a major decline in world economic activity. Indeed, the decline in economic activity in Canada was one of the severest in the world, and the recovery among the slowest relative to the late twenties. Data on national income for seventeen countries indicate that the decline in Canada from 1929 to 1932 was exceeded only by that in the United States. The

[1] Gross national expenditure and gross national product are henceforth referred to as GNE and GNP. The data in this paragraph refer to the current dollar series.

shortfall of national income in Canada in 1937, compared to 1929, exceeded that for all but three countries.

Canada's closest economic ties are with the United States and the United Kingdom. The over-all downswing in the former was only a little severer than that in Canada, with the decline in GNE amounting to 46 per cent in 1929-33. As in Canada, the subsequent recovery in 1937 still left GNE 13 per cent below the 1929 level. In the United Kingdom, by contrast, national income fell only 11 per cent to 1933, and by 1937 it exceeded the 1929 level by 11 per cent.

In analysing this period, primary emphasis has usually been placed on the very large role of external factors in the Canadian economy. Many important factors can be cited to support this thesis: a large proportion of current production was exported; many of the most important resources could not be efficiently exploited unless large surpluses were produced for export, and alternative markets were not available for these surpluses in Canada; a large part of domestic investment took place in the export industries such as transportation which derived a large share of their income from the export and import trade; and sudden shifts in the terms of trade could have disastrous effects on incomes, the balance of payments, and monetary conditions. This reasoning was extended to foreign transactions generally, particularly to heavy imports of capital to finance investment, and to the psychological effects of close ties with important trading partners through affiliated companies and financial markets.

Such considerations go a long way toward explaining economic fluctuations in Canada and will be given a great deal of weight in this study. They do not fully account, however, for the great severity of the decline or, more particularly, for the incomplete nature of the recovery. The study of cyclical change, even in an "open economy" such as Canada's, requires a broader framework than that which has usually been used for this period. Such a framework should recognize that the determinants of economic activity are varied, and that they are related to developments over a considerable period of time. Only by such an analysis can one hope to explain, for example, why investment in durable assets by 1937 was less than half the 1929 level, while exports of goods and services had almost attained the 1929 level and there had been a growing surplus in the current account after 1933.

In order to build on the work already done on this period, a study of economic fluctuations will require emphasis in three areas. First, as an intensive study of a particular cycle, or part of it, it needs an approach which combines theory, statistics, and history, in order to examine developments in the past and the structure of the economy, and to determine how these affected the period. Secondly, the effects of external transactions on the domestic economy should be examined rigorously. Thirdly, the determinants and role of domestic investment have not been very thoroughly analysed for this period, and they clearly warrant careful consideration.

We shall elaborate each of these points in turn before formulating our preliminary hypotheses about the recovery problems of the thirties. Before doing so, however, a brief look at the structure of the economy is necessary, since the nature and the extent of fluctuations in any country are closely related to this.

The Structure of the Canadian Economy

Canada sold and purchased abroad a very large amount of goods and services, and certain commodities and countries dominated this trade. In 1928 merchandise exports and exports of goods and services were 22 per cent and 29 per cent respectively of GNE, while merchandise imports and imports of goods and services were 20 and 30 per cent. In 1928 the United States took 38 per cent of Canada's merchandise exports and the United Kingdom 22 per cent; the proportion of exports going to these two countries was usually even higher than this in the period under review. On the import side, fully 67 per cent of total imports in 1928 were purchased from the United States, and 16 per cent from the United Kingdom. There was usually a current account surplus with the United Kingdom and other overseas countries, the proceeds of which were available to help settle the large current account deficit with the United States. A few commodities which bulked large in exports were either exported in a natural state or were processed before export, but generally not into highly manufactured commodities. In the period 1926-9 over half of total exports consisted of wheat and flour, newsprint, pulp wood and wood-pulp, and non-ferrous metals and products. Prominent among imports were industrial materials and fuels, such as cotton, wool, coal, and petroleum; many types of industrial and farm machinery, and motor vehicles and parts; and agricultural products not available in Canada.

The second factor of great importance in the economic

structure is the large amount of foreign capital in Canada. In 1930 foreign long-term capital in Canada amounted to $7,613 million, of which $4,660 million was held in the United States and $2,766 million in the United Kingdom. About 30 per cent of the total foreign investment was in railways, and about one-fifth in each of manufacturing and government securities. Non-resident ownership of manufacturing and steam railways was 40 per cent and 56 per cent respectively in 1930.[2] The effects of such large amounts of foreign capital on the determinants of investment, income payments abroad, monetary conditions, and government policy, deserve careful analysis in any study of fluctuations in Canada.

Related to these is the heavy investment necessary per capita in a country with a great area and a small population, particularly if it is to exploit most advantageously its more abundant staple products. The opening of the prairies for wheat production, and the provision of transportation and handling facilities to move the crop to seaboard; the development of non-ferrous metals; the manufacture of newsprint paper; all of these required large amounts of capital. The same was true of a number of highly manufactured products such as automobiles, with the related heavy investment in roads and other facilities. Large overhead costs must be incurred in a relatively short period for such developments, and returns are dependent on an uncertain future. If that future involves a serious price deflation, the burden of overhead costs will create severe strains in the economy. Where, as in Canada, much of this capital was in the form of bonded debt, underwritten by governments, and payable to non-residents, the implications for anti-depression policy become highly important.

Another significant point is the large proportion of the population engaged in agriculture. The civilian labour force in 1931 was estimated at 4,105,000, of which 12 per cent were unemployed. Of the employed group, agriculture accounted for 29 per cent, manufacturing industries 15 per cent, and service industries 13 per cent.[3] Although agriculture's relative

---

[2] Canada, Dominion Bureau of Statistics, *Canada's International Investment Position, 1926-1954*, pp. 34, 72, 78. The Dominion Bureau of Statistics is henceforth referred to as D.B.S.

[3] D.B.S., *Canadian Labour Force Estimates, 1931-1950*. It should be noted that if employers, self-employed, and unpaid family workers are included by industry, the shares of manufacturing and services are increased to about 17 per cent and 20 per cent respectively, while that for agriculture is unchanged. See D.B.S., *Canada Year Book, 1937*, p. 145. This publication is henceforth referred to as *C.Y.B.*

contribution to employment had fallen steadily from about 45 per cent of the total in 1891 to about 30 per cent in 1931, the agricultural industries were clearly still of major importance. Furthermore, agriculture was highly concentrated as to cash income; in 1926 and 1927 wheat accounted for about 40 per cent of farm cash income, and cattle, calves, and hogs for another 20 per cent. A large proportion of some of the more important agricultural products was exported. This was particularly true of the largest crop of all, namely wheat, of which over 70 per cent was exported in the form of wheat or flour in the late twenties.

Although there is no *a priori* reason why agriculture generally should lead to cumulative, self-reversing, and more or less rhythmic fluctuations of the type we have in mind,[4] its importance in the Canadian economy requires that it be studied closely. Some attention will be given, therefore, to the interaction of agriculture and industry, the special factors leading to instability in agriculture and its role in the transmission of external developments to the domestic economy.

These comments by no means exhaust the aspects of the structure of the economy which need to be kept in mind when considering economic fluctuations. Other aspects will be developed as the analysis proceeds, as will such important institutional factors as the organization of the banking system and the attitude of government to its role in dealing with fluctuations.

The Approach to Economic Fluctuations

It was noted that the intensive study of a particular cycle requires the use of theory, statistics, and history.[5] The use of theory is (or should be) common to all analysis of fluctuations. Unless one is to be bogged down hopelessly in the many events and statistics, assumptions must be made, their effects reasoned out, and the resulting hypotheses tested. The intelligent use of statistics is necessary not only to measure the actual behaviour of the economy, but also to examine the hypotheses as they apply to the period under review. Finally, a broad historical picture of the actual environment in which the fluctuations took

---

[4] Except for some specific commodities.

[5] For a statement of the method of the "quantitative-historical" approach, see Robert A. Gordon, "Business Cycles in the Inter-war Period," *Papers and Proceedings of the American Economic Association*, especially pp. 54-6.

place is necessary since the historical background determines the particular nature of each cycle to an important degree. Furthermore, hypotheses can never be "proved" in a definitive sense; judgment must be exercised, and this is impossible without a knowledge of the historical circumstances. Such an approach clearly involves close attention to developments in the important sectors of the economy, as well as the use of aggregative measures of activity. The conclusions are intended to apply only to the period covered, although similarities to other cycles will be evident.

Finally, no study of this type can begin in a vacuum. The fluctuations in any period are related not only to current developments, but also to those in the immediately preceding period and to trends over a considerable period of time. Although no attempt will be made here to separate precisely the cyclical and trend movements, some consideration will be given to the inter-relationships between them as they affected this period.

Some Comments on External Transactions

It was stated above that this study will place a considerable emphasis on the impact of external transactions. However, not only must their role be carefully defined, but also a theory of external determinants, as an explanation of Canadian economic fluctuations, must not be pushed beyond certain limits.

One might question, for example, the relevance of the concept of business cycles for Canada, with her large primary and processing industries and important external ties. Might not the fluctuations in Canada be regarded as the result of the transmission of fluctuations in activity from more highly industrialized countries? This view is correct if it implies that the pattern of cyclical change in Canada is determined, to an important degree, by events outside the Canadian economy, and that the theoretical structure developed to explain such fluctuations in highly industrialized countries is not entirely relevant to the Canadian economy. With respect to the former point, however, it should be noted that recurring fluctuations of a self-reinforcing nature have appeared wherever certain characteristics have dominated an economy: money transactions, the profit motive combined with the making of decisions distributed among many individuals and organizations, and the use of large aggregations of capital in a highly complex and interdependent production process. Moreover, in a richly endowed young country experiencing rapid surges in the development of resources and industrialization, fluctuations are bound to occur unless perfect judgment on the part of entrepreneurs and governments can be assumed. Fluctuations in Canada, and especially the major turning points, will be greatly influenced by those occurring abroad, but this is not to say that fluctuations are not inherent in the Canadian economy itself. Neither the extent of fluctuation nor the timing of turning points follows a set pattern as between Canada and her main trading partners.[6]

Theoretical explanations of cycles, as developed for more highly industrialized economies, must undergo certain modifications if they are to be used to explain fluctuations in Canada. More emphasis must be placed on the balance of payments, the relative importance of investment determinants will vary, and the emphasis on domestic investment typical of many theories will have to be shared with exports. Any consideration of the limitations and effects of policy decisions will have to take more account of external factors. However, the presence of a largely private enterprise economy, the durability of capital investment, a high standard of living and a wide variation in distribution of income, and the industralization of some sectors of the economy, all suggest that much of the theoretical structure developed elsewhere will be relevant to a discussion of Canadian cyclical fluctuations.

Perhaps this problem can be put in perspective by defining three types of economic activity found in Canada. First, certain industries and regions, engaged mainly in the production and processing of primary products for export, are directly dependent on export activity. Wheat, newsprint, and non-ferrous metals are the most important examples. A second type of economic activity is not directly related to export activity. Much of the secondary manufacturing industry, for example, was developed largely to serve the domestic market. In the housing industry also many determinants exist which are not directly related to the export market. All forms of this type of activity are affected, of course, by changes in income in the export sector, and some of the manufacturing industries are subject to competition from imports as well. Finally, some types of economic activity parallel developments abroad. Major international events, such as wars and their aftermath, will tend

6 This view is emphasized by the findings of Vernon M. Malach. See his *International Cycles and Canada's Balance of Payments, 1921-33*, particularly p. 47.

to have similar effects on both Canada and her main trading partners. An extension of this type of activity may be noted in the automobile industry. The introduction of the industry, its growth, and changes in it will tend to parallel similar events in the United States, partly because the Canadian industry is an outgrowth of that in the United States, and partly because some of the forces affecting the industry in each country are similar.

Let us pursue the question of dependence on external factors a little further. Clearly the importance of exports as a determinant of investment cannot be interpreted in a rigid current sense. In the period 1900-14, investment rose by leaps and bounds; exports, however, although well over the levels of the previous decade, were relatively stable from 1900 to 1905. They were relative stable once more from 1906 to 1911, but at a higher level. It was not until *after* 1911, when the investment of the previous decade had taken effect, that exports rose rapidly. Exports were stable from 1925-9 when investment rose very rapidly once more; the one exception was in 1928, when the largest wheat crop in Canadian history was harvested.[7] To expect a simple relatonship, in the form of rising exports leading to rising investment over short periods, would be to accept a very crude form of the multiplier and accelerator. Exports clearly have to be fairly high, and they must not experience a severe setback; but they do not necessarily have to rise rapidly, or at all, in order to help create the proper conditions for an investment boom.[8] Export prospects must be favourable, or rather judged to be favourable, but with this consideration we have moved from current trends in sales to expectations with regard to an uncertain future. Current export sales, and those expected in the near future, should not be over-emphasized as a determinant of investment even in the

[7] It should be added that exports in the second half of the twenties were well over those of the first half, reflecting particularly the recovery in the agricultural sector. Exports were also fairly stable from 1947 to 1950 inclusive at a time when investment rose rapidly. The Korean War and heavy wheat crops raised exports to higher levels thereafter.

[8] It is worth noting, however, that there was an export balance in each of the three periods *preceding* the investment booms. The picture is complicated by the effect of war and post-war disturbances, which contributed to export balances in the two later periods referred to in the text and the previous footnote. It would appear, however, that periods of great prosperity in Canada have usually been associated with deficits (except in war) and those of lesser activity with surpluses. See K. W. Taylor, *Statistics of Foreign Trade*, Vol. II: *Statistical Contributions to Canadian Economic History*, pp. 3-5.

great primary exporting and related processing industries; they represent only one of the factors taken into account to gauge prospects in an uncertain long-term future, especially if the industry is young. For many of the secondary industries, furthermore, such factors as tariffs, growth of population, and urban development will play a greater role than whatever export outlets they may develop – with the important proviso that the over-all levels of exports must be broadly sustained.[9]

One should note also the large part of the investment programme which is reflected in imports. Does the cumulative reciprocal interplay of investment with consumption, which has been emphasized in business cycle theories for more self-contained economies, have a role in a country like Canada? Not many statistics are available on this, but the following are suggestive. The greatest relative import content for the components of GNE is likely to be in expenditures for machinery and equipment. Imports of machinery and equipment in the late twenties were probably 30 to 40 per cent of total Canadian purchases of machinery and equipment.[10] This was at the height of the boom in Canada. The direct import content of expenditures for construction would be well under this, perhaps about 10 to 15 per cent, since most of the necessary materials would be produced in Canada and the high labour content would be almost wholly domestic.[11] The import content of non-

[9] This dependence on economic activity abroad, and particularly on that in the United States, is of course not unique to Canada. Rapid development is highly unlikely in most trading countries, even highly industrialized countries, given a major depression in the United States. For the impact of the United States on world activity in the inter-war years, see United States, Department of Commerce, *The United States in the World Economy*. The international synchronization of business fluctuations is shown in Wesley C. Mitchell, *Business Cycles: The Problem and Its Setting*, pp. 424-50, and Gottfried Haberler, *Prosperity and Depression*, pp. 266-7.

[10] The import content of Canadian purchases of machinery and equipment in 1929 is given as 21 per cent in Canada, Department of Trade and Commerce, *Private and Public Investment in Canada, 1926-1951*, p. 23 (henceforth referred to as *P.P.I.*). Some related indicators suggest this figure may be low. Another study concluded that "approximately 40 per cent of the domestic disappearance of machinery and equipment from 1926 to 1930 was imported." See Kenneth Buckley, *Capital Formation in Canada, 1896-1930*, pp. 36-7 and 99. Some part of the difference between these two figures reflects the use of gross investment data for total machinery and equipment expenditures in the former estimate, in contrast with the flow at producers' prices in the latter.

[11] See Buckley, *Capital Formation in Canada, 1896-1930*, p. 36.

farm inventories was probably higher than that for construction, but a measure of it is not available. It is clear that, while investment would lead to considerable "leakages" via imports, the major part of the direct effects would be on Canadian income and employment. Rising consumer expenditures, a result of the increase in investment, would also spill over into imports; part of the effect of such expenditures on induced investment would, therefore, be felt abroad. But there would be enough effect in Canada to yield a cumulative interplay of investment and consumption. The difference between the Canadian economy and more self-contained economies lies in the relatively larger import leakages and in the possible complications in the balance of payments which may develop in a rapid upswing.

Another factor of great importance is the heavy inflows of capital from abroad which have developed in periods of rapid investment in Canada. These have had tremendous effects, not only by permitting a degree of development beyond the capacity of the domestic economy, but also in the borrowing of highly developed technology and the integration of commodity and financial markets. While acknowledging and emphasizing the great importance of such flows, we must keep in mind the sequence of events and motivation. Viner's classic study emphasized that the capital inflows led to an increase in reserves; that domestic prices rose more than export prices, and both rose more than import prices; and that, consequently, an import surplus developed.[12] Later analysis has not only added the effects of income changes on imports (in addition to the effects of differing changes in price levels), but also pointed to determinants of income other than capital imports.[13] The work of Innis and others has emphasized the "real" forces inherent in the rapid development of domestic investment, the effects of technological changes combined with vast primary resources, and the rigidities and other maladjustments which an investment boom may leave in its wake. Attention has been shifted, in other words, to large changes in autonomous investment, whether financed in Canada or from abroad. This type of analysis must supplement the balance of payments aspects if a proper understanding of cyclical changes (as against the transfer mechanism) is to be achieved.

[12] Jacob Viner, *Canada's Balance of International Indebtedness, 1900-1913.*

[13] C. G. Meier, "Economic Development and the Transfer Mechanism," *Canadian Journal of Economics and Political Science.* This journal is henceforth referred to as *CJEPS.* See also p. 17.

Even where foreign capital has provided a major share of the financing necessary for domestic investment, some distinctions should be made with respect to making decisions and taking risks. Decisions concerning the inflow of capital for direct investment, as well as the retention of profits in Canada by subsidiaries, certainly reflect the policies of parent companies abroad. The initiative for investment financed by new issues sold abroad, however, generally rests with Canadian corporations and governments. In terms of the decision-making process, new issues play a permissive rather than an activating role. In those direct investment companies which are fully owned abroad, all the capital risks are normally borne by the parent company. Where foreign financing involves capital in the form of new issues only, however, control of the operation rests with residents. The risks involved for the non-resident then consist of exchange losses, if the issue is payable in Canadian currency, and the possibility of default. These risks were often minimized by the issue of securities which were optionally payable in foreign currencies and by government guarantees.

The Role of Domestic Investment

Two analytical devices should be described briefly. One is the multiplier. An increase in investment in plant, for example, will lead to a greater increase in income than the actual expenditure on the plant, because of the induced effects on consumer spending. An increase in government spending or exports (or the export balance at similar levels of total trade) will have the same types of consumer re-spending effects. Just how far such a process goes depends, among other things, on the size of the initial outlay and whether it is repeated; the extent to which increased savings, taxes, and payments abroad (resulting from the higher income) create leakages from the flow of income; the stage of the cycle; and any possible adverse effects associated with the initial increase in spending.

Part of the effect on income lies in the stimulus given to investment by the increase in consumer spending. The accelerator is an analytical device for examining the relation between production of producers' or consumers' durables and final consumption or sales.[14] Since such durables give a stream of goods

---

[14] There is a considerable literature on the multiplier and accelerator principles, part of which is referred to in CHAP. VI. For an excellent brief analysis, see Robert Aaron Gordon, *Business Fluctuations*, CHAPS IV and V.

and services over time, a given increase in consumption will lead to a much greater rise in the production of the durable good itself – if expectations as to the future course of demand and other factors lead to a decision to increase production of the durable good. The degree to which the output of the durable good increases depends on the durability of the investment required to produce the commodity and the importance of other production costs for the commodity. If there were a fixed relation between the amount of change in the output of the final product and the output of the capital equipment necessary for its production, a fall in the absolute amount of increase of final output could lead to a fall in the absolute level of related investment.

In this rigid sense the theory is not applicable to reality. The relation of final demand and investment is not fixed since it depends on expectations as to the future course of demand, the availability of capital, cost-price relations, and other conditions, as well as changes in current demand. Excess capacity will modify the relationship, since an increase in final demand may lead only to greater use of existing facilities. Statistical tests of the accelerator have generally been unfavourable.[15] The basic concept is a useful one, however, since changes in output are one factor affecting decisions about the expected future profitability of some investment. The concept also helps explain the greater swings in the production of investment goods than of final output. The usefulness of the concept is increased if it is limited to specific industries and longer periods of time.[16]

The durability of investment and the uncertainty of the return together give investment its instability. Durability means that replacement can be postponed and that investment will give services over a considerable period of time. This, in turn, may lead to a bunching of investment by various industries when opportunities are favourable, and very little investment (apart from minimum replacement) when conditions deteriorate. The uncertainty of the return on investment is, of course, a reflection of the fact that a large commitment must be made in the present which may or may not be justified later by the course of events.

Here we are at the crux of the question of what determines

---

[15] For a list of tests and a discussion of the accelerator principle, see A. D. Knox, "The Acceleration Principle and the Theory of Investment," *Economica*.

[16] Gordon, *Business Fluctuations*, pp. 104-7 and 118.

investment. The expectation of profit in the future is, in general, the determinant of private investment. But what determines expectations with respect to future profitability?

It is convenient to distinguish two types of investment. Some investment is *induced* by changes in aggregate income in the immediate past, the present, and those expected in the near future. *Autonomous* investment, on the other hand, is not closely related to such changes in income.[17] The former type of investment will play a relatively greater role in older industries, in the absence of rapid technological change in such industries. One can grant the usefulness of a modified acceleration principle, as in induced investment, and still point out that autonomous spurts in investment are the dynamic factor in an economy. Such a concept is particularly useful in explaining investment in new industries undergoing rapid expansion.

The reaction of autonomous investment in Canada to its determinants resembles that in highly industrialized and more self-sufficient countries: it tends to come in spurts and bunches, it can fall off as rapidly, and it may get under way without an increase in current output. It differs from these other countries, however, in that the accelerator is even less applicable in Canada because the country is less developed; in such a country, much investment may at times be determined by the prospects over a very long period for vast sections of the country.[18] Another difference, of course, is that much more of the output of autonomous investment must eventually be exported.

The most important single factor affecting autonomous investment is innovations.[19] By this we mean not only techno-

[17] Some objections can be voiced to these concepts. See T. Wilson, "Some Reflections on the Business Cycle," *Review of Economic Statistics*, p. 245; and M. J. Ulmer, "Autonomous and Induced Investment," *American Economic Review*, p. 587. It will be admitted that there is a constant interplay between the two types of investment, and also that the classification is not a very thorough one. It is useful for preliminary analysis, however, particularly as it directs attention to the dynamic aspects of investment in relatively new industries or those older ones undergoing extensive change.

[18] Stewart Bates has made this point in his review of Haberler's *Prosperity and Depression* in *CJEPS*, p. 602.

[19] For an analysis of this concept and its relevance to economic fluctuations see Gordon, *Business Fluctuations*, pp. 327-32 and Alvin H. Hansen, *Business Cycles and National Income*, pp. 72-6 and 190-4. Joseph Schumpeter gave a central role to innovations in his analysis of cycles, and H. A. Innis has emphasized their place in Canadian economic development. Malach has used the concept to good effect in analysing Canadian turning points in the twenties and early thirties.

logical change, but also new markets (including export markets), exploitation of new resources, settlement of new areas, and other important developments leading to greatly increased expectations of future profits. The innovations may have been developing for a while, but the full impact is likely to be fairly sudden and large, leading to a cumulative upswing via the multiplier-accelerator model. It is the impact of innovations which wrecks any attempt to relate investment to current sales or income and which plays the dynamic role in Canadian cyclical change.

A comprehensive analysis of investment would bring in a number of other factors affecting business expectations as to the profits to be derived from investment. These include availability of funds at home and abroad, cost-price relationships, the amount of debt already incurred, the stock of capital and its degree of utilization, the desire to maintain the competitive position of the firm, government policies, expectations as to the general outlook and, of course, the rate of change in current sales. Autonomous investment will be undertaken in a particular industry given an innovation and if the climate for investment, as determined by the above factors, is favourable. Changes in current sales are clearly not enough, even for induced investment; there may be excess capacity, or wide fluctuations in the recent past may make firms hesitate to undertake large commitments. Investment by governments will have somewhat different determinants because much more than the profit motive is usually involved. Decisions made by governments about future developments also involve difficult judgments about the prospects over very long periods, especially if the governments are actively assisting the settlement and development of a country.

Some Preliminary Hypotheses

Canadian economic fluctuations cannot be explained by a simple model. Export changes are very important, but so are changes in autonomous domestic investment (whether for eventual home or foreign consumption). As we look at the record, these two dynamic variables must be given close attention. In particular, we shall look closely at the impact of the former on the economy and at the various determinants of the latter. In order to give a fuller explanation of this period, some important aspects of domestic consumption and government policy will also be considered.

Why was the recovery of the Canadian economy so incomplete in the thirties? Our major preliminary hypotheses can be summarized as follows.

(1) The international downswing struck Canada at a time when the major phase of western settlement had largely been completed. The great surge of autonomous investment before the war, based primarily on wheat and railways, had lost some of its impetus in the twenties.

(2) Several large and relatively new industries developed rapidly in the twenties. Their impact on the thirties was limited by the fact that investment opportunities had been so thoroughly exploited in the twenties. There were no extensive backlogs of investment opportunity in the major industries, old and new, to cushion the downswing and expedite the recovery.

(3) The severe downswing deserves careful analysis because it left a host of problems in its wake which slowed recovery. The severity of the downswing in Canada was primarily a function of the extent of the collapse of exports and domestic investment. The Canadian economy, as developed over several decades, was peculiarly vulnerable to the type of international collapse which occurred, a collapse involving an exceptionally severe industrial and financial collapse in the United States, a sharp decline in world primary prices, and the demoralization of the world trading and financial mechanism. The downswing in Canada was accentuated by a number of cost rigidities, financial excesses in the preceding Canadian boom, and monetary crises elsewhere.

(4) The beginning of recovery in Canada reflected primarily the impact of recovery abroad although a number of internal adjustments occurred in the downswing which eased the start of recovery. The recovery of exports to their previous levels, and a growing export surplus, left the economy well below full employment levels by 1937, however, with a particularly large gap in domestic investment relative to 1929. The cumulative interplay of exports with domestic spending components, as indicated by the multiplier-accelerator model, was weak. The three major factors in the incomplete recovery of the economy are noted below.

The damage to the world trading and financial mechanism was only partially repaired in the upswing. The slow and erratic recovery in the United States was an important factor in the

Canadian recovery.[20] It is true that total exports of goods and services rose to about the 1929 level, particularly with increased gold production and larger sales to the United Kingdom. The nature of the recovery in exports, however, suggests that the effects on income were modified in several ways. There was little recovery in primary export prices until late in the upswing, and the terms of trade did not return to the level of the late twenties till 1937. It was a highly uneven recovery, with little improvement taking place in the important wheat trade. The strongest growth in exports was in metals, but the multiplier effects in this sector were probably relatively small.

Secondly, the effects of the downswing lingered into the upswing and retarded recovery. Many of the uneven price-cost declines were not fully corrected for much of the upswing. A strong desire for liquidity and reduction of debt prevailed after the unhappy experience of the downswing, and because of a large continuing burden of debt. The tremendous excess capacity which prevailed, and continuing high inventory ratios, limited for a time the effect of rising sales on induced investment.

Thirdly, the recovery in domestic investment was quite incomplete. As noted earlier, the extent of recovery in long-term investment depended not only on current sales, but also on the extent to which investment opportunities had been exploited earlier, how far corrective adjustments were made in the downswing, the degree of excess capacity, and the effects of these and other factors on business men's expectations about future profitability. The failure of autonomous investment to revive was closely related to the previous thorough exploitation of investment opportunities, as noted in (1) and (2) above. The cautious approach to both induced and autonomous investment should also be related to the developments in the downswing and upswing, as noted above, which weakened the incentive to invest.

(5) The downswing in Canada was more severe, and the

[20] It should be clear from the previous paragraph that the use of the term "slow" here is relative. The actual percentage increases from the low point of 1933 were substantial. But the recovery by 1937 was well short of both the full employment level and the previous peak in the late twenties, and the ratio of national income in 1937 compared to 1929 was low relative to that of most other countries. The term "slow" in this context, therefore, refers to the incompleteness of the recovery. I am indebted to Mr. Gideon Rosenbluth for drawing my attention to the need to emphasize this distinction.

recovery slower, relative to 1929, than in many other countries. As a preliminary explanation of this, three points are suggested. First, the collapse of world primary prices and the restrictions on world trade would affect Canada more seriously than many other countries, both because of the large role played by exports and because of the degree to which exports consisted of primary products. Secondly, the international collapse occurred at a time when new investment opportunities had been exploited for some years at a rate which had few parallels elsewhere, and when the major phase of western expansion was coming to an end. Thirdly, one of the most severe downswings and most incomplete recoveries occurred in the United States. The aggregate swings in Canada and the United States were not greatly different. In part this reflects the close economic ties which Canada has with the United States. In part, however, it was the result of factors which cannot be related closely to current developments in the United States.

Antecedents of the Depression of the Thirties

The course of the depression and recovery cannot be properly understood without some study of developments which took place long before the thirties. Our immediate task, therefore, is to outline briefly economic change in the preceding decades, noting particularly several developments which were to affect the course of the depression profoundly.

Three distinct periods of development can be delineated after 1895. From about 1895 to 1913 the settlement of the west dominated the economic scene. The wheat boom and the extension of the railway system are the main themes of this period. The war of 1914-18 consolidated the growth in these sectors of the economy and gave a strong impetus to several relatively new industries. During the twenties these new industries were pushed forward vigorously, easing for a time some problems of adjustment which were becoming evident in the older industries.

The settlement of the West [1]

For approximately twenty years before 1895 the growth of the Canadian economy was slow. Although there were some outstanding achievements, such as the construction of the Canadian Pacific Railway, falling prices and relatively slow progress abroad severely hindered economic development.

Two basic national decisions made at this time were to have important repercussions on the future. One was the decision to use tariff protection as a stimulus to industrialization, a decision given effect in the tariff of 1879. The second decision

---

[1] The most inclusive source on this period is Canada, *Report of the Royal Commission on Dominion-Provincial Relations*, especially Book I, *Canada: 1867-1939*, CHAP. III, and Appendix III by W. A. Mackintosh, *The Economic Background of Dominion-Provincial Relations*, CHAPS. II-IV. This report and its appendixes are henceforth referred to as the *Rowell-Sirois Report*. The writer has used this very able report extensively for historical background, particularly in the period up to 1930. For an excellent recent analysis see Buckley, *Capital Formation in Canada*, CHAPS. I-VI.

was to build the Canadian Pacific Railway by an all-Canadian route. In effect, this meant higher construction costs and, accordingly, need for greater aid from the Dominion government.

When the west finally began to open up, a third policy was added to and integrated with these two, namely, deliberate attempts by governments to aid and expedite the settlement of the west by immigration policy, aid to transportation, and other means. These three basic decisions were closely related. The tariff was intended to preserve much of the new western market for Canadian industry, and industrialization would increase the east-west traffic so crucial for the railways.[2]

The rapid development which took place in Canada after 1895 was dependent on a number of changes in Canada, West-Europe, and the United States.[3] The increased rate of world industrialization and the trend to urbanization led to large increases in the demand for raw materials and foodstuffs. Prices were generally rising after 1895, and the prices of Canada's exports rose more rapidly than those of her imports, particularly of the iron and steel imports necessary for the investment programme. Interest rates were low, and the capital market in the United Kingdom was once more willing to make large amounts of funds available. Transportation costs fell with the building of transcontinental lines, government regulation to ensure low rates for the movement of grain, the deepening of the St. Lawrence canals, and improvements in ocean transportation. Finally, it should be noted that the best lands of the United States plains had been settled, but excellent free land was still available in Canada. Problems of production were conquered in part by borrowing technology, such as the dry farming techniques and irrigation methods developed earlier in the United States to cope with lack of rainfall. The development in Canada of early maturing varieties of wheat made it possible to move northward into areas with shorter growing seasons.

The boom which accompanied the conjuncture of these economic developments was very strong. Forces were set loose which led to the development of the west and, more slowly, of the mining and forest frontiers; a rapid growth of manufactur-

2 *Rowell-Sirois Report*, Appendix III, p. 20.
3 *Ibid.*, pp. 22-3 and Book I, pp. 66-7; V. W. Bladen, *Introduction to Political Economy*, CHAP. V; D. C. Corbett, "Immigration and Economic Development," *CJEPS*, p. 365; Buckley, *Capital Formation*, CHAP. II. Buckley associates the timing of this major turning point primarily with favourable market conditions for wheat and the closing of the United States frontier.

ing and service industries; and rapid growth in population and urbanization. The speed and direction of development were, to an important degree, determined by government policies, while capital imports and immigration gave an elasticity to the boom it could not otherwise have had.

The development of wheat on the prairies for export was the most important single factor in this boom. One million people from other parts of Canada and from other countries moved to the prairies between 1896 and 1913, and the proportion of the total population living on the prairies rose from 7 per cent to 20 per cent. The development of wheat necessitated large investments in railways, farms, and towns and gave a great impetus to manufactures in the east.

The pattern of development was, to an important degree, inevitable. Much of the west was better suited to wheat than to any other product once the technological changes necessary for its development had been made, and the wheat produced was of the very highest quality. Canada was simply pursuing on a vast scale the principle of comparative advantage through specialization and trade. But certain consequences were involved. A very heavy transportation burden was assumed by the country. The specialization of the prairie economy meant instability at times for all of Canada because of dependence on fluctuating export prices in the face of relatively fixed costs, because of dependence on weather, and because of the relative immobility characteristic of agricultural regions. This instability was to be aggravated later by the optimism of the period for, particularly after 1908, the dry belt of south Saskatchewan was turned to field crops as well.[4]

Something like an industrial revolution occurred in Ontario and Quebec, where the bulk of manufacturing activity developed. Manufacturing expanded rapidly under the impetus of the growing western market and the general increase in population, combined with protective tariffs which directed most of the demand to the home market. Although the growth of manufacturing was distinctly oriented to the home market, in some manufacturing industries important export outlets were to develop. Borrowing of advanced technology through branches and subsidiaries of foreign companies or by other arrangements also played an important role in the development of manufacturing. The trend to larger and more integrated production units was quickened in this period.

[4] *Rowell-Sirois Report*, Book I, p. 68.

Two of the most marked characteristics of this period were the growth and urbanization of the population.[5] In the decade 1901-11 population increased at the rate of 3 per cent per annum. Net immigration from 1910-11 was 715 thousand, compared with a natural increase of 1,120 thousand. "At no other time between 1851 and 1941 did migration add much more than one-fourth as much as natural increase."[6] Apart from increases in population there were large shifts in population under the impact of frontier settlement, industrialization, and urbanization. The two most notable changes in the distribution of population were the shift to the prairies and urbanization. In spite of the many new farms brought into existence, the ratio of urban to rural population rose from 32 per cent to 45 per cent from 1890 to 1910.

The three basic national policies noted earlier had a substantial impact on this period, both as a stimulus and as a major factor determining the nature of development. Railway policy in particular deserves brief comment, since its lingering effect on the thirties is given some emphasis below.[7]

The availability of staples and of cheap water transportation made it inevitable that Canada would produce a few staples on a large scale for export. Very heavy outlays were necessary, however, in order to span the west and to handle its produce as it moved to world markets. The distances and areas to be covered, and the fact that the dominant eastward movement of wheat was seasonal, meant a tremendous overhead combined with relatively unused capacity in some periods and peak loads at others.[8]

Canada entered this period with one transcontinental railway (the Canadian Pacific Railway), the Intercolonial Railway for the Maritimes, and the Grand Trunk for Quebec, Ontario,

[5] For an analysis of population changes and their effects, see Corbett, "Immigration and Economic Development," pp. 360-8; N. Keyfitz, "The Growth of Canadian Population," Population Studies; and M. C. MacLean, "The Correlation between Population Density and Population Increase in Canada," Proceedings of the Canadian Political Science Association.

[6] Corbett, "Immigration and Economic Development," pp. 362 and 364.

[7] See the Rowell-Sirois Report, especially Book I, pp. 69-72, and Appendix III, pp. 32-4.

[8] H. A. Innis has developed the impact of innovations in transportation in relation to the production of staple products, and examined their effects on government finance and other factors. See his Problems of Staple Production in Canada, particularly CHAP. I; and "Unused Capacity as a Factor in Canadian Economic History," CJEPS.

TABLE 1

GROWTH IN THE ECONOMY, 1900-13
(Millions of dollars)

Item	1900	1905	1910	1913
Merchandise exports	156	205	281	443
Merchandise imports	177	264	429	655
Current account balance	− 37	− 87	− 251	− 408
Net long term capital movement	+ 30	+ 110	+ 308	+ 542
Home investment (a)	86	158	273	405
Steam railway mileage	17,657	20,487	24,731	29,304
Capital employed in manufacturing (b)	447	834	1,248	1,959
Wheat acreage (000)	4,225	—	8,865	11,015
Terms of trade (export price as percentage of import price) (c)	100	103	114	111
Wholesale price index	100	113	125	133
Population (000)	5,322	5,992	6,917	7,527

SOURCE: *Rowell-Sirois Report*, Appendix III, p. 25, and *C.Y.B.* for various years.

(a) This series is from Buckley, *Capital Formation*, pp. 126-31. It represents the flow of construction materials and machinery and equipment at producers' prices. In 1901-10, according to Buckley's quinquennial estimates, the flow of these products at producers' prices amounted to about 60 per cent of gross domestic capital formation (excluding inventories). More inclusive data on capital formation in this period appear in Table 4 below.

(b) Capital employed in manufacturing includes establishments with five persons or more; the figure of $1,959 million is for 1915, and includes establishments with an output of $2,500 or more regardless of number of persons employed. It should be emphasized that Canadian manufacturing series include processing of raw materials as well as production of finished goods.

(c) Terms of trade are those estimated by Taylor, *Statistics of Foreign Trade.*

and to Chicago. It emerged from it with two largely completed additional transcontinental lines, the National Transcontinental and the Canadian Northern Railway. These were in part incorporated with lines already existing, but involved extensive duplication both with one another and with the Canadian Pacific Railway. In addition, the Dominion government had undertaken the construction of the Hudson Bay Railway, although it was not completed till much later. The provinces, furthermore, by giving aid or guarantees, had pressed the building of local lines.

The object of federal policies was to help open up the west and to link the various regions. But the Dominion government also emphasized, as it had during the earlier construction of the Canadian Pacific Railway, the desirability of all-Canadian routes and termini in preference to less costly routes which passed through or ended in United States territory. The desire to expedite and control railway construction involved governments in heavy financial obligations and substantial grants of land. In addition to railways, other transportation facilities received extensive government aid.

It is not simple to give the reasons for the tremendous growth in railway mileage in this period. Governments and others desired to lower rates, to link the various regions of Canada,[9] to open new areas, and to provide facilities for moving the rapidly increasing flow of products. Regional pressures for lines were a powerful factor in the extensive building programme; political exigencies could not fail to be important where it was necessary to retain the favour of those who provided guarantees for loans.[10] Along with this complex of economic and political factors, the tremendous optimism of the period should be mentioned.[11] The settlement of the prairie region in the United States was a constant example, government revenues were rising rapidly, traffic and settlement were booming, and the rapid development of the period was expected to justify the construction programme. By 1914, however, Canada was left with great parallel stretches of track over what even today are largely unproductive areas. The cost was not burdensome when customs revenues and income generally were rising and new

9 It would be difficult to understand, however, why this linking would involve three lines which duplicated one another to such an extent.

10 E. W. Beatty, "The Canadian Transportation Policy," *Papers and Proceedings of the Canadian Political Science Association,* especially p. 111.

11 In this connection Innis has stated, "It would be heresy to ask whether rapid development which involves mortgaging the resources of a young country is desirable. New countries are not in a position to ask whether capital investments are sound in the long run. They proceed in an atmosphere of boundless optimism on the assumption that there are no limits to the country's possibilities." See his *Problems of Staple Production in Canada,* p. 56.

capital was available to finance the old, but with the benefit of hindsight one can note that other circumstances were to lead to a severe burden and to limitations on the policy of the central government.

It has been stated that "The most fundamental characteristic of the period was a high rate of investment induced by improved expectations of profit from the exploitation of natural resources, newly tapped by the extending railways, subjected to new production techniques, or converted into profit possibilities by favourable shifts in costs and prices."[12] It was the prospect of greater profits from sales in the future, sparked by the innovations noted above, which must be regarded as the dominant motivating factor in the investment boom. A whole new area was being opened up in the west, and the older areas were undergoing radical changes in manufacturing and service industries.

Two points need to be emphasized here. The results of the boom could not be foreseen; its justification lay in the distant future. It would be a mistake, then, to attempt to relate the rapid rise in long-range investment projects too closely to current changes in sales. Like all strong booms, this was primarily a surge of autonomous investment which induced further investment through its effects on income and consumption. It was not till 1912 and 1913, after production capacity had been greatly increased, that really rapid increases in exports could, and did, take place. It was twelve years before the level of exports doubled the 1900 total; in the same period imports rose about three and a half times, and investment four and a half times. Although the rise in export prices and values was an important indicator of favourable prospects, emphasis must be put on other factors as well.

Another point to be considered is the role of foreign capital in the boom. It has been estimated that from 1901 to 1915 capital imports were more than half as large as domestic savings.[13] The capital inflow both contributed to and financed the growing deficit in the current account. The United Kingdom supplied $1,750 million of the inflow of capital from 1900 to 1913, and the United States supplied another $630 million.[14] The bulk of the inflow of capital was in the form of fixed-interest securities, which were mainly sold abroad by the gov-

[12] *Rowell-Sirois Report*, Appendix I, p. 24.
[13] Buckley, *Capital Formation*, p. 63.
[14] Viner, *Canada's Balance of International Indebtedness*, CHAP. VI, especially pp. 126 and 134.

ernment or guaranteed by it. United States capital, however, largely took the form of direct investment in manufacturing and some of the primary resource industries.[15]

Viner's study of the transfer mechanism emphasized the dominating role of capital inflows and corroborated the price-specie-flow mechanism of adjustment in the balance of payments. More recently, changes in income have been given more emphasis in the adjustment of the balance of payments, and somewhat more attention has been paid to determinants of income other than capital imports. It has been stated that "It is significant that the noticeable acceleration of growth in the Canadian economy after 1895 did not initially depend on the inflow of foreign capital. Not until 1905 did foreign borrowing reach significant proportions, although marked expansion commenced a full decade earlier. As we shall argue below, foreign investment reinforced and prolonged the expansion, but it was the opportunities provided by the earlier expansion which originally attracted foreign capital."[16] In effect, the opportunities were created by a number of innovations discussed earlier. The preliminary exploitation was undertaken in Canada, but guarantees by governments and the prospects for wheat were key factors in attracting foreign capital. The fact that the bulk of financing abroad was in the form of public or guaranteed fixed-interest securities, rather than direct investments, suggests clearly that the decisions and risks lay very heavily with the governments and corporations in Canada.[17] The size of the boom can be clearly related to the fact that a whole frontier was available for exploitation, which meant large shifts in population, and that immigrants and foreign capital were also available.[18]

---

[15] Of the companies in Canada in 1934 which were "controlled by or definitely affiliated with American firms" 66 had been established before 1900, while 273 of them had been established from 1900-13. Herbert Marshall, Frank A. Southard, Jr., and Kenneth W. Taylor, *Canadian-American Industry: A Study in International Investment*, pp. 19-21.

[16] C. G. Meier, "Economic Development and the Transfer Mechanism," *CJEPS* p. 3.

[17] In this context, it is interesting to note Buckley's comment in *Capital Formation* (p. 34): "Government intervention rather than the profitability of railroading in Canada was responsible for the large flows of foreign capital attracted to the railway field." He goes on to state that wheat was the prime mover in railway development in this period.

[18] A. F. W. Plumptre, "The Nature of Political and Economic Development in the British Dominions," *CJEPS*, p. 494.

So great was the boom in long-term investment that Canada appears to have felt only mildly some of the brief downswings abroad in this period.[19] The annual data which are available indicate that home investment did not fall in Canada during the downswings in the United States in 1904 and 1911. Exports declined moderately in 1904, imports rose, and investment was stable. In 1911, exports rose moderately while both imports and investment rose rapidly. In the downswing of 1908 in the United States all three Canadian aggregates weakened and declined somewhat, and in the 1914 downswing in the United States all three fell considerably. In the latter decline, however, the investment boom may have been tapering off in any case, and the immediate effects of the war were depressing in Canada as well.

The period 1895 to 1913 was one not only of great expansion but also of increased specialization and interdependence. A large domestic market was built up by the increases in population, but heavy economic dependence on exports of foodstuffs and raw materials in some regions, and the interdependence of regions, led to greater vulnerability to outside factors. A great deal of the investment was financed from abroad. The first test the economy would have to meet would be that of selling the vast amounts of wheat abroad and developing an export surplus (sufficient to finance and repay the loans) to the extent that new inflows were not forthcoming or desired. One cannot think of the decisions in this period as being taken with an eye to all the immediate inter-relations and consequences involved, not to mention the possible consequences in the far future. But these decisions were to have some dominating influences on that future. Wheat and railways in particular, as they developed, meant vastly increased wealth; they also meant

[19] This statement must be considered as tentative since only a few annual series were considered. For dates of United States cyclical swings, see Wesley C. Mitchell, *What Happens during Business Cycles*, p. 12. The annual figures for domestic investment referred to in this paragraph are those of Buckley, as noted in Table 1. The estimates of home investment by A. K. Cairncross lead to a similar conclusion; see Meier, "Economic Development and the Transfer Mechanism," p. 3. It is of interest to note that the United Kingdom, Germany and France skipped the downswing of 1911 but not that of 1904; see the data from the National Bureau of Economic Research as presented in Gordon, *Business Fluctuations*, p. 562. It is also of interest that Willard L. Thorp, through a reading of business annals, dated recessions in Canada in 1907-8 and 1913-14, but not 1904 or 1911; see Wesley C. Mitchell, *Business Cycles: The Problem and Its Setting*, pp. 392 and 432-4.

increased vulnerability to fluctuations in income, and rigidities in the overhead costs of the economy. While prices and incomes were rising with the investment boom, and the terms of trade improving, the burdens of these debts and policies could be borne. Differences of interest between regions on protective tariffs and other matters, moreover, were less pressing. If demand abroad did not develop to expectations or fell, and if prices collapsed, the full costs of the structure erected in these years would be evident.

The War and Its Immediate Aftermath

The Canadian economy by 1913-14 was experiencing difficulties and passing from a period of rapid internal growth to one in which a great need for markets abroad was evident. The war made it possible to effect this transition, although it left in its wake a great many other problems. A short post-war boom and a severe but brief deflation afterwards preceded the long upswing of the twenties.[20]

The period from 1914 to 1922 has many interesting aspects, but for our purposes certain highlights only need be touched. By 1913-14 the long investment boom was beginning to slow down. Domestic investment in 1913 was equal to or moderately above the 1912 level, in spite of a very large rise in both exports and capital inflows. In 1914 both domestic investment and several other types of expenditure declined. Recession in the United States, falling prices, higher interest rates and growing difficulties in borrowing from London, and the disturbance to international trade caused by the war, all contributed to the interruption of economic growth.

This interruption was brief, however, as the demand for foodstuffs and munitions in particular began to soar. In some ways the war and immediate postwar period continued and accentuated the developments of the previous two decades. In addition, a number of relatively new industries were expanded, and this momentum set the stage for their contribution to the boom of the twenties.

Some of the more striking changes brought about by the war were the rapid shift to current account surpluses in 1916,

[20] See Alice W. Turner, "Sequence of Economic Events in Canada, 1914-1923," and B. H. Higgins, "The War and Postwar Cycle in Canada, 1914-1923," in Canada, *Advisory Committee on Reconstruction; and Rowell-Sirois Report*, Book I, CHAP. IV and Appendix III, CHAP. IV.

1917, and 1919, in contrast to the unbroken string of deficits since 1900; the sharp collapse of domestic investment, which had been the driving force of the previous boom; and the great rise in prices. Heavy demands for foodstuffs from the Allies, reduced acreage in Europe, and the high freights confronting competitors such as the Argentine and Australia led to rapid increases in Canadian farm output. The increase in wheat acreage from 1913 to 1920 equalled the increase in the much longer period from 1900 to 1913, and post-war demands in war-torn Europe increased acreage sharply again. Meat and dairy products received a great boost as well. Heavy debts were contracted at high agricultural prices and rising land values, and much relatively marginal land was brought into production at the high prices. The position of the prairies as the great export region was consolidated, and dependence on wheat was accentuated.

The tremendous demand for munitions was the most important factor in the rapid rise of manufacturing output; domestic prosperity, combined with reduced supplies from Europe and an increase in the tariff, also contributed to the increase. The scale

TABLE 2

SELECTED ECONOMIC SERIES, 1913-22
(Millions of dollars)

Series	1913	1918	1920	1922
Merchandise exports	443	1,209	1,267	884
Merchandise imports	665	922	1,429	745
Current account balance	− 408	− 82	− 323	− 47
Domestic investment	405	427	653	362
Steam railway *mileage*	29,304	38,484	38,976	39,360
Capital employed in manufacturing	1,959(a)	2,927	3,372	3,244
Wheat *acreage* (000)	11,015	17,354	18,232	22,423
Wholesale price index (1900 = 100)(b)	133	266	325	203

SOURCES: *Rowell-Sirois Report,* Appendix I, pp. 25 and 41; various issues of the *C.Y.B.*; and Buckley, *Capital Formation.*

(a) Refers to 1915 rather than 1913 and includes only establishments with an output of $2,500 or more. Later figures include all establishments.

(b) The effect of very great changes in prices on the value series, as indicated approximately by the wholesale price index, should be kept in mind.

and variety of wartime manufacturing experience added to the maturity of a number of industries.

Relatively newer industries were assisted by the direct or indirect effects of the war. Pulp production more than doubled from 1913 to 1920, and the percentage of pulpwood production used in Canadian mills rose markedly. The major factors in these changes were the growth in the consumption of newsprint paper in the United States and the shift to manufacture in Canada. The existence of the railways, growing industrialization in Canada and abroad, and new uses for metals had led to considerable exploitation of ore bodies before the war. The production of non-ferrous metals was speeded up by wartime demands and high prices, and the transition was begun from export of ore to further fabrication in Canada. The automobile industry had been established in Canada in the early years of the century. In 1907 registration of motor vehicles was 2,000; this increased to 51,000 in 1913 and 276,000 in 1918. Although such rates of growth could hardly be equalled later, the largest absolute increases were to come in the decade or so after the war.

A few other wartime developments must be mentioned to fill in the historical background of the thirties. The war period saw the culmination of one phase of railway growth in Canada. Early in the war two of the transcontinental railways so lavishly aided by governments ran into difficulties.[22] The Railway Inquiry Commission of 1916 recommended that they be taken over by the government. It was feared that bankruptcy and default, although these would eventually lead to a reduction in their heavy fixed costs, might also lead to a financial panic and damage the credit of the country. They were merged with other government railways to form the Canadian National Railways. This solution of the railway problem, posing two railway giants in competition against each other, was to have important effects on the course of investment in the twenties and of economic policy in the thirties. On the merger itself, another Royal Commission later commented:

All the debenture liabilities of the companies, including as well those on which there had been no guarantee and those guaranteed by the provinces, as well as those which the Dominion had guaranteed, were assumed by the Dominion. Practically

21 See footnote 19 of this chapter.
22 See the *Rowell-Sirois Report*, Book I, pp. 103-5 for a further discussion of these developments.

the whole of the capital expenditures on the newer roads had been financed by the sale of these fixed interest securities. There was virtually no equity investment. The entire cost of these misguided ventures was, therefore, loaded on the shoulders of the taxpayer with very little loss to the private investor. Thus a heavy overhead on the economy undertaken at private risk was converted into fixed charges of government.[23]

The great inflation of the war and post-war period was, in part, a direct reflection of the methods used to finance the war. Inflationary issues of notes and advances from the banks were used extensively. Rapid expansion of loans to individuals and corporations and rising external prices added further to the inflationary forces. One of the major developments in this period was the very successful flotation of several large war loans in Canada, the first long-term financing of any consequence within Canada by the government.[24] The tremendous rise in Dominion government debt in the period reflected not only war and demobilization costs but also expenditures on capital account, and the assumption of certain railway liabilities as well. Between 1913 and 1921 the Dominion government's debt (including railways) rose from $521 million to $3,520 million, that of the provinces and municipalities from $790 million to $1,437 million.[25]

The actual transition from war to peace was effected rapidly, but with some violent fluctuations.[26] The first few months after the war were a period of hesitancy and uncertainty, associated particularly with the drop in war orders and exports. Beginning in the spring of 1919, however, a brief but marked boom developed in response to rising government deficits, high export values, and the large liquid assets and expenditure backlogs associated with the war. The chief characteristic of the boom

23 *Ibid.*, p. 104. Other parts of this *Report* properly place more of the responsibility with governments than is implied by this quotation.
24 *Ibid.*, p. 98.
25 *Ibid.*, p. 105. The figures include a small amount of duplication between governments. For an examination of monetary policy and inflation in this period, see Higgins, "The War and Post-war Cycle in Canada," pp. 13-15 and pp. 21-8.
26 A detailed analysis of economic fluctuations in Canada after the war is not relevant here. See Higgins, "The War and Postwar Cycle in Canada," pp. 29-69 and Turner, "Sequence of Economic Events in Canada," pp. 12-21. A thorough analysis of the forces responsible for the revival in 1921 appears in Malach, *International Cycles and Canada's Balance of Payments*, CHAP. II.

was its highly speculative and inflationary nature, reflecting not only the strong demand factors referred to above but also various shortages in supply. The index of industrial production rose from 66 in 1919 to only 70 in 1920, while wholesale prices rose from 134 to 155.[27]

This very speculative boom was short-lived. The downswing, which began about the spring of 1920, was related particularly to the decline in export volume and (with a lag) value, and the considerable reduction in the federal government's deficit. Furthermore, there was a widespread feeling in the business and financial community that the deflation was inevitable in view of the rapidity of the previous price increase. The major characteristic of the downswing was the great decline in prices. The fall in export and import prices was particularly notable, especially those of agricultural products. Industrial production fluctuated more moderately than wholesale prices and recovered earlier. A general recovery was under way in the second half of 1921.

The comparative brevity of the downswing and the impetus to recovery can be related to two major sets of factors.[28] With recovery abroad, the price decline ceased and exports began to increase. The underlying long-term prospects in Canada, moreover, were favourable. While agriculture was relatively depressed for a few years, a number of fairly new industries were beginning a very strong expansion. In newsprint, automobiles, and electric power, for example, the volume of production in 1922 exceeded that of 1920, and in each case a substantial increase occurred in 1923. The construction industry had been severely depressed in the war, but with a backlog of housing, road building, and other investment projects, and the sharp deflation in costs, the stage was set for further rapid expansion. The volume of construction, on an annual basis, fell only moderately in 1921 and recovered sharply in 1922.[29]

---

[27] The base year throughout this study in 1926, unless otherwise specified.

[28] Malach, *International Cycles*, CHAP. II, considers the commercial application of innovations and early rise in exports as the major factors in the turning point. As less significant factors he includes replacement demand, an increased rate of growth in consumption, the fall in money wage rates, and the larger inflow of long-term capital.

[29] For the indexes referred to in this paragraph and below on the period to 1925, see D.B.S., "Recent Economic Tendencies in Canada, 1919-1934," and "Twelve Years of the Economic Statistics of Canada, by Months and Years, 1919-1930," *Monthly Review of Business Statistics*.

The post-war boom and slump were very similar to those in some other countries, particularly that in the United States.[30] This was true not only of the timing and extent of fluctuation, but also of its patterns in several types of expenditure. In chapter I it was anticipated that the close ties between Canada and her main trading partners would impart a great deal of similarity to fluctuations in Canada and abroad. The similarity in change arising from the effects of fluctuations in foreign trade was greatly enhanced by parallel fluctuations in other variables, mainly because of similar experiences in Canada and abroad in response to wartime demands. Some of the common factors involved were the backlog of demand, monetary inflation to finance the war, the large liquid assets, the pattern of change in government deficits, and the investment opportunities available from such industries as automobiles.

The Upswing of the Twenties

The first few years of the twenties were a period of some uncertainty for Canadian development, a period of adjustment to wartime distortions and the post-war boom and collapse. There were, however, strong underlying forces at work, which will be examined shortly.

The downswing of 1920 and part of 1921, and the upswing in the next two years, have already been noted. From 1923 to 1924 economic activity levelled out, but a strong increase occurred again in 1925. The retardation of expansion in 1924, which was slight and specialized, was probably caused by the decreases in a number of exports, particularly to the United States, and a decrease in construction activity. For the year as a whole, a fall of 6 per cent in industrial production in the United States contrasts with one of less than 2 per cent in Canada.[31]

In spite of a sharp but brief downswing in 1920-1 and some specialized setbacks in 1924, the first half of the twenties showed significant advances in output. Agriculture, it is true,

---

[30] For analyses of cyclical fluctuations in the United States in this period, see R. A. Gordon, "Cyclical Experience in the Inter-war Period," in *Conference on Business Cycles:* and Thomas Wilson, *Fluctuations in Income and Employment*. For the United Kingdom as well, see League of Nations, *Economic Fluctuations in the United States and the United Kingdom*, 1918-1922.

[31] The Canadian index includes construction, which declined in 1924, while the United States index excludes construction.

experienced great difficulties in this period. Some idea of the progress in these years, however, can be derived from the following figures:[32]

	1919	1920	1923	1925
		(1926=100)		
Industrial production	66	70	84	90
Manufacturing production	71	71	86	93
Output of consumers' goods	74	72	82	91
Output of producers' goods	65	75	85	87
Export volume	78	66	81	97
Wholesale prices	134	155	98	103

In the fourth quarter of 1924 the index of industrial production began a prolonged and strong upswing which reached a peak in the first quarter of 1929. This peak was almost double the level in the third quarter of 1924.[33] The index of industrial production failed to show an increase in only three quarters in this long period of upswing. It levelled out in the first quarter of 1926 and fell in the third quarter of both 1926 and 1927. Neither of the two decreases, which were about 5 per cent each, lasted more than one quarter.[34]

To properly understand the recovery problems of the thirties, it is necessary to inquire into the reasons for the long upswing of the twenties, its nature, and whether any weaknesses

32 Data are from D.B.S., "Recent Economic Tendencies in Canada, 1919-1934."

33 For purposes of comparison with the figures immediately before this paragraph, it is worth noting that industrial production in the third quarter of 1924 was about 70 per cent of the average for 1926.

34 Again there is some similarity to fluctuations in the United States. The Canadian index of industrial production includes construction, however. In both the first and third quarters of 1926 the construction component fell very sharply. The monthly data suggest this was due to a bunching of contracts in particular months; for the year 1926 as a whole, the index of construction volume rose by 25 per cent. The mild recession in the second half of 1927 in the United States was associated, to an important degree, with the closing of the Ford plants. Expenditures in constant dollars for residential construction and producers' durables both declined in 1927, while those for business construction levelled off. Automobile output was sharply reduced in Canada also. Exports, moreover, fell by about 5 per cent, but those to the United States were higher. In contrast to the United States, expenditures for residential construction, and particularly for business construction and producers' durables, were all higher in constant dollars in 1927. While GNE in constant dollars rose by 8 per cent in Canada, in the United States the increase for the year was only about 1 per cent.

developed. Certain developments preceding and at the upper turning point in 1929 need examination since their effects in the thirties were profound. Some general comments on the twenties will help set the background for a more intensive analysis of these developments.[35]

Appendix Table 50 indicates the striking changes which occurred in national income in the late twenties. It is interesting to note that income originating in agriculture was high but not greatly changed from 1926 to 1928, in spite of a record wheat crop in 1928, and that it fell sharply in 1929. The decrease in 1929 was large enough to lower national income, in spite of increases in most other groups. Income originating in mining rose by 35 per cent in 1926-9; in construction, by 45 per cent; in manufacturing, by about 30 per cent; and there were sharp increases in a number of service industries also.

No major component of GNE rose as rapidly in the late twenties as investment in durable assets. The sharp percentage increases by industry are shown in Table 3. The longer-term changes in domestic investment are shown in Table 4. Both of these sets of data will be used extensively in our analysis.[36]

At the same time that substantial investment was being made in some of the older industries during the twenties, rapid progress was occurring in a number of relatively new industries. These new industries generally had been founded before the war, but their major absolute effects on income and investment took place after the war. Their development hinged on the

[35] Study of the twenties is hampered by the lack of official National Accounts data prior to 1926. Private estimates exist, but the concepts used and methods of compilation differ from those available from 1926 on and detail of components is lacking.

[36] The available data on capital invested, or the stock of capital, are subject to so many problems of classification, valuation and coverage that they are used very sparingly in this study. It is interesting to note, however, two points brought out by a comparison of capital invested in 1920 (in some cases 1921) and that in 1930. First, the stability of capital invested in agriculture from 1921 to 1930 was in marked contrast to considerable increases in capital invested in several other sectors of the economy. Secondly, five groups (mining, pulp and paper, steam railways, central electric stations and streets and highways) accounted for about 65 per cent of the increase in capital invested in (roughly) the combined areas of agriculture, mining, manufacturing, transportation and other utilities, and government investment. See *Rowell-Sirois Report*, Book I, p. 116. It should be added that, apart from the problems noted at the beginning of this footnote, the level of prices in 1920 was considerably higher than that in 1921, which in turn exceeded that of 1930.

TABLE 3

Gross Domestic Investment (Excluding Inventories) by Industry, 1926-9
(Millions of dollars)

Industry	1926	1927	1928	1929	Percentage change 1926-9
Agriculture	89	109	139	121	36
Mining, quarrying, oil wells	17	18	32	46	171
Manufacturing					
Pulp and paper	44	47	49	26	− 41
Other	178	234	276	348	96
Construction	14	15	25	34	143
Steam and electric railways and telegraphs	92	117	127	199	116
Other utilities	82	87	119	145	77
Trade	24	27	50	68	193
Commercial services, finance & insurance	27	46	54	64	137
Housing	212	217	236	247	17
Government depts. (a)					
Engineering	65	82	95	110	69
Other	21	29	35	42	100
Other (b)	52	59	59	69	33
Total private and public investment	917	1,087	1,296	1,518	66

Sources: D.B.S., *National Accounts, Income and Expenditure, 1926-1950*, p. 54 (henceforth referred to as *National Accounts*) and various tables in part II of *P.P.I.*

(a) Investment by government business enterprises is included with the appropriate industries.

(b) The residual category includes rounding error.

availability of resources in Canada, technological change, demand for their products at favourable prices, lower transportation costs, and availability of capital from abroad. Several very important industries, based on development of resources, were geared mainly to export markets. Others were clearly developed for the domestic market, although in some export outlets took an important share of their production. In discussing the prewar period, emphasis was laid on wheat and railways as the most important factors in the investment boom. In the twenties the emphasis shifted, at least in relative terms, to newsprint, metals, electric power, and developments related to the spread of the automobile. Rapid growth in these industries, as well as in the service industries, gave a tremendous impetus to investment and also determined to an important degree the nature of developments after 1929.

During the first half of the twenties some of the dislocations to the world trading and monetary system occasioned by the

TABLE 4

QUINQUENNIAL ESTIMATES OF CAPITAL FORMATION IN CANADA, 1901-30 (*a*)
(Millions of dollars)

	1901-1905	1906-1910	1911-1915	1916-1920	1921-1925	1926-1930
Gross domestic capital formation	1,283	2,287	3,279	4,033	3,641	5,831
Selected sectors						
Prairie farm investment (*b*)	221	319	463	370	245	454
Railways	165	473	682	423	386	583
Automobles (*c*)	4	19	73	178	257	503
Selected sectors as percentage of gross capital formation						
Prairie farm investment (*b*)	17.3	13.9	14.1	9.2	6.7	7.8
Railways	12.9	20.7	20.8	10.4	10.6	10.0
Automobiles (*c*)	0.3	0.8	2.2	4.4	7.1	8.6

SOURCE: Buckley, *Capital Formation,* Appendix and Tables 8, 14 and 15. The figures are in current dollars, reflecting both price and volume changes.

(*a*) The method used to estimate these figures differs from that used in the official National Accounts data. Buckley's method is based on commodity flows, while the estimates in the National Accounts are based on capital expenditures reported by corporations.

(*b*)Includes housing and other buildings, equipment, trucks and inventories, but excludes passenger cars. Grain and livestock inventories were 66, 92, 282, 49, 50 and 38 millions of dollars respectively.

(*c*) Includes highways, bridges, and producers' automobiles.

war and the post-war cycle were being repaired.[37] Exports
from Canada had fallen in value by over one third in 1921. By
1926 exports were again at the 1920 value, even though export
prices were more than one-third less than those of 1920. In
other words, a sharp increase in the volume of exports occurred
between 1921 and 1926 to help set the stage for the upswing
of the twenties. A current account surplus reappeared in 1923
and continued until the investment boom changed it to a deficit
in the late twenties.

While the high level of exports was a necessary factor in the
boom, one should not regard the heavy investment of this period
as being induced solely by current exports. Export volume rose
during the first half of the twenties, thus giving an impetus to
some investment. In the period 1926-9, however, when the investment boom was under way, export volume and value were
remarkably stable at high levels – except in 1928 when a very
large wheat crop was harvested.[38] Consumer expenditure rose
strongly in this period, and personal saving as a percentage of
disposable income fell in both 1927 and 1929. Government
spending on goods and services rose particularly sharply in 1929
and 1930. Increases in population, including net immigration in
the last half of the twenties, played a role also. The rise in urban
population was very striking, accounting for 77 per cent of the
increase in population from 1921 to 1931. The application and
extension of technological change involved heavy investment
in a number of industries.

Capital imports played a much smaller role in the investment boom of the twenties than they did before the war.[39] But
new issues placed abroad and direct investment inflows (along
with retained earnings) continued to play an important part in

[37] The international background of the twenties is well known and
need not be dealt with here. See League of Nations, *Course and
Phases of the World Economic Depression*, CHAPS. I-IV inclusive,
and Joseph A. Schumpeter, *Business Cycles*, vol. II, CHAP. XIV.

[38] The one sector of GNE to fall in 1929 as a whole was exports.
This was due to wheat. Exports of merchandise, excluding wheat
and flour, rose in both 1928 and 1929.

[39] See Buckley, *Capital Formation*, pp. 62-8, for estimates of the
considerable decline in the ratio of the current account deficit
to private domestic savings over the two periods. It should be
added that ratios of foreign to domestic capital, including those
used in the text above, must be considered as approximate, both
because of statistical problems and difficulties in relating financial flows to domestic investment. In addition, the important
gaps in information on the nature and effects of parent-subsidiary
relationships limit any analysis of the full impact of foreign
capital.

financing domestic investment and supplying technology and market connections.[40] From 1926 to 1930 the net borrowing from abroad, as represented by the current account balance adjusted for retaining earnings, was equivalent to about 25 per cent of net private and public investment. If outflows of capital from Canada are disregarded and only direct foreign participation in domestic investment considered, the long-term inflows and retained earnings were equivalent to perhaps half of the net domestic investment.[41] At first sight such large percentages might suggest a very strong causal relationship from foreign financing to domestic investment. With respect to inflows of direct investment and the use of retained earnings by non-residents, a good case can be made for such a causal relationship.[42] With this type of foreign financing, the non-resident took both the initiative and capital risk through the establishment of the subsidiary company and through continuing influence on the subsidiary's policies. In our discussion below of saturation of investment opportunities, particularly as it applies to the automobile industry and to some firms in newsprint, this point needs to be kept in mind. It is important to note, however, that the bulk of the inflow of long-term capital in the late twenties was in the form of new issues. The initiative for borrowing and much of the risk in these were assumed by Canadians. Furthermore, it is important to examine the reasons for the investments financed by such inflows. From the point of view of both Canadian and foreign lenders, these centred around the profitability of the investments as reflected in the complex of factors determining the outlook for the country.

The result of these factors was to enlarge investment opportunities considerably and lead to heavy gross and net investment. Toward the end of the upswing, the rapid rise in stock prices gave a speculative impetus to the underlying investment boom. The investment increase was far in excess of replacement needs. If depreciation charges are used as a very approximate measure of replacement, private net investment in durable assets from 1926 to 1930 was about 45 per cent of private

[40] See Table 51 below.
[41] A. E. Safarian and E. B. Carty, "Foreign Financing of Canadian Investment in the Post-War Period," *Proceedings of the Business and Economic Statistics Section, American Statistical Association.*
[42] Within the framework, of course, of the Canadian climate for investment, as determined by opportunities, government policy and other factors.

gross investment.[43] In effect, a large amount of replacement was undertaken and substantial additions to capacity were made. Most industries participated to some degree in this process, with the result that in many of them there was little backlog for the thirties unless new developments occurred.[44]

In the period before and during the war, the Dominion government had actively encouraged the direction of economic activity. Partly because of the heavy debts it incurred in the process, its role in economic development in the twenties was relatively smaller. Both the Hudson Bay Railway and the new Welland Canal, begun before the war, were completed in (or shortly after) this decade by the government. These were, in effect, consolidations of the pattern of investment necessitated by the wheat economy. But provincial and municipal governments took over enthusiastically. While the federal debt fell in per capita terms in this decade, that of the municipalities and provinces rose 20 per cent and 70 per cent respectively. Provincial and municipal governments played the important role in highways and roads, were responsible for much of the investment in utilities, and incurred rising costs for social services.[45]

Developments in Selected Industries in the Upswing[46]

A thorough analysis of investment can be undertaken only by examining specific industries. The following comments on in-

[43] See Table 37 below. Depreciation charges are the only measure of replacement now available, but they are not a very precise measure. Such charges will tend to exceed actual replacements in a period of rapid increase in the stock of capital, and also when prices are rising. In the period 1926-9 the stock of capital rose rapidly, while prices were stable or slowly falling: the use of depreciation charges as a measure of actual replacement in this period has probably understated net investment. Depreciation charges are also not an adequate measure of depreciation at current cost, that is, capital consumption, particularly in a period of rapidly changing prices. It should be recognized also that, in any society where obsolescence plays a large role, the distinction between replacement and additions to stock becomes blurred. For comment on these factors and a list of sources, see Safarian and Carty, "Foreign Financing of Canadian Investment."

[44] See Malach, *International Cycles*, pp. 22, 32, 57 and 119 for a brief but suggestive analysis of the role of innovations and of domestic investment in the twenties.

[45] For an account of public investment from 1900 to 1930, see Buckley, *Capital Formation*, CHAP. V.

[46] The reader may wish to refer to Tables 40 to 47 in connection with these industry studies.

dustries help set the background for the analysis of problems in industry in the thirties and point to certain weaknesses in the twenties which contributed to those problems.

The Wheat Economy[47]

The war severely reduced European production, and revolution in Russia removed one important source of wheat exports. With rapidly rising prices, acreage expanded in the United States, Canada, Argentina, and Australia. The severe fall in wheat and cattle prices after 1920 exerted a deflationary effect on agriculture until about 1924. The rise in agricultural prices after 1923, combined with a slower rise in agricultural costs for a period and the lowering of freight rates made possible by the Panama Canal, led to a renewed expansion in agriculture.[48] Yields were larger in the last half of the twenties, particularly in 1928. International trading and currency relationships had achieved some stability after the unsettled post-war conditions.

In comparison to the preceding decades, agricultural growth was decidedly slowing down. Seeded acreage in wheat had risen from 4 million acres in 1900 to 10 million acres in 1914 and 18 million acres in 1920. The next year it rose to 23 million acres. But from that year until 1928, acreage fluctuated narrowly between 22 and 23 million in all but one year. It was not until 1928 and 1929 that further important increases in acreage appeared, partly in an attempt to offset lower prices. Approximately the same picture appears for all field crops.[49]

Such a slowing down in the long-term rate of growth can have important implications for investment, under certain circumstances.[50] But two factors partly offset the effects of slower growth on investment in agriculture and in industries serving

[47] The analysis of agriculture has been restricted largely to wheat. In the peak year of 1928 farm cash income from the sale of wheat was $451 million, amounting in itself to 7.4 per cent of GNP. In the period 1926-9 farm cash income from the sale of wheat was three-fifths of all cash income from the sale of field crops and 40 per cent of total farm income. Not only its size, but its volatility and its effects on other parts of the economy justify close attention to this product. See D.B.S., *Handbook of Agricultural Statistics*, Part II.

[48] *Rowell-Sirois Report*, Book I, p. 115.

[49] Absolute and percentage changes in quinquennial wheat output are shown in Tables 9 and 10.

[50] See pp. 11-12 on the accelerator and induced investment. It is interesting to note that the absolute increases in wheat production were about the same in the first and second halves of the twenties. See Table 9.

agriculture. One was the succession of excellent yields from 1925 to 1928, combined with large export outlets at prices which, while falling, were well over those of 1921-3. The second factor was the technological change associated with the combustion engine. Between 1921 and 1931 tractors on prairie farms increased from 38,000 to 82,000, motor cars and trucks from 73,000 to 155,000, and combines from none to 9,000. Nevertheless, gross domestic investment in agriculture rose more slowly than that in many other industries from 1926 to 1928-9. More significantly, prairie farm investment fell sharply as a percentage of gross capital formation compared to pre-war, and even in absolute terms (and in spite of higher prices) in 1926-30 it barely equalled the level of 1911-15.[51]

Agriculture experienced a slowing down or maturing in its longer growth while still, with good yields and technological change, contributing to the prosperity of the last half of the twenties. Although the role of agriculture was decreasing relatively, it was still the single most important industry in the country. High wheat prices and good yields were necessary to carry the costs of debt incurred for construction, land, mechanization, and other purposes – and to yield sufficient revenue to the prairie governments to meet the debts which they had incurred for development.[52]

[51] See Tables 3 and 4. It should be noted that inventories of grain and livestock fell considerably in the quinquennial periods mentioned here, while farm machinery expenditures doubled. These opposite changes were partly related. See Buckley, *Capital Formation*, CHAP. II, for a thorough analysis of investment in the wheat economy to 1930, including the slowing down of extensive investment after 1915-20 as the wheat frontier diminished, and the continuing role of intensive investment associated with mechanization and the combustion engine. Note also the following statements: "At the close of this decade the settlement of the Western plains was virtually completed, and the area was provided with the capital equipment and the community facilities adequate for a high standard of living." *Rowell-Sirois Report*, Book I, p. 121; and "With the disappearance of the frontier, the rate of western expansion, although obscured by the effects of the war, and the effects of technological change in the Panama Canal and the use of the combustion engine, slowed down. In the depression the consequences of an abnormal period of growth made their appearance." F. J. Westcott, "An Approach to the Problem of Tariff Burdens on Western Canada," *CJEPS*, p. 215.

[52] In 1931, more than one-third of the "fully-owned" farms (excluding those partly owned and partly rented) had mortgages, which averaged 41 per cent of the value of the mortgaged farms. *C.Y.B., 1934-35*, p. 298.

There were, however, very distinct clouds on the horizon.[53] In the last few years of the upswing there was a clear tendency to world over-production of wheat, which would probably have led to a further price decline after 1929 even without the cyclical downswing. Acreage outside Europe had been greatly increased during and after the war. Reconstruction in Europe was proceeding, however, and Russia re-entered world markets. The large world crops toward the end of the decade led to falling prices after 1926 and accumulation of stocks late in the decade. At the same time, however, per capita consumption of wheat was falling, and some shift to other foods appears to have been under way. From 1925 on there was a conscious policy in several European countries to encourage domestic production. In the United States the tariffs of 1913, 1921, and 1922 led to gradually rising duties on farm products, which were to reach a peak in the Smoot-Hawley Tariff of 1930.[54] Clearly, such a situation was potentially dangerous for a country like Canada which, in the last half of the twenties, was exporting over 70 per cent of her wheat crop as wheat and flour and was supplying about 40 per cent of world wheat exports.

In Canada in 1929 the belief that the price of wheat would rise with the expected short crops led to a widespread withholding policy and a speculative rise in price in mid-1929. The considerable decline of wheat exports in 1929 can be traced partly to the short crop of that year, and partly to a holdback which raised prices above world prices and helped reduce the Canadian share of world exports. The wheat pools held back their supplies rather than sell on a falling world market, and at the end of the year were left with increased stocks. The collapse in wheat prices below the initial payment of $1.00 by the pools put them in serious difficulty. Continued decline in prices worsened the situation, and the federal government stepped in finally to assume control of the pools' selling agency.[55]

[53] See League of Nations, *Course and Phases of the World Economic Depression*, pp. 38-49.

[54] C. B. Davidson, "Recent Legislation affecting International Trade in Farm Products," *Proceedings of the Canadian Political Science Association*.

[55] See Bladen, *Introduction to Political Economy*, pp. 142-3; C. P. Wright, "Report of the Royal Grain Inquiry Commission, 1938," p. 231; H. L. Griffen, "Public Policy in relation to the Wheat Market," *CJEPS*, p. 484.

Newsprint

Before the first half of the twenties was over, the relatively new pulp and paper industry had become the largest manufacturing industry in Canada in terms of value of production. The development of its major sector, newsprint, deserves close examination.[56]

Production of newsprint in the United States was about the same in 1913 and 1929 at 1,300-1,400 thousand tons, in spite of the rapid increase in consumption of newsprint in that country. The increased demand was supplied by imports, which rose, from 220 thousand tons in 1913 to 2,421 thousand tons in 1929. Given the proximity of Canadian resources to the large northeastern United States market, and abundant coterminous supplies of cheap wood, water, and water power, it was inevitable that Canada would play the major role in supplying the United States. In 1913 newsprint was put unconditionally on the United States free list. Embargoes on the export of pulpwood from Crown lands expedited the development of the newsprint industry in Canada.

The expansion in Canada was phenomenal. From 1913 to 1920 Canadian production tripled to 867 thousand tons; in the next nine years it tripled again to 2,725 thousand tons. In 1929 Canada accounted for about 65 per cent of world exports of newsprint. Of the 1929 output 90 per cent was exported, and 90 per cent of this was exported to the United States. Although gross investment in durable assets in the pulp and paper industry in 1926-9 was only 4 per cent of all private and public investment, its importance was greater than this alone would suggest. To take only one striking effect on other or related industries, by the end of the decade this industry was producing or purchasing the equivalent of more than one-quarter of all the water power capacity in Canada.[57]

After 1926 the industry was in difficulties. By 1923 the New York price of newsprint had fallen from the high level of 1920 to $82 per ton; by 1926 and 1927 it was down to $70,

---

[56] On the newsprint industry in the twenties and later, see especially Bladen, *Introduction to Political Economy*, CHAP. VI. See also E. A. Forsey, "The Pulp and Paper Industry," *CJEPS*, p. 501; C. P. Fell, "The Newsprint Industry," *The Canadian Economy and Its Problems*, eds. H. A. Innis and A. F. W. Plumptre; various issues of the *C.Y.B.* in this period; and the *Financial Post* for March 12 and October 1, 1932.

[57] *C.Y.B.*, 1930, p. 365. This is a minimum estimate.

and in 1929 it was $62. The operating ratio in 1926 was 86 per cent; during the succeeding three years it fell to between 73 and 75 per cent. This situation was bound to create difficulties for an industry whose mills were mainly capitalized (and contracted for power and wood) to operate at well over 90 per cent of capacity and $75 pr ton.[58]

The decrease in operating ratios reflected the fact that the rise in capacity was more rapid than that in sales. The capacity of the industry was doubled from 1925 to 1930. Profits had been large, sales were rising, funds were readily available, and provincial governments made it easy to secure timber rights. Although prices were falling, costs also fell because of technological improvements such as the greater use of water power in operations.[59] A marked movement towards merger developed in the late twenties. To finance mergers and to expand capacity, large amounts of funds were raised, mainly by the issue of bonds, debentures, and preferred shares. Thus, heavy rigid charges were incurred, charges which rose rapidly per ton as operating ratios fell.

The structure of the industry added to its problems. It may be described as an oligopoly with a fringe of smaller but still powerful companies. With falling operating ratios and heavy fixed costs, the instability of such a situation became apparent. Attempts to agree on prices and allocate output failed under the temptation of cutting prices to secure large contracts.[60]

The industry had obviously over-expanded and would have required considerable adjustments even without a depression. Gross investment in durable assets in the pulp and paper industry was $47 million in 1927 and slightly higher in 1928; it fell

[58] See *Financial Post*, October 1, 1932, p. 11, and Forsey, "Pulp and Paper Industry," p. 503. Operating ratios can mean different things, depending on the definition of capacity. Those used above appear in Bladen, p. 159.

[59] See Bladen, *Introduction to Political Economy*, p. 157, for a list of the technological changes affecting the industry.

[60] Three large companies controlled about half the output, and another dozen or so the remainder. The situation was made more difficult by the presence of large buyers who could offer substantial contracts and thus play off one firm against another. It was further aggravated by the practice of the trade; not only were contract prices renewed yearly or half yearly, but under the contract the purchaser was entitled to any lower price established in any other contract made by mills with a capacity of 100,000 tons or more per year. In effect, a producer who cut his contract price forced all others to follow suit. See Bladen, *Introduction to Political Economy*, pp. 159-83, for industrial structure, competition, and attempts at control in the industry.

to about half this level in 1929 and was negligible by 1933. Yet the volume and value of newsprint exports was rising in the period 1926-9 and fell only in late 1929 and later.

Mining

Another industry which gave a tremendous impetus to development in the twenties was mining.[61] The most important developments occurred in the field of metallic minerals.

Most sectors of the industry increased their production very rapidly in the two decades before World War I.[62] The output of precious metals lagged during the war, but during the twenties gold output tripled and silver production doubled. The post-war slump drastically reduced the output of non-ferrous metals from the high wartime levels, but new production records were set in the last half of the twenties. Copper output tripled from 1923 to 1929. Annual lead production had exceeded 50 million pounds only a few times between 1900 and 1920; by 1929 it was over six times this volume. Nickel production fell from 93 million pounds in 1918 to only 18 million pounds in 1922, but from 1928 to 1930 it was about 100 million pounds a year. Zinc output also rose rapidly.

The non-metalic minerals and iron generally did not show any such phenomenal changes. Much of Canada's large reserves of these minerals could not be economically exploited at that time. Thus, Canada was importing almost all of the ore used in her iron and steel industry, half or more of her coal consumption, and almost all of the crude oil used in her refineries.[63]

But "in contrast with her weak position in the production of coal, iron, and petroleum, Canada, in 1929, stood first among the countries of the world in the production of nickel and asbestos (90 per cent and 65 per cent of world output respectively), second in the production of gold, aluminium, cobalt, and the platinum metals, third in silver, gypsum, and mica, fourth in copper and lead, and fifth in zinc.[64] Apart from the availability of excellent ores, there were various reasons for this strong Canadian position. Technological change in the

---

61 See *C.Y.B.*, 1931, CHAP. XII; Innis, *Problems of Staple Production in Canada*, CHAP. III; H. A. Innis, *Canadian Frontiers of Settlement*, Vol. IX, *Settlement and the Mining Frontier*; and E. S. Moore, "The Mining Industry and the Depression," in *The Canadian Economy and Its Problems*.

62 See Table 9 for long-term production series.

63 Moore, "Mining Industry and the Depression," pp. 34-5.

64 *Ibid.*, p. 35.

industry and adaptation of transportation facilities were crucial. The science of metallurgy made rapid strides, for example, the development and use, in the twenties, of the selective flotation and electrolytic processes. The separation of ores permitted the recovery of a larger proportion of metal and commercial treatment of complex ore bodies. The slump in nickel production after the war was overcome by the development of new alloys for commercial uses.[65] Rapid growth in some world industries, such as those producing automobiles and electrical machinery, created increasing demands for metals. The application of technological changes in transportation, particularly the use of gasoline engines, aircraft and tractors, opened up areas not accessible by rail. Water power also played an important role in mechanical techniques of production.

The effects of these changes were widespread. Power, construction, railway branch lines, and supplying industries such as lumber, chemicals, and machinery all benefited. There were other less direct effects. As new areas were opened, speculation in mining shares rapidly increased, especially in 1928 and 1929. This was not the only element of instability in the industry. The boom psychology was particularly evident in the earlier stages of mining exploitation. The post-war depression had indicated the instability of prices of a producers' material. Many of the metals were largely exported and thus closely related to industrial production and tariff policy in the United States and elsewhere. But the continued activity in mining (especially gold) in the depression was to give support to areas and industries hard hit by the virtual collapse and slow recovery of many other sectors of the economy.

Utilities

Private and public gross domestic investment in durable assets from 1926 to 1929 inclusive totalled $4,818 million. About one-fifth of this investment was in utilities. Fully three-quarters of the latter investment was in steam railways and telegraphs ($498 million) and central electric stations and gasworks ($227 million).[66]

Some characteristics of this type of investment should be mentioned. Both governments and private enterprise are im-

---

[65] See the *Financial Post*, February 27, 1937, for the substantial programme of expansion in nickel, a programme virtually completed by 1930.
[66] *P.P.I.*, Tables 41, 47 and 52.

portant participants in such investment. In 1929, for example, 57 per cent of new investment in all utilities was in privately owned public utilities. The same percentage applied in central electric stations, while in steam railways and telegraphs the figure was 47 per cent.[67] A very large capital investment is required, with heavy interest charges, and the projects generally require a relatively long period of time to complete. Although all investment in durable assets requires consideration of long-term prospects, this type of investment can be expected to require consideration of even longer-term and broader developments. A new railway may open up a whole area, and a central electric station may drastically reduce costs and attract new industries to a region – but neither may happen with the speed or to the degree expected. Such large and partially completed investment cannot be terminated suddenly in the face of a downswing. Once completed, however, the absence of new projects of this type leaves a large gap in investment.

Hydro-electric power was developed more rapidly than any other utility in this period. The central provinces of Canada, which have the bulk of the manufacturing industries, did not have coal but were well supplied with water power. The impetus to develop hydro-electric power came from a number of sources, but the rapid growth of the pulp and paper industry was the main one. Over 90 per cent of the machinery of this industry was driven by electric power derived from water.[68] The mining industry also was an important user of hydro-electric power; the rapidly developing aluminum industry represented, in effect, the import of bauxite and the export of power. Other manufacturing industries were increasing their use of power in the war and post-war period. Rates were lowered by the growing availability of hydro-electric power, and by improvements in generation, transmission, and electric appliances and motors. Growing domestic and commercial uses also provided an impetus to expansion. Direct exports to the United States were also a factor, amounting by 1929 to 8 per cent of the electric energy generated in central electric stations. In spite of the rapid increase in the capacity of central electric stations, the ratio of output to their maximum capacity rose

67 *Ibid.*, pp. 72-84.
68 *C.Y.B.*, 1932, p. 290. See also p. 43. Actual water power capacity in this industry by the end of the decade far exceeded that of all other industries combined (excluding the central electric stations), and it purchased large amounts of power from the central electric stations.

from 42 per cent in 1922 and 1925 to about 50 per cent in 1927-9.[69]

Hydro-electric power was at the base of much of the expansion of the twenties. The co-existence of low-cost power and wood and metal resources, and the ease of transmission to industrial, commercial, and domestic users, had many important effects on investment which cannot be measured easily. While the growing use of hydro-electric power stimulated the development of such power, the very existence or prospect of low-cost power in turn reacted on industrialization. The provision of power involved heavy investment in generation, transmission, and distribution facilities. Total capital invested in central electric stations rose from $485 million in 1921 to $1,056 million in 1929. The comparable figures for all manufacturing industries (excluding central electric stations) showed a much slower rate of increase, namely, from $2,698 million to $4,005 million.[70]

The rate of expansion in other utilities, as well as in manufacturing, was slower than that in power. The absolute increase in the number of telephones in use between 1911 and 1920 was equal that in the twenties; in other words, the rate of increase

TABLE 5

SELECTED STATISTICS ON UTILITIES, 1900-30

	Installed hydraulic turbine horse-power (000)	Telephones (000)	Electric railways (single-track mileage)
1900	173	n.a.	553(a)
1910	977	303(b)	1,047
1920	2,516	856	1,699
1925	4,338	1,143	1,738
1930	6,125	1,403	1,509

SOURCE: C.Y.B., 1932, pp. 290, 560 and 614.
(a) Refers to 1901.
(b) Refers to June 30, 1911.

[69] D.B.S., Central Electric Stations in Canada, various issues.
[70] The 1921 data for manufacturing, furthermore, exclude capital invested in the non-ferrous smelting industry. Data are from various issues of the C.Y.B.

declined. Electric railway mileage reached its peak in the 1923-5 period and actually declined after that, although total car mileage increased. The growing competition of the auto-mobile was a factor here, but the relatively small increases in mileage after 1915 would suggest the major growth period of this industry had passed in any case.[71] By contrast, the absolute increase in the twenties in horse-power installed far exceeded that before 1920.

Much of the financing of the heavy investment in such utilities was undertaken by foreign capital, a considerable part of it in the form of fixed-interest securities payable in foreign currency.[72] Provincial and municipal ownership meant guar-antees of interest on much of the debt and rigidity in public finance.

When the depression struck, a number of large hydro-electric and other projects were under way. More than half of the total installations for hydro-electric power at the end of the decade, for example, had been put in place since 1922; yet there were projects under construction, or "actively projected" at that time, which would have added as much power as had been installed since 1922.[73] Many of these projects were com-pleted in the years 1930 to 1932, thus maintaining investment somewhat in the downswing. No new installations were under-taken, however, for several years after early in 1931. When many of the projects already undertaken were completed, in-vestment simply collapsed, there was excess power (given the difficulties of such important users as the newsprint industry), and new investment was not forthcoming for several years.

As indicated above, more than half of all investment in utilities and about a tenth of all gross domestic investment in durable assets from 1926 to 1929 were in steam railways. In an earlier section it was noted that the financial difficulties of a number of railways had led the federal government to assume their debts and merge them into the Canadian National Rail-ways (CNR) in 1923. The nationally owned system found itself in direct competition with a well-built, unified private system, the Canadian Pacific Railway Company (CPR).

The CNR was already burdened with a vast debt when it

---

[71] Single-track mileage was 1,590 miles in 1915. See also Buckley, *Capital Formation*, p. 33.

[72] Non-resident ownership of capital in utilities (excluding steam railways) rose from 32 to 36 per cent between 1926 and 1930. See D.B.S., *Canada's International Investment Position*, p. 78.

[73] *C.Y.B.*, 1930, p. 364.

began operating as a unit in 1923, much of the debt representing assets built at high cost, or through unproductive territory, or duplicating other lines. Both systems undertook heavy investment programmes in the twenties. The losses of the CNR in the period 1923-31 totalled $456 million, including $288 million for interest on government loans. By contrast, the CPR's net income substantially exceeded interest throughout the period, and large dividends were paid.[74]

The immediate problem is to suggest the reasons for the substantial increase in investment and indicate the difficulties in which it placed the railways by the end of the decade. Steam railway mileage had risen from 17,657 miles to 30,795 miles between 1900 and 1914 and rose to 38,806 miles by 1920. In the next decade there was only a small increase, relatively and absolutely, to 42,075 miles in 1930. Furthermore, the amount of rolling stock (locomotives and freight cars) declined in the twenties after substantial increases in the previous two decades. Such measures are imperfect guides to railway investment.[75] Nevertheless, Table 4 shows that railway investment not only fell sharply in relative terms after 1911-15, but also remained below its previous quinquennial peak in absolute terms.

While the longer-term growth of railway investment was decidedly slackening, such investment was a significant part of total investment and rose from the first to the second half of the twenties. While net investment in road construction in the twenties never attained the pre-war level, rising expenditures for replacement of road offset part of this decline. In addition, the substitution of heavier and more specialized equipment in the twenties (along with replacement demands arising from the heavy pre-war investment) resulted in a much better maintenance of expenditures for equipment than for road construction.[76]

A full analysis of railway expenditures in the twenties requires some consideration of the structure of the industry. The CNR attempted in the twenties to make an integrated and

---

[74] See Canada, *Report of the Royal Commission to Enquire into Railways and Transportation in Canada, 1931-32*, pp. 16-17. (This report is referred to below as *Railways Report, 1931-32*.) The ratio of stock to long-term debt, however, was substanially higher in the CPR and its fixed charges correspondingly lower.

[75] See Buckley, *Capital Formation*, CHAP. III, for a discussion of this point, and a comprehensive analysis of investment in transportation to 1930.

[76] *Ibid.*, pp. 29-31.

powerful system out of the patchwork of companies which it controlled.[77] The CPR met the competition by extending and improving its own services in order to prevent the loss of revenue. In the first two decades of the century, an excessive trunk-line mileage had been laid down; in the third decade, there occurred an extensive duplication of branch lines in the prairies, and of hotel, steamship, and other services. It is not suggested that competition was the only force at work, although other expenditures such as replacement needs and improvements in locomotives and cars have a competitive cost aspect. But it is clear from statements by the railways to the Royal Commission of 1931-2 that aggressive competition played a major role in maintaining investment.[78]

The effects of the competitive struggle were greatly enhanced by the fact that the CNR, as a publicly owned system, had access to public funds. The CNR was subject to immense political pressure to bring services to various areas. "Running through its [the CNR's] administrative practices, however, has been the red thread of extravagance. The disciplinary check upon undue expenditure, inherent in private corporations because of their limited financial resources, has not been in evidence. Requisitions of the management have been endorsed by governments, and successive parliaments have voted money freely, if not lavishly."[79]

Two other factors should be noted briefly. Although the railways had largely adjusted themselves to the competition of water transport, the loss of high paying traffic to motor vehicles was something relatively new and increasing rapidly.[80] Secondly, the relatively stable structure of freight rates was one of the rigidities of the Canadian economy, with particularly dam-

---

[77] Innis, *Problems of Staple Production in Canada*, Part II, has a discussion of this CNR policy.

[78] See also footnote 35, CHAP. VII. The trend of earnings or traffic could hardly justify much of the heavy expenditure. The CPR was able to pay large dividends and add to surplus through the twenties, but not by inordinate amounts. The CNR was unable to cover its interest charges to the public alone from 1923 to 1929, except for two years. Revenue ton miles were fairly stable (except in 1928) for both lines, and passenger traffic was falling as competition from the automobile increased. See D.B.S., *The Canadian Pacific Railway Company, 1923-1952*, pp. 6-7 and 10-11, and D.B.S., *Canadian National Railways, 1923-1952*, p. 8-12 and 18-19.

[79] *Railways Report, 1931-32*, p. 13.

[80] *Ibid.*, pp. 54-9 and Appendix II; and J. B. Rollit, J. L. McDougall and A. W. Currie, "Aspects of the Railway Problem," *CJEPS.*

aging effects in the thirties on some areas exposed to a sharp fall in export prices.[81]

A Canadian railway system could be expected to have severe problems because of the low density of traffic associated with a vast but sparsely populated country, and the highly seasonal movement of the important grain crop. To these inevitable problems were added those occasioned by mistakes of judgment extending over the first three decades of the century, and the growing threat of motor competition. These problems were affecting the railways long before the collapse of demand, in the downswing, for the products they carried.

Automobiles

The increasing use of the motor vehicle was one of the outstanding developments of this decade. Two important characteristics of the structure of the industry should be noted. First, it was a smaller scale model of the United States industry, the subsidiaries of the three large United States companies dominating the Canadian market.[82] Second, it had enjoyed continuous and substantial tariff protection since 1907.[83]

The rapid long-term increase in automobile investment, as measured by expenditures on producers' automobiles and highways, is evident from Table 4. In addition, expenditures on consumers' automobiles rose continuously from $18 million in 1906-10 to $92, $360, $420 and $760 million respectively in succeeding quinquennial periods.[84] It will be noted that registration of all types of motor vehicles tripled in the twenties. From 1918 to 1924 inclusive, domestic consumption of automobiles was relatively stable at about 80 thousand per year, except for a slump in 1921. Beginning in 1925, however, domestic consumption rose sharply to a peak in 1928.[85] Better roads, lower prices, and rising incomes were all factors in these increases. It will be noted also that exports, mainly to countries

[81] In the view of the railways the inelasticity of some rates contributed to their problems. See, for example, J. L. McDougall, "Evidence Presented to the Duff Commission," CJEPS, p. 204.

[82] See O. J. McDiarmid, Commercial Policy in the Canadian Economy, p. 258; and Marshall, Southard, and Taylor, Canadian-American Industry, p. 64.

[83] McDiarmid, Commercial Policy in the Canadian Economy, pp. 266 and 356-7.

[84] Buckley, Capital Formation, p. 33.

[85] The data for 1927, and subsequent increases in both domestic consumption and exports, reflect in part the closing down and change-over in model of the Ford Company.

Table 6

SELECTED STATISTICS ON AUTOMOBILES, 1905-30(a)
(Numbers, to nearest thousand)

	Production	Imports	Exports	Apparent domestic consumption (b)	Registrations (c)
1905					1
1910					9
1920	94	9	24	80	409
1925	162	15	74	102	724
1926	205	29	75	159	832
1927	179	37	58	158	940
1928	242	47	80	210	1,069
1929	263	45	102	205	1,187
1930	153	23	45	131	1,232

SOURCE: *C.Y.B., 1937*, pp. 668-9.
(a) Passenger cars and trucks, except for registrations.
(b) Include changes in inventories.
(c) Passenger cars, commercial cars or trucks, motor buses, and motorcycles. In 1930 registrations of motor buses and cycles amounted to 12 thousand.

(other than the United Kingdom) enjoying British preference tariffs, formed an important share of total sales.

The social and economic effects of these changes were profound. Construction of highways and roads was hampered by the war, but after the war large building schemes were pushed forward by provinces and municipalities. Total provincial and municipal assets, accounting for their outstanding debt, rose by about one billion dollars from 1921 to 1930; highways, streets, and bridges accounted for over a third of this increase.[86] One reason for extending and improving roads and highways was to attract the tourist trade from the United States, a trade which was growing with the rapidly increasing use of the automobile in that country. The growth of urban and suburban areas, in part associated with the automobile, gave a strong stimulus to construction and to the organization of retail trade. Those directly affected by the upsurge in motor vehicle sales included suppliers, such as refineries and parts manufacturers. The automobile industry itself became an important contributor to

[86] *Rowell-Sirois Report,* Book III, pp. 10-19.

employment and income. Capital invested in the industry (excluding suppliers) rose from $40 million in 1921 to $98 million in 1929, while in terms of gross value of production the industry rose from eighth to fourth place among the manufacturing industries of Canada.

Two additional points are of significance to fluctuations after 1929. First, the automobile not only gave an impetus to consumer spending, but it also increased the importance in consumption of durables. Durables are postponable, and give, to part of consumption, fluctuations similar to those of investment. Secondly, by 1930 the capacity of the industry was 400,000 vehicles a year.[87] Even the high production level of 1929 was well below this. Under such conditions, the stimulus to expand investment would be limited simply because a large capacity had already been built to exploit the existing opportunities.

Residential Construction

Gross domestic investment in residential construction in the years 1926-9 amounted to about one-fifth of all private and public investment in durable assets. The difficulties which hampered housing construction in the thirties warrant close attention to the developments of the twenties.[88]

Between 1921 and 1931 the population of Canada rose by 18 per cent, but regional increases varied widely. The west coast showed the greatest increase, at 32 per cent; Quebec and the Prairies were next at about 20 per cent each, with Ontario showing a 17 per cent increase, and the Maritimes remaining almost stationary. In this period of industrialization, development of resources, and urbanization, shifts of population were to be expected. The spread of the automobile, furthermore, speeded suburban construction. Such changes, along with rising incomes, could be expected to lead to increases in housing investment.

Statistics on money flows created by housing construction indicate relative stability from 1922 to 1925 (except for a decrease in the 1924 recession) and two higher plateaux in 1926-7 and 1928-9. The relatively small increases in 1927 and 1929 are in contrast to the strong increases in a number of other components of investment, even if one keeps in mind the ten-

[87] *Financial Post*, August 27, 1932, p. 13, and the Canadian Bank of Commerce, *Monthly Commercial Letter*, October 27, 1932.
[88] Most of the data in this section are from O. J. Firestone, *Residential Real Estate in Canada*.

dency for the latter to fluctuate more widely than housing over the business cycle. There was, however, a considerable increase in residential construction from the first to the second half of the decade.

The number of dwellings completed from 1921 to 1930 inclusive was 496 thousand, while net family formation has been estimated at 358 thousand. Other sources of housing needs (and of effective demand also, in some degree) arise from destruction of the housing stock and the increase in non-family households; these have been estimated at 128 thousand for the decade. Thus the actual number of dwellings constructed in the twenties covered the purely physical need, as measured above.[89]

Apart from the factors noted above, housing investment can be affected by the cost of housing and the size and age of the stock of houses. If prices are considered in a relative sense, in terms of change, they do not appear to have been a deterrent to current effective demand, except possibly in 1929. Prices for newly built houses fell sharply in 1922 from the high levels attained after the war and slowly throughout most of the period up to 1928; they advanced by 2 per cent in 1928 and almost 5 per cent in 1929.[90]

The trend to relatively fewer owner-occupied dwellings in the twenties may be evidence that prices (or financing terms) were too high, thus forcing increased rental occupancy.[91] Both this trend, however, and the growing number of multiple dwellings can be attributed in part to the growing mobility of a country experiencing rapid development, urbanization, and the growing use of the automobile. The slow increase in expenditures for gross residential construction in the second half of the decade was partly due to this marked shift to multiple housing units, for the average cost of a multiple dwelling unit is substantially lower than that for single unit housing.[92]

89 From 1926 to 1929 inclusive completed dwellings were 240 thousand, while housing need as measured above was 230 thousand. It should be added that the over-all physical need, in the sense noted, is not an adequate criterion of the physical need resulting from shifts in population.

90 See Firestone, *Residential Real Estate*, p. 99, for an index of prices of newly built homes. Both wage rates in building and prices of materials were rising in 1929, the former more rapidly.

91 In 1921, 67.3 per cent of occupied dwellings were occupied by owners, but by 1929 the figure was 62.4 per cent. Firestone, *Residential Real Estate*, p. 45.

92 *Ibid.*, pp. 407-8.

Table 7

SELECTED DATA ON HOUSING, 1921-30

	Dwellings completed (000)	Residential construction		Vacancy rate(b) (%)
		Gross	Net(a)	
		(millions of dollars)		
1921	34	160	66	2.7
1922	42	174	87	2.7
1923	43	180	89	5.6
1924	39	157	67	6.3
1925	45	180	90	5.7
1926	55	212	120	5.2
1927	57	216	122	5.1
1928	63	236	136	4.7
1929	65	247	140	4.7
1930	53	204	97	4.1

SOURCE: Firestone, *Residential Real Estate.*
(a) Excludes depreciation (wear and tear and obsolesence). Current replacement cost estimates of depreciation were used.
(b) Vacancy rates represent empty dwellings as a percentage of total available dwellings.

As for the stock of dwelling houses, one should note that building had been proceeding at a very rapid rate in Canada during the first two decades of the century. The large and relatively recently built stock of houses was further increased in the twenties, though at a reduced rate per thousand population.[93] In spite of this long period of construction activity, vacancy rates in the twenties were not inordinately high in relation to "normal" rates and were falling after 1923-5.[94]

The data presented above contrast with the experience of the United States and United Kingdom. The number of dwellings completed in the United States fell after 1925, and a definite decline began in the United Kingdom in 1928.[95] Comple-

[93] See Table 8.
[94] "An average vacancy rate of 4 per cent . . . was considered a desirable vacancy rate to provide flexibility necessary to meet Canadian housing requirements in ordinary time." Advisory Committee on Reconstruction (1944) as quoted by Firestone, *Residential Real Estate*, p. 50, footnote 2.
[95] Firestone, *Residential Real Estate*, p. 73. For Canada and the United Kingdom dwellings completed, but excluding conversions, were used. For Canada and the United States non-farm permanent housing was used, with dwellings completed for Canada and started for the United States.

tions in Canada rose slightly in 1929 and declined only in 1930.[96] Housing construction in the United States was clearly overextended. The index of rents in the United States fell by about 15 per cent from 1924 to 1929; in Canada, the rent index was fairly stable from 1923 to 1928 and rose in 1929 and 1930.[97]

The strong rate of residential construction over previous decades had supplied a large and fairly new stock of houses. Construction in the twenties kept pace with the new over-all physical need for houses. Although investment in residential construction did not rise as rapidly as most other types of investment in the last half of the twenties, it did reach a plateau well above the levels of the first half of the twenties. These points, and the level of vacancy rates in the twenties, suggest that there was no pressing backlog of housing demand to carry into the thirties. However, the data do not suggest that residential construction in Canada exerted deflationary influences, as it clearly did in the United States.

The above comments on industry by no means cover all the important developments of the twenties. Nevertheless, the industries selected are important enough, and sufficiently different, to permit some evaluation of the behaviour of domestic investment in the thirties.

96 The peak in Canadian dwellings constructed, and perhaps in the value series as well, may have been earlier than the data used in this section suggest. The method which was used to arrive at the basic dwelling series was to distribute the change in dwellings between the decennial census years by using "an index of domestic disappearance of building materials primarily or largely used in new residential construction." Some of these building materials would also enter non-residential construction, however, so that the derived pattern of housing construction could have been affected by the pattern of non-residential construction —which was strongly upward in the late twenties. There is, of course, no a priori reason why the peak in residential construction need be the same as that for non-residential construction. Firestone tests his derived series by comparing them with various housing series, but some of these are themselves affected by non-residential construction, and some others could be interpreted as giving a peak in 1928. See Firestone, *Residential Real Estate*, part IV, section 13. In any case, the Canadian experience in housing was evidently considerably better than that in the United States.

97 Data for the United States from Gordon, "Investment Boom of the 'Twenties," p. 204, and for Canada from D.B.S., *Prices and Price Indexes, 1913-1936*, p. 103.

Some Longer-Term Considerations

In this study, no attempt has been made to fit trend lines to the inter-war period and study deviations from these lines.[98] But some percentage changes in five-year averages of volume were computed by industries, thus yielding a combined cyclical and longer-term picture. The length of the period covered above, namely, since 1895, is such that consideration has generally been restricted to "intermediate" trends.

A few questions need to be resolved before proceeding to the statistics. What, exactly, is the significance of a declining rate of growth, such as those shown in some series in Table 10 and elsewhere in this chapter? An industry can typically be expected to go through a period of rapid growth after the product has been accepted and its use spreads. As the market becomes saturated, however, the rate of growth in output slows down or declines. New markets for a product, or new uses for it, can lead to a new growth in output. This pattern in rate of growth can be taken to reflect simply the arithmetic fact that large percentage changes are easier to accumulate on a small than on a large absolute base. The effects on employment and income of an increase in coal output are greater for a change from 1,000 to 2,000 tons than from 200 to 600 tons (all other things being constant), but the percentage change in the former is much less. The absolute levels must be kept in mind, therefore, and they have been shown separately in Table 9.

The significance of a declining rate of growth can be utilized in two ways. First, the decline may be the result not of saturation of the market through the typical growth pattern of an industry (barring innovations), but of such factors as the loss of international markets due to tariffs or high costs, or new competitive products. Secondly, the accelerator principle can be used to explain longer-run changes in particular industries if the principle is not applied rigidly and exclusively. The period 1900-29 was one of relatively full employment (except for 1913-14 and a few years after 1920). This test for the accelerator, therefore, is met in a broad sense. But the slowing down of the rate of increase in output need not affect invest-

---

[98] The implications in this approach that trend and cycle are separate forces, and that the trend line represents the norm which would occur if cycles were absent, appear to be questionable and in some ways misleading. See Gordon, *Business Fluctuations*, pp. 218-21.

ment, via the accelerator, if technological change occurs, and replacement needs may maintain investment for a time.

Turning to statistics, the following points stand out. A number of series show declining rates of growth in the twenties, some of them in absolute terms. The rate of population growth slowed down considerably after the rapid increase from 1905-14. The rate of increase in railway mileage slowed down considerably in the twenties; the absolute increases themselves were much smaller than those in any five-year period since early in the century and were exceeded by most absolute increases right back to 1870. On a per capita basis the percentage change was negative in the twenties. Even the increases in 1900-14 were relatively small per capita, but they were large in absolute terms. As was noted earlier, investment by railways continued to be large in the twenties because of replacement of equipment and road, growing hotel and steamship facilities, and some branch-line construction on the prairies. It was also noted that the aggressive competition associated with the formation of the government railways, and political factors, both played an important role in these extensions. In spite of these factors and the higher price level, railway investment remained below the pre-war level.

The rate of increase in wheat production was considerably slower after 1914. The absolute increases in both the first and second halves of the twenties, while substantial, were about the same. Acreage increased up to 1921, but was relatively stable thereafter until 1928; there were excellent yields, however, in the last half of the twenties. Although the growth trend in this industry had slowed down, mechanization gave some impetus to investment. Even with good yields and mechanization, however, prairie farm investment in the last half of the twenties barely equalled that of 1911-15. The declining rate of increase in dwellings completed, per thousand population, is quite noticeable in the twenties.[99] In the selected utilities shown in Table 5 only electric power shows a rising *absolute* increase;

[99] The same applies to the previous decade, but this includes the wartime decline of construction activity. It should be noted, however, that Buckley's data on housing investment expenditures show an increase from $568 million in 1911-15 to $742 and $1,060 million in 1921-5 and 1926-30, with housing a fairly stable proportion of gross construction by quinquennial periods from 1900 to 1930. See Buckley, *Capital Formation*, p. 38. In addition, the level of these estimates of housing investment may be too low. See Buckley, "Capital Formation in Canada," in *Problems of Capital Formation*, pp. 109 and 116.

telephones indicate a constant absolute increase in the twenties compared to the previous decade, and electric railways an absolute decline. Only the first of these three utilities had a larger absolute effect on income (as measured by these series alone) in the twenties than in the previous decade.

Table 8

ANNUAL AVERAGE COMPLETIONS OF DWELLINGS PER DECADE, 1881-1940

	Completions (000)	Per thousand population	
		Number	% Change
1881-1890	15	3.2	—
1891-1900	21	4.0	+ 25
1901-1910	49	6.8	+ 70
1911-1920	47	5.3	— 22
1921-1930	48	4.6	— 13
1931-1940	40	3.5	— 24

SOURCE: *Firestone, Residential Real Estate*, p. 478.

For metals, interpretation of the statistics is complicated by the effect of very large percentage increases in the initial stages of exploitation, the effects of large new discoveries in the last years of the nineteenth century, and the effects of the downswing after the war. Keeping these factors in mind, it can be said that the rate of growth in metallic minerals was quite strong in the last half of the twenties, and an upward trend in growth was indicated.[100] Coal mining, on the other hand, was clearly a declining industry. Other strong intermediate trends appear in the newsprint and automobile industries.

In some industries, accordingly, there was a distinct slowing down in the rate of growth of output and, in some, even in the absolute increases. If the accelerator were to be applied rigidly, a slowing down in the absolute growth of output would lead to a fall in the absolute amount of investment. In so far as investment is related to current output, a stable or even slowly rising absolute output will not sustain growing net investment in the industry. But neither gross nor (it would appear) net

[100] A better impression can be secured in this case if the average output data are combined and compared by decades over the period 1900-39.

investment fell in these industries in the late twenties since other factors intervened to maintain and increase investment for a time.

The significant point here, however, is that these slower rates of growth (or slower absolute growth and absolute declines in some cases) must be related to the recovery period of the thirties. Agriculture suffered in the thirties from low yields and low prices; had there been a strong upward trend in investment in agriculture, as in the pre-war period, the effects of even a major cycle would have been modified. The same reasoning would apply to some other industries. All of these industries had special problems as well and suffered from the downswing in economic activity; but the slowing down of their intermediate growth trends was also a factor which retarded the upswing of the thirties. On the other hand, the rapid growth characteristic of new industries, and their large effect on income after the initial stages of development, offset much of this in the twenties. The strong recovery of output in some of these relatively new industries in the thirties was in part related to the underlying upward rate of growth.[101]

It should be noted that no attempt has been made above to suggest a general theory of secular stagnation for the economy as a whole. The problem of very long-term trends for the whole economy and their relation to 1929 and later has not been examined. With reference to intermediate trends for specific industries, rather than long-term trends of a more general nature, we have noted the development of relative maturity in some specific industries and some of the effects involved.

[101] Along with the question of slower growth in certain industries, a case might be made for the view that the industries which contributed greatly to the pre-war boom required (at a roughly comparable stage of development) larger amounts of investment than those which were expanding rapidly in the twenties. See the suggestive comments in Buckley, *Capital Formation*, pp. 11 and 31-3, which indicate, among other things, that gross domestic capital formation was a higher percentage of GNP in 1901-15 than in 1926-30. It is difficult to resolve this question fully, not only because of the lack of data on the stock of capital and of criteria for determining the investment directly and indirectly required by various industries, but also because a major international downswing occurred after 1929 and cut short the investment boom. No attempt has been made here to come to a firm conclusion on this point as it relates to the investment recovery of the thirties; for reasons to be noted later, neither the newer nor the older industries showed striking investment recoveries in the thirties relative to the levels of the twenties.

Comparisons with the United States and United Kingdom

Canadian cyclical experience in the twenties had many factors in common with that of the United States, as was suggested earlier with respect to fluctuations in 1919-23, 1924, and 1927. The forces behind the long upswing of the twenties were also similar in many respects. Among the more important factors, one can note the part played in both countries, directly and indirectly, by the expanding use of the automobile and of electric power, and the rapid progress in some other relatively new industries; the great activity in the construction industries; the backlog of demand, due to the war, in the earlier years of the twenties; and the strong increases in consumption.[102] Some of the contrasts in experience in Canada and elsewhere are worth noting briefly, as a background to analysis of cyclical experience after 1929.

Foreign trade plays a far larger part in the Canadian economy than it does in that of the United States. After the early years of the twenties, the importance of foreign trade to cyclical fluctuations in the United States was greatly reduced. In Canada, however, the substantial increase in the volume of exports from the first to the second half of the twenties was a necessary factor in the great prosperity of the country.[103] The decline of wheat and flour exports to $300 million in 1929, from $400 and $500 million in 1927 and 1928 respectively, acted as an important deflationary pressure in Canada. World over-production of a number of primary products in the late twenties, and the attendant price fluctuations, had consequences for Canada far beyond those for the United States. It is perhaps not too great a simplification to state that while the United States had one very volatile form of expenditure, domestic investment, Canada had two (partly related) ones – both of which formed a large proportion of GNE in Canada.

102 For analyses of the United States experience in the twenties, see Gordon, *Business Fluctuations*, pp. 371-89, and "Investment Boom of the 'Twenties"; and Wilson, *Fluctuations in Income and Employment*, CHAPS. XV and XVI. For the United States and the United Kingdom, see Schumpeter, *Business Cycles*, CHAP. XIV.

103 By contrast, the United Kingdom's export situation was far less favourable as a result of industrialization elsewhere, and because of the high cost of her exports associated with the return to the former gold parity. The value of United Kingdom exports in 1927-9 was only about half the inflated 1920 level and some 10 per cent less than in 1924-5.

Table 9

FIVE-YEAR AVERAGES OF VOLUME OF OUTPUT AND OTHER SERIES, 1890-1939
(Thousands of units, except as noted)

	Population	Railway Mileage	Wheat production (million bu.)	Telephones in use(a)	Electric power generated (million hours)(b)	Automobile production	Newsprint production (tons)	Gold (fine oz.)	Nickel (million lb.)	Copper (million lb.)	Lead (million lb.)	Coal (million tons)
1890-94	4,881	14	43					49	3	8	2	4
1895-99	5,126	17	48					444	5	13	27	4
1900-04	5,529	19	76					1,051	10	36	39	7
1905-09	6,387	22	121	415				515	21	55	50	10
1910-14	7,419	27	196	625				631	42	68	33	13
1915-19	8,100	37	254	957	7,128	88(c)	740(c)	811	75	104	43	14
1920-24	8,883	39	341	1,264	14,210	108	1,080	1,143	46	73	97	16
1925-29	9,649	41	431	1,283	17,803	210	2,130	1,832	83	167	303	16
1930-34	10,494	42	349	1,283	17,803	96	2,254	2,752	82	302	294	13
1935-39	11,052	43	312	1,311	26,173	173	3,052	4,190	194	510	379	15

SOURCES: Data were compiled from various issues of the C.Y.B. and from D.B.S. *Monthly Bulletin of Agricultural Statistics* (September 1936), p. 315. Some production series for earlier years are not available, but certain impressions may be gained from related series in Table 5 on selected utilities and Table 6 on motor vehicle registration.

(a) Telephone calls were not available for years before 1911-14. The first average for telephones in use refers to 1917-19.

(b) Central electric stations only.

(c) Refers to 1917-19.

Table 10

LONG-RUN PERCENTAGE CHANGE IN VOLUME OF OUTPUT AND OTHER SERIES, 1890-1939
(Change in five-year averages on a per capita basis)

	Population	Railway mileage	Wheat production	Telephones in use	Electric power generated	Automobiles	Newsprint	Gold	Nickel	Copper	Lead	Coal
1890-94	+ 5.4	+ 15	+ 12					− 23				
1895-99	+ 5.0	+ 9	+ 6					+ 770	+ 28	+ 57	+ 1,338	+ 42
1900-04	+ 7.9	+ 4	+ 47					+ 118	+ 106	+ 163	+ 35	+ 9
1905-09	+ 15.5	+ 4	+ 37					− 57	+ 85	+ 33	+ 11	+ 66
1910-14	+ 16.2	+ 6	+ 40					+ 5	+ 70	+ 6	− 42	+ 21
1915-19	+ 9.2	+ 25	+ 19	+ 40				+ 18	+ 61	+ 39	+ 19	+ 15
1920-24	+ 9.7	− 4	+ 22	+ 40		+ 13	+ 34	+ 29	− 44	− 36	+ 104	− 4
1925-29	+ 8.6	− 5	+ 16	+ 22	+ 84	+ 79	+ 82	+ 47	+ 65	+ 112	+ 189	− 3
1930-34	+ 8.8	− 5	− 26	− 7	+ 15	− 58	− 3	+ 38	− 8	+ 66	− 11	− 28
1935-39	+ 5.3	− 4	− 15	− 3	+ 40	+ 73	+ 29	+ 45	+ 124	+ 61	+ 23	+ 10

SOURCE: Derived from Table 9.

The financial abuses which greatly accentuated the United States downswing were also present in Canada. In both countries the speculative optimism and the ease of access to funds led to much unwise financing and over-expansion. Common stock prices almost doubled from 1926 to 1929 in Canada and the United States, while in the United Kingdom and many other countries the rise in stock prices was far more moderate. However, because of legal prohibitions, banks in Canada did not become involved in mortgages as they did in the United States. The general strength of the Canadian banking system would tend to ameliorate the downswing, relative to that of the United States. But a very large part of Canadian private and public debt of this and earlier periods was incurred abroad in fixed-interest securities, and payable in foreign currencies. Although deflation struck bonded debtors everywhere, exchange depreciation in Canada for a time put a severe additional burden on Canadian debtors.

Canadian economic development in the twenties as a whole, and particularly in the second half of that period, was far more rapid than that of most other countries.[104] Between 1923 and 1929 the index of manufacturing production rose by 37 per cent, and that of mining production by 60 per cent. The comparable United States figures were 13 per cent and 11 per cent. The increase in economic activity in the United Kingdom was also more moderate than that in Canada, the index of industrial production rising by only 12 per cent from 1924 to 1929. In both the United States and United Kingdom, moreover, much of the increase occurred in the last year of this period, while the gains were more evenly distributed by years in Canada. National income in the United Kingdom, in current dollars, was remarkably stable in the second half of the twenties. The export problem and the over-valuation of the pound, the strike in 1926, and special problems in declining industries such as coal, combined to limit her progress. The constant dollar series for GNE in the United States indicate a fairly stable and high

104 The Canadian upswing was apparently less intense than that in the United States in the first half of the twenties. See Malach, *International Cycles*, p. 20. For data on industrial production by countries, see League of Nations, *Course and Phases of the World Economic Depression*, pp. 17 and 111, and various issues of the *Statistical Year Book*. The data in this paragraph refer to the Federal Reserve Board revised index for the United States, and the Board of Trade index for the United Kingdom. The former is described in the *Federal Reserve Bulletin*, December 1953. It has been used throughout this study, although in a few cases where it seemed appropriate the old index has also been given.

level from 1923 to 1925, and stability again at a higher level from 1926 to 1928, with a sharp rise in 1929.[105] GNE rose by 1 per cent in both 1927 and 1928, then by 7 per cent in 1929. The Canadian constant dollar series are quite different, showing a rise of 8 per cent in both 1927 and 1928, and no increase at all in 1929. While a number of important components of expenditure increased in 1929, Canadian exports of goods and services decreased by 6 per cent with the sharp fall in exports of wheat.

The over-all rate of development in Canada was greater than that in the United States in 1926-9, as indicated by an increase in constant dollar GNE by 17 per cent and 10 per cent respectively. One should note particularly that the increase in private and public investment in durable assets was far greater in Canada; from 1926 to 1929 the increase in constant dollars was only 4 per cent in the United States and fully 60 per cent in Canada.[106] This statement should be qualified for the United States, because of the decline of expenditures for residential construction after 1926. The broad picture in the United States for expenditures on construction and producers' durable equipment, nevertheless, is mainly one of a high but fairly stable level from 1926 to 1928, with a spurt in 1929 for some types. By contrast, constant dollar estimates for Canada show residential construction rose by close to 10 per cent from 1926 to 1928 (and levelled off in 1929), while from 1926 to 1929 other private construction almost doubled, producers' durable equipment rose by 70 per cent, and government investment by 75 per cent.

If one turns to particular industries, the striking differences in durable investment stand out even more.[107] Between 1926 and 1929 there was an increase in investment in manufacturing plus mining of 80 per cent in Canada, and about 15 per cent in the United States; railway investment more than doubled in

[105] The United States data are those presented by Simon Kuznets in *National Product since 1869*, pp. 35-52. For data on the United Kingdom, see A. R. Prest, "National Income of the United Kingdom, 1870-1946," *Economic Journal.*

[106] If inventories are included, the increases become 10 per cent for the United States and 46 per cent for Canada, reflecting an increase in the rate of inventory accumulation in the United States in 1929 and the reverse in Canada. The 1929 decline in inventories in Canada, however, was due solely to a decline in agricultural inventories; the absolute rise in non-agricultural inventories was greater in 1929 than in each of the three preceding years.

[107] Data on investment by industry in the United States are presented in Gordon, "Investment Boom of the 'Twenties," p. 183.

Canada, but declined in the United States; while investment in public utilities rose by 73 per cent and 17 per cent respectively. The differing behaviour of investment in residential construction has already been noted. The similarities in the experiences of the two countries in the last half of the twenties must be viewed in the context of more rapid changes in investment in Canada, changes characteristic of a country engaged in rapid exploitation of resources, industrialization, and the related investment in utilities.

This difference in the behaviour of investment is significant in several ways. On the aggregate level, private and public investment in durable assets by 1929 was 18.7 per cent of GNE in the United States and 24.6 per cent in Canada.[108] This type of expenditure is the most variable one in both countries; given a collapse of investment expectations, whatever the reasons for it, Canada could expect more severe fluctuations if only this one point is considered.[109] True, for a number of both old and new industries it appears that investment opportunities were relatively more plentiful in Canada in the second half of the twenties.[110] Many of these opportunities were already well exploited, however, and investment in such industries could hardly go on at the previous rate, even if sales continued to rise. The development and extent of the international collapse was undoubtedly the major factor in the strong reversal of the growth of investment. But the abundant stock of new capital and some over-investment were to act as a very important brake on the extent of the subsequent recovery.

Concluding Comments

The great pre-war investment boom had centred around wheat and railways. These sectors of the Canadian economy were greatly expanded during and immediately after the war. The investment boom of the twenties reflected the rapid expansion of a number of relatively new industries, particularly metals,

108 Kuznets' series for the United States.
109 But it should be noted that consumers' durables in 1929 were 12 per cent and 9 per cent of total consumer expenditures in the United States and Canada respectively. The data for Canada do not include a number of miscellaneous durables, but the discrepancy in the two proportions would probably still exist if data on these were available. The import content of investment goods is considered on pp. 101-3.
110 Either that, or they must have been far more fully exploited than in the United States.

pulp and paper, water power, and the automobile, and the consolidation of growth in the older industries. A considerable manufacturing sector had developed, mainly to serve the greatly enlarged domestic market. Interdependence of the various sectors, however, meant the domestic industries were also subject to fluctuations in export income.

Two consequences of the long period of development have been given particular emphasis above. First, with respect to the structure of the economy, these changes involved both increased vulnerability to large fluctuations in income and heavy rigid costs. The former can be related to the uncertain yield of wheat, to the nature and concentration of exports, and to certain weaknesses in international trade and finance which were to strike hard at countries heavily engaged in international trade. Canadian exports were concentrated largely in metals, which are subject to great fluctuations in price and volume, and in wheat and newsprint, where capacity had greatly expanded. This concentration, moreover, involved regional specialization and quite differing regional ability to withstand the shock of depression. Finally, for these products exports comprised a large part of both Canadian production and of world trade – a combination of factors which involved great sensitivity to the vicissitudes of international depression and tariffs.[111] If anything, the Canadian economy had become even more susceptible in the twenties to any collapse in world export demand.

International trade and finance had made a partial recovery from war and post-war dislocations, but several problems remained which were to accentuate the international downswing. These included tendencies to over-supply of some primary products, increasing protectionism, continued problems with reparations and war debts, the accumulation of large and mobile short-term funds, and a decline in long-term capital flows after 1928.

The large and rigid Canadian cost structure was inevitable to an important degree, reflecting the heavy capitalization required for efficient productive processes and by the vast distances to markets. These costs were increased by political

[111] In 1930 Canadian exports of wheat were 32 per cent of world exports (and more than this in earlier years); Canadian newsprint exports, 63 per cent of world exports; aluminum, 31 per cent; and copper, lead, and zinc 12-14 per cent. *Rowell-Sirois Report*, Book I, p. 126. That these large proportions generally involved very little control of market prices (except at the risk of large losses in sales volume) will be evident later.

decisions, such as the all-Canadian routes for railways, and by over-enthusiasm about the expected rate of growth of the economy. A very large portion of the debt required by these investments was in fixed-interest securities held abroad, much was payable in foreign currency at the option of the holder, and a considerable portion was guaranteed by the government.

The second major consequence of the long period of development concerns changes in the stock of capital. Canada entered the thirties with a large and relatively new capital stock. In spite of specific factors which kept up their investment for a time, the longer-term rate of growth in some of the major older industries was slowing down. The strong pre-war expansion of the west was not available to modify the effects of the international collapse. Moreover, the existing investment opportunities in some of the newer industries had also been very thoroughly exploited. In newsprint, for example, a complex of factors led to over-expansion. In the automobile industry the existing investment opportunities appear to have been temporarily saturated. In other industries, such as housing, sufficiently large additions had been made to the stock of capital that there was probably no substantial backlog of investment opportunities. It is clear that a country such as Canada could not withstand the major collapse in exports and the severe disorganization of international trade and finance which characterized the downswing. These developments were bound to effect seriously the outlook for investment in an economy in which exports comprised over 20 per cent of GNE. To fully comprehend the problems of the thirties, however, one should add to the collapse of demand the types of supply problems noted earlier. One could not expect the very large investment of this period to go on indefinitely. It was Canada's misfortune that the adjustments had to be made in a period of rapid disintegration in foreign trade and finance, unlike the adjustment after 1913 which was eased by wartime demands.

A few other points, which were passed over above, should be noted. The speculation of the late twenties, and the collapse of the stock markets, also were to accentuate the deflationary impact of the downswing. Canadians participated not only in the rapidly rising Canadian market, but in the United States stock boom as well. The merger movement of the last half of the twenties was related in part to the boom in the stock market. Consolidations and reorganizations led frequently to flotation of new issues, which often raised interest costs sharply. In conjunction with stock splits, new issues to shareholders at special rates, and other practices of the boom, these devices led many companies into serious financial difficulties in the down-swing.[112] When prices fell, the Canadian economy suffered greatly from the heavy fixed debts accumulated on perfectly justifiable grounds in terms of the investment outlook. It suffered also from financial abuses born of over-optimistic speculation, and of too rapid expansion in some industries.

The increasing importance of durables in consumption lent greater variability to income, since the purchase of such durables as the automobile is postponable. Offsetting this to some degree was the rising trend of expenditures on services, which show greater cyclical stability than either durables or nondurables.

The emphasis above has been not on cyclical changes as such, but on somewhat longer periods of time and specific developments which affected the thirties. No attempt has been made to relate the developments outlined above too closely to the specific turning point in 1929. Our analysis does suggest that, even if world conditions had not sharply deteriorated, some tapering off in economic activity might have occurred.[113] In fact, it would appear that the actual peak of activity in Canada may have preceded that in the United States.[114] While the decline in exports to the United States played an important role after the United States downturn, the immediate downturn in Canada was related to other factors. Thus one writer has concluded that "The deadlock in wheat and the decline of

---

[112] See Canada, *Report of the Royal Commission on Price Spreads*, CHAP. III, for a discussion of the merger movement and financial abuses in the twenties.

[113] One must make the qualifications that replacement needs would have been large in some cases, investment opportunities were still buoyant in some industries (such as metals), and innovations might have initiated a new set of stimuli. In connection with the last of these points, however, one should note that the major impact of innovations occurs some time after they have appeared on the scene; see Gordon, *Business Fluctuations*, p. 279. As for replacement, much of the capital stock in the newer industries was fairly recent, and much replacement had already taken place in railways.

[114] Malach, in *International Cycles*, CHAP. IV, places the Canadian cyclical peak in May 1929, compared to June and July for the United States and United Kingdom, respectively. His deseasonalized export peak is July 1928, but total exports remained at high levels into the first few months of 1929; exports to the United States turned down after the Canadian cyclical peak.

investment opportunities seem to be the major causes of Canada's early downturn. Before these two problems could be solved the rest of the world had also suffered set-backs so that what might have been but a minor recession for Canada developed into a major depression."[115]

115 Malach, *International Cycles*, p. 32. It might be added that the psychological and other effects arising from close corporate, financial and commercial relations between Canada and the United States are such that major developments in the latter may affect the outlook in the former even before a strong decline in exports to the United States gets under way. The peak in exports to the United States in this case, however, was apparently well after the over-all peaks in the two countries.

CHAPTER THREE

The Downswing
from 1929 to 1933

The period of the thirties was characterized by a world-wide downswing of exceptional length and severity, followed by a very slow recovery. Among those countries for which similar measures of economic activity are available, Canada experienced one of the worst downswings and most incomplete recoveries relative to 1929. In this chapter, the international background of the downswing will be considered briefly, the major developments in Canada examined, and the experience in Canada compared with that of some other countries.

The International Background of the Downswing

Two events of major international significance should be noted.[1] One was the severity of the decline in the United States, reflecting not only an industrial downswing but also severe financial problems. The other was the collapse of world trade and finance, culminating in the international financial crisis of 1931. The decline was aggravated by such factors as the heavy burden of debts, the differing degree of price decline, rigidities in a number of cost items (particularly investment costs), and a temporary exhaustion of investment opportunities in a number of industries in several countries.

That the decline in the United States had severe ramifications abroad is hardly surprising. A severe decline in that country affected other countries by considerably reducing imports, especially imports of raw materials. This effect was accentuated by a sharply increased tariff and by lower capital exports. From 1926 to 1929 the supply of United States dollars to other countries, from purchases of goods and services and from new

[1] The international aspects of the downswing have been examined by a number of authorities. See particularly: League of Nations, *Course and Phases of the World Economic Depression*, CHAPS. IV-VIII; Schumpeter, *Business Cycles*, pp. 906-54; Gordon, *Business Fluctuations*, pp. 389-95 and 405-8; W. Arthur Lewis, *Economic Survey, 1919-1939*, CHAP. IV; the annual publications of League of Nations, *World Economic Survey*; League of Nations, *International Currency Experience*; U.S., Department of Commerce, *United States in the World Economy*.

investment abroad, varied between $7.3 and $7.5 billion; in 1932 it had declined to $2.4 billion. Although the foreign transactions of the United States were not often of great importance to that country, they played a large part in world trade and capital movements.[2] In addition, there were important psychological effects from such events as the stock market crash.

The severity of the downswing also reflected the breakdown of an orderly system of trade and finance. In particular, severe repercussions followed the over-supply of a number of world primary products, the fall in long-term capital exports, a multiplication of restrictions on trade, the large international shifts in short-term capital, and the culmination of these developments in the international financial crisis of 1931.

The international downswing had several stages. Broadly speaking, industrial production in most countries was falling in the second half of 1929. The decline in agricultural income began earlier, but was intensified by the decline in industrial production. The stock market crash in the United States speeded up the decline in that country in the fourth quarter of 1929. In the early months of 1930 there was a retardation of the decline in most countries, which proved to be short-lived, however, particularly because expectations of recovery were discouraged when prices of primary products collapsed.[3] A number of countries such as France and the United Kingdom, whose industrial production had not been greatly affected before mid-1930, now experienced sharp declines in output. The international downswing accelerated in the second half of 1930.

The increasingly serious problem of debtor countries producing primary products should be noted. The growing over-supply of a number of primary products led to rising stocks and falling prices in the late twenties. The decline in such prices accelerated in 1930. On both domestic and international markets, prices of manufactured commodities fell less than those

---

[2] In 1929 the United States accounted for 16 percent of world exports and 12 percent of world imports. Her share in imports of raw materials was far larger than this. The foreign loans floated in the United States in 1919-29 exceeded those floated in all other lending countries combined. See Department of Commerce, *United States in the World Economy*, pp. 5-6 and 29-31.

[3] Lewis appears to consider the disruption of primary commodity markets, due to an excess supply in relation to population growth and industrial production, as the most important factor in the problems of the thirties. See Lewis, *Economic Survey, 1919-1939*, pp. 196-7.

of primary commodities.[4] Moreover, long-term capital exports to such countries declined; those from the United States fell as early as mid-1928, while those from France and the United Kingdom fell in 1929 and 1930 respectively. Precisely when their export receipts were falling and their terms of trade deteriorating, the debtor countries were unable to cover their substantial import and foreign income payments by borrowing. This led not only to severe financial and other problems for such countries, but also to widespread cuts in imports of manufactured products and a growth of pressures contributing to the financial crisis of 1931. Along with the problems just noted, the plethora of restrictions on trade, set off by the Smoot-Hawley tariff and agricultural protectionism in Europe, greatly reduced the volume of international trade and speeded up the decline in prices of internationally traded commodities.

In spite of these unfavourable circumstances, a slight recovery began in several countries, including the United States and Canada, early in 1931. It soon faded, however, mainly because of the growing international financial crisis. International shifts in very large short-term balances were the main immediate factor in this crisis. These shifts, in turn, partly reflected some fundamental weaknesses in the international financial mechanism of the twenties. The crisis was also partly due to strains which developed in the downswing, particularly the sharp price declines already noted for primary export products. The greatest pressure from flights of capital developed after the failure of the largest Austrian bank in May 1931. This, in turn, raised doubts about the position of Germany, and much of the short-term capital loaned earlier to that country was withdrawn. The pressure shifted to the United Kingdom, particularly when doubts arose as to the liquidity of substantial short-term loans that country had made to Germany and other countries. Large outflows of gold forced the United Kingdom to abandon the gold standard on September 21, and sterling and a number of other currencies depreciated. Flight of capital and loss of gold from the United States followed, as well as internal drains, and led to tighter money conditions and a worsening of the situation of the banks in that country.

The general uncertainty and pessimism generated by the financial crisis of 1931 restricted domestic and foreign lending

---

[4] Both the over-supply and the inelasticity of supply of a number of primary products, especially agricultural products, were major factors in depressing prices. Other reasons for differential price changes are outlined on pp. 163-9 of League of Nations, *Course and Phases of the World Economic Depression*.

·even further, and the decline continued until about mid-1932. In the summer of that year a renewed expansion began in most countries. This time the expansion continued, so that the world recovery is generally dated from this period.[5]

The Downswing in Canada

Almost one-fifth of the labour force in Canada was without jobs and seeking work by 1933.[6] The severity of the downswing in Canada was related to three broad groups of factors. First, the international downswing was long and severe, with consequently sharp decreases in Canadian exports and income. Secondly, the downswing was accentuated by heavy rigid costs, financial abuses, over-expansion, and other legacies of the past. Thirdly, these and other factors led to a collapse of long-term profit expectations, which in turn led to a very severe collapse of domestic investment. Some aspects of the decline in consumption, and of government policy, were also significant. Before examining these factors individually, however, let us look briefly at the broad statistical picture.

Between 1929 and the low point in 1933 GNE fell by 42 per cent in current dollars. The sharpest percentage change was in domestic investment, which fell to 11 per cent of the 1929 level (or 18 per cent if inventories are excluded). Exports and imports of goods and services also fell drastically, although relatively less than investment did. Consumer expenditure was much more stable, while government expenditure showed the smallest relative decline. The decline in constant dollars was significantly less, except in some of the components of investment. This, of course, was a reflection of the severe price deflation which struck the economy, particularly through the serious fall in the price of Canadian exports.

The outstanding shifts in the composition of expenditures were the sharp fall in investment and, to a lesser extent, in exports, as a percentage of total expenditure, while consumer and government expenditures played a larger relative role because of their smaller relative decrease. Imports of goods and services fell more rapidly than exports, reflecting in part the severe decline in domestic investment. While international

---

[5] A further banking crisis in the United States took some series to further low points early in 1933, and adversely affected Canadian recovery as well. Developments in 1932 and early in 1933 are covered in detail in the next chapter.

[6] D.B.S., *Canadian Labour Force Estimates, 1931-1950*, p. 15.

transactions in goods and services were in balance by 1933, in contrast to substantial deficits earlier, this balance was achieved at a much lower level of transactions.

In terms of current dollars, GNE fell by 11 per cent in 1930.[7] The significant declines were in exports of goods and services and durable investment, each of which fell by a fifth; about half the decline in the former reflected price declines, while the fall in durable investment was almost wholly a fall in volume. Such declines in exports and investment, unless offset by strong and independent increases in consumer or government expenditure, can lead to magnified effects through the multiplier-accelerator model referred to earlier. Actually, expenditure by governments on goods and services rose sharply in 1930, and a large deficit took the place of the previous year's equality of revenue and expenditure. Consumer spending fell by only 4 per cent; personal saving (excluding change in farm inventory) fell by $325 million to $42 million in 1930.

These effects were not strong enough to offset the deflationary impact of sharply falling exports and domestic investment. The decline in GNE accelerated to 18 per cent in 1931, with exports and durable investment once more showing the largest relative decreases. The effects were now being felt more strongly elsewhere, however, for consumer expenditure fell sharply and government expenditure declined moderately. GNE continued to fall at about the same rate in 1932. Two significant points, to be elaborated later, should be noted. Government expenditure had risen in 1930 and fallen only slowly in 1931; it now fell sharply, particularly because of the completion of government investment projects and a cut in relief works. This lag in the completion of large projects also accounts for an exceptionally sharp fall in non-residential construction in 1932. The low point in the annual GNE was 1933, when the decrease was only 6 per cent, or one-third of the decreases in the two previous years.[8] A number of decreases

---

[7] See Tables 11 and 49 for data on GNE in the downswing. From 1928 to 1929 GNE rose by only 1 per cent in current dollars and was unchanged in constant dollars. As noted earlier, this reflected the sharp drop in exports of wheat and flour; other major components of GNE, including non-wheat exports, continued to rise.

[8] It is well to keep in mind here the limitations of annual data for short-term cyclical analysis. For example, although several series show decreases for 1933 as a whole, they could easily have been rising for a good part of the year. Many series fell in the first and fourth quarters of 1932 and 1933, but were rising rapidly in mid-1933. The annual data might show this only as a slower rate of fall in 1933 than in 1932.

Table 11

CHANGES IN GROSS NATIONAL EXPENDITURE, 1929-33

Component	1933 as a percentage of 1929		Components as a percentage of current dollar total	
	Current dollars	Constant dollars(a)	1929	1933
Consumer expenditure	65.7	82.9	71.2	81.3
Government expenditure	77.1(b)	84.1	11.1	14.8
Gross domestic investment				
Including inventories	11.3	10.5	22.6	4.4
Excluding inventories	18.0	21.1	21.6	6.7
Residential construction	30.8	39.3	4.0	2.1
Non-residential construction	16.3	19.6	7.9	2.2
Machinery and equipment	14.1	15.5	9.7	2.4
Exports of goods and services	50.6(c)	74.7	26.5	23.3
Merchandise only—				
excluding gold	45.2	73.3	19.1	15.0
Imports of goods and services	42.6	57.7	31.5	23.3
Merchandise only	28.9	43.3	20.6	10.4
Gross National Expenditure	57.6	70.7	100.0(d)	100.0(d)

SOURCES: *National Accounts,* Tables 2 and 3 p. 17. Volume of foreign trade derived from D.B.S., *Export and Import Price Indexes, 1926-1948.*

(a) 1935-9 dollars.

(b) 1933 as a percentage of the peak in 1930 was 69 per cent.

(c) The low in 1932 as a percentage of the peak in 1928 was 45 per cent.

(d) Does not total 100 per cent exactly because of rounding and residual error.

were less in absolute and relative terms than in the previous two years, including those in consumption, private investment in durable assets, and the change in inventory value. Two changes were notable. Export of goods and services actually rose in value by 3 per cent; with a further fall of imports of goods and services, the current account was approximately balanced. But while these comparatively favourable developments occurred, government expenditures on goods and services now fell more, relatively and absolutely, than in 1931 and 1932. Again this reflects in part the lag in decreases in government investment, with the result that its largest deflationary effect was felt in the year in which recovery was beginning. Combined government deficits had reached a peak in 1931; their size decreased, for both federal and provincial-municipal governments, in 1932 and especially in 1933.

The decline in exports reflected a sharp and extended drop in both prices and volume. Merchandise exports, excluding gold, were only 45 per cent of the 1929 level by 1933; in terms of constant dollars, they had fallen to 75 per cent of the 1929 level by 1933. The declines were larger if measured relative to the 1928 peak for exports. The basic elements in Canada's exports (including non-monetary gold) in the period 1926-9 are quite simply stated; agricultural and animal products were 58 per cent of the total, with wheat and flour alone accounting for 32 per cent of total Canadian exports; newsprint, wood pulp, and pulpwood were 15 per cent together; and non-ferrous metals and gold were 10 per cent. While ultimate consumers' goods bulked large in exports, and declined relatively less in volume than the producers' goods which dominated imports, the price situation in many of Canada's major exports was extremely weak.[9] Foodstuffs were subject to extreme price fluctuations because of the growing tendency to over-supply of cereals toward the end of the twenties, inability to decrease output in the downswing, and increased agricultural protectionism in the downswing and earlier. Newsprint was in a highly vulnerable price position as a result of over-expansion and the pricing structure of the industry. Industrial raw materials such as non-ferrous metals were subject to sharp declines in both price and volume, partly because of over-expansion in some items (such as copper), partly because of tariffs, but mainly because of the very sharp declines in industrial production and investment in export markets.

The greater decline in imports than in exports was primarily a reflection of the larger role of producers' goods in the former. In addition, a large number of Canadian imports of a highly manufactured or processed nature betrayed very little price fluctuation in the downswing. This was true, for example, of a whole range of items in the iron and products group, particularly for such important imports as machinery, equipment, and automobiles and parts.

[9] See Table 31 for the volume and price declines in exports and imports.

The decline in exports would lead, *ceteris paribus*, to a decline in income greater than the initial decline in exports. This would occur in three ways. First, in those export industries where investment was closely related to current sales, investment might be reduced – depending also on whether the drop was expected to continue and what was happening to other determinants of investment. With the drop in income and investment in the export industries, consumer respending would likely be affected; in turn, still other declines in investment might take place.[10] A third effect of the export decline was that it helped worsen the outlook for autonomous investment.

We must look more closely at the decline in domestic investment, and particularly at two questions. Why did the decline occur? Why was it so severe?

It was noted earlier that in the period before the war investment, on an annual basis, did not fall in response to two export declines. In 1920-1, moreover, extensive opportunities for investment existed to shorten the downswing, and a number of costs were quickly and sharply cut. In the early thirties the circumstances were quite different. The international collapse was severe and prolonged. Investment opportunities had been well exploited. In some respects, the boom of the twenties may not have been as strong as that before the war. Finally, many costs showed a high degree of rigidity.

One cannot, broadly speaking, attribute the initial decline in investment to a lack of foreign capital, since the inflow of long-term capital rose markedly in 1930. The lack of long-term capital from abroad was to have some restrictive effects later in the downswing; by that time, however, investment plans had already been sharply reduced. The reversal of total investment was related to two factors. The decline in wheat exports in 1929, and in other exports in 1930, reduced investment by the multiplier-accelerator process. This process would apply particularly to those older industries where the rate of growth had slowed and investment was more closely related to current sales – especially when it became evident that the decline in

10 Some idea of the extent of dependence of protected manufactures on sales to exporting regions can be derived from a study of sales of 23 manufacturing industries in Ontario and Quebec. In 1929, 18 per cent of their sales were in the Prairies, 5 per cent in British Columbia, and 6 per cent in the Maritimes. The remaining 71 per cent of domestic sales were in Ontario and Quebec, of course, but part would be to export industries in those provinces. See the *Rowell-Sirois Report*, Appendix III, p. 87.

sales was not temporary, and other determinants of investment (such as changes in costs) were unfavourable.

The other factor in the reversal of total investment was the drop of autonomous investment as long-term profit expectations worsened. This, in turn, was related to two broad sets of forces. One was the deterioration in the international situation, which became progressively worse as world industrial production, stock prices, and primary export prices fell; trade was restricted; and financial crises occurred. The internal impact of such changes was bound to be severe. The other point, which was emphasized in the study of the twenties, is that the expansion of some relatively new Canadian industries in the twenties was so rapid that, by the end of the period, there was no extensive backlog of investment opportunity. The decline in autonomous investment would have magnified effects on income, as did that in exports.

The above factors in the reversal of investment also suggest some of the reasons for the severity of the decline. Private investment in durable assets had risen from 15 per cent of GNE in 1926 to 22 per cent in 1929. An export economy which is subjected to a severe international collapse when investing so heavily will experience a considerable decrease in investment, both because of the effects of reduced exports on income and on economic prospects, and because of the postponable nature of much investment. These effects will be enhanced if heavy and rigid debts have been incurred (particularly to non-residents), other costs fall slowly, and speculation has led to financial abuses. They will be enhanced even further if the longer-term growth of some older industries has slowed, and investment opportunities in the newer industries have been heavily exploited. Analysis of the twenties, the exceptional severity of the fall in investment, and the fact that the subsequent recovery of investment was so incomplete – all suggest that much more was involved in the decline of investment than postponement because of reduced sales.

The above comments have not referred specifically to the role of inventories. An unplanned accumulation of business inventories occurred in 1930 as sales fell faster than output. With prices falling and expectations low, business men would attempt to reduce output below sales in order to decrease inventories; otherwise, large inventory losses would occur. Attempts to reduce inventories would, of course, put further pressure on prices and reduce employment and income. In fact, business men were not very successful in reducing inventories as sales fell faster than they anticipated, and farmers increased wheat acreage to offset lower prices and uncertain yields. In some agricultural and several raw material products, such as base metals, large world stocks accumulated with new acreage or new producers, and the existence of these helped depress world prices.

The above factors do not fully account for the extent of the decline. Closer attention must be given to two other aspects of the downswing, namely the uneven nature of decline (and the related rigidities) and the financial problems of the downswing.

It was the unevenness of decline which posed some of the most serious problems of the depression. The large decline in export and import prices was bound to lower internal prices in a country where such a large part of income was from foreign trade. This in itself would have created problems, for example, because of fixed debts and other relatively fixed costs. The fall of export prices was greater than that of import prices, which meant a deterioration in the terms of trade; in 1932 it took about 16 per cent more in volume of exports to buy the same volume of imports than in 1926 (and in 1929 approximately). This difference was, in effect, the higher cost of production, relative to sales prices, for the economy as a whole in relation to the rest of the world. Another very important consequence, related in part to the differing degree of fall in export and import prices, was the difficulty of meeting external debt charges. A very large part of the investment boom of the twenties in Canada was financed by borrowing from abroad in fixed-interest securities. From 1926 to 1930, fully 47 per cent of total interest paid on bonds and debentures was paid to non-residents.[11] In 1926-30 interest paid abroad was 10 per cent of total current account receipts; as current receipts fell, the ratio rose to 20 per cent in 1931-3.[12]

It is well to point out here that the problem of meeting fixed debt charges was by no means limited to the external charges. The external charges were an aspect of the over-all fixed debt incurred in Canada, which had serious consequences with falling prices and income no matter where it was held. It has been estimated, for example, that over one-fifth of all the capital in Canadian private industry was bonded debt, and that nearly

[11] D.B.S., *Canada's International Investment Position, 1926-1954*, p. 41. Footnote 25 below is also of interest here.
[12] The comparable ratios for interest and dividends paid abroad were 18 and 34 per cent respectively.

Table 12

PRICE CHANGES IN CANADA, 1926-37
(1926 = 100)

Index	1929	1933	1935	1936	1937	1933 as percentage of 1929
GNE, implicit price index	98.3	79.9	81.4	84.0	86.4	81.3
Wholesale prices						
Total	95.6	67.1	72.1	74.6	84.6	70.2
Consumers' goods	94.7	71.1	73.6	74.7	79.5	75.1
Producers' goods	96.3	63.1	69.5	72.4	86.1	66.5
Building and construction materials	99.0	78.3	81.2	85.3	94.4	79.1
Farm prices	100.8	51.0	63.5	69.4	87.1	50.6
Commodities and services used by farmers	97.6	72.7	76.0	77.4	82.3	74.5
Export prices	91.2	57.1	62.3	66.1	76.7	62.6
Import prices	90.5	64.5	67.1	68.3	75.0	71.3
Terms of trade	100.8	88.5	92.8	96.8	102.3	87.8

SOURCES: D.B.S., *Prices and Price Indexes, 1913-1940, Price Index Numbers of Commodities and Services used by Farmers, 1913-1948*, and *Export and Import Price Indexes, 1926-1948*.

30 per cent of prairie farm capital was borrowed at fixed charges.[13] What gave an added importance to the external debt was, first, its size relative to the total debt of Canadians; second, the fact that much of it was payable, at the holder's option, in foreign currencies at a time when the exchange rate had depreciated; and third, the fact that this occurred as part of a general situation of collapsed export prices and sales which led Canada into current account deficits, and when the terms of trade had shifted markedly against Canada.

There were other rigid charges. Farm wholesale prices fell more than all wholesale prices; this is another way of saying the terms of trade turned against the farmer. If prices for commodities and services used by farmers are considered, the comparison becomes more apt and the difficulties of farmers more apparent. An important reason for the differing behaviour of farm and non-farm prices lies, of course, in the organization

[13] *Rowell-Sirois Report*, Book I, pp. 146-7.

of the industries concerned. The farm industry has many units of production; it must compete, to an important degree, on world markets; mobility may be limited because of lack of alternative occupations, or because of the family structure of the enterprise. These factors make it difficult to control production.[14] In manufacturing, the opposite is frequently true. Oligopolistic market structures, centralized control, product rather than price competition, collusion, and other factors often lead to relatively little price competition. In the face of declining sales, output and employment are cut. In addition, much of Canadian manufacturing industry was protected by tariffs. These were increased sharply in 1930 and 1931, thus accentuating the tendency to greater price rigidity in this sector.

One further type of rigidity should be mentioned. The rigidity of wage rates was particularly evident in the first year or two of the downswing; not until 1932 did widespread cuts in wage rates appear in the annual data. Particularly notable, for present purposes, was the rigidity in rates in such sectors as the building and metal trades, which are of special importance in the costs of investment. The rise in most rates in 1930, when investment expectations were collapsing, was also notable. Prices of building and construction materials were also less flexible than other prices in the downswing. Prices of producers' equipment were even more inflexible.[15]

The significance of the rigidity in wage rates is difficult to gauge, particularly since no allowance has been made in the data for changes in productivity. The maintenance of wage rates tends to maintain purchasing power, but also keeps costs high. Which of these has the greater effect on income at any one time depends on a number of circumstances. In an open economy such as Canada's, moreover, one must take into account not only the net effect on domestic income, but also the related necessity of meeting export and import competition. If a major downswing is under way and is expected to continue, it is not likely that cuts in wage rates will have much effect in maintaining investment. They may have favourable effects on investment in the subsequent recovery, however, but only if a backlog of investment opportunities exists.[16] In any case, any

14 As noted in the industry studies in chapter VII, government intervention was unable to prevent a severe decline in wheat prices, given the large world stocks and the necessity of selling most of the Canadian crop on world markets.

15 See Tables 12 and 39.

16 See League of Nations, *Course and Phases of the World Economic Depression*, CHAP. VI, and Lewis, *Economic Survey*, p. 55.

positive effects which wage cuts might have had in the down-swing were considerably weakened by dragging them out over much of the downswing.

In view of the unevenness of decline, it is not surprising that within Canada there appeared very marked differences in ability to withstand the depression. Perhaps the best comment on these differences is that of the Rowell-Sirois Commission: "In Central Canada and Nova Scotia, where the amounts obtained from salaries and wages in tariff-protected industries and naturally sheltered occupations and from fixed interest investments were relatively the greatest, the total incomes fell least. In Western Canada, where the proportions of the receipts from export production were the highest, the total incomes fell most. The Prairie Provinces, almost wholly dependent upon the export of wheat, suffered the most severe declines."[17]

Another important factor in the degree of decline was the extent of monetary deflation. This was in part the inevitable consequence of the desire for liquidity. Consumers deferred purchases of major durables as incomes fell. Inventories were reduced where possible, in order to cut inventory price losses. These and similar reactions accentuated the decline in prices. Repayments to banks as loans fell due and the reduced demand for new loans would tend to raise cash reserves relative to deposits.[18] Companies lending on mortgages would also find fewer borrowers. These institutions, because of a lack of acceptable borrowers and because they were desirous of security in assets, turned increasingly to government bonds as investment outlets for their funds. In effect, funds were used increasingly to repay debt, to build a liquid position, or to finance government deficits, rather than to undertake physical investment. The rigidity of interest rates, and their rise after September 1931, cannot be considered the full measure of capital stringency. Not all borrowers could get funds at these rates, either in Canada or in New York. Funds were available, obviously, as several Dominion government issues in Canada in the downswing were over-subscribed, and the Dominion and some provincial gov-

---

[17] *Rowell-Sirois Report*, Book I, p. 150.

[18] The ratio of cash to Canadian deposits in commercial banks was virtually unchanged, at from 8.1-8.3 per cent, from 1929 to 1931. It was only in 1932 that it rose to 8.8 per cent (partly in response to government action) and to 9.9 per cent in the next year. Bank of Canada, *Statistical Summary, 1950 Supplement*, p. 7. There appears also to have been some pressure by the banks to reduce credit in the downswing. See Malach, *International Cycles*, pp. 38, 131-2.

ernments were able to borrow in New York. But not all borrowers would be considered such prime risks.

But more was involved in the monetary deflation than the desire for liquidity. The speculative nature of the last stages of the boom accentuated the extent of monetary deflation. Borrowing had been over-extended in a number of industries, and financial abuses had been common. In addition, the decline was accentuated by the exposure of weaknesses in monetary systems. Canada avoided a banking or monetary crisis, but not the effects of such crises elsewhere. The exchange rate did not depreciate until after the sterling crisis of 1931. Long-term interest rates in Canada were highly rigid in the first two years of the downswing. With the departure of sterling from gold, the Canadian dollar depreciated in terms of the United States dollar, but appreciated in terms of sterling. Bond prices fell and yields rose sharply. Apart from the general shock they gave to confidence in the financial markets, these two specific factors now further affected Canadian activity. The rise in yields meant that those who were attempting to borrow to complete projects found they were charged higher rates for new capital –

TABLE 13

INDEX NUMBERS OF SELECTED INTEREST RATES, 1929-37

	Long-term investments		Short-term investment	Private mortgage loans(b)
	Government bonds	Corporation bonds	Government bonds	
1929	100.0	100.0	100.0	100.0
1930	95.9	99.4	91.2	98.7
1931	93.9	106.2	82.9	95.8
1932	103.8	124.3	95.1	99.4
1933	93.3	122.2	77.7	96.8
1934	80.5	99.2	54.5	94.1
1935	72.6	89.6	42.9	85.8
1936	66.1	77.6	30.1	82.0
1937(a)	68.5	74.4	36.1	—

SOURCES: Stanley E. Nixon, "The Course of Interest Rates, 1929-1937," *CJEPS*, p. 422.

(a) Data for 1937 refer to first four months only.

(b) Private mortgage loan interest is a "weighted average of rates charged in Ontario and Montreal on new business and renewals by a representative company."

TABLE 14

DISPOSABLE INCOME AND CONSUMPTION, 1929-37
(Millions of dollars)

Item	1929	1933	1935	1936	1937
National income at factor cost	4,789	2,452	3,188	3.487	4,062
Add transfer payments	111	209	236	238	251
Add transfer portion of interest on public debt	143	174	176	176	173
Deduct earnings not paid to persons(a)	− 386	8	− 227	− 324	− 444
Equals personal income	4,657	2,843	3,373	3,577	4,042
Deduct personal direct taxes	− 68	− 69	− 80	− 95	− 112
Equals personal disposable income	4,589	2,774	3,293	3,482	3,930
Deduct consumer expenditures	− 4,393	− 2,887	− 3,243	− 3,457	− 3,777
Equals personal saving	196	− 113	50	25	153
Personal saving excluding change in farm inventories	325	− 80	51	81	164
Consumer expenditures					
Durable goods	387	150	229	259	313
Non-durable goods	2,459	1,609	1,830	1,962	2,154
Services	1,547	1,128	1,184	1,236	1,310

SOURCE: *National Accounts,* Tables 5 and 36.

(a) Includes undistributed corporation profits, withholding taxes, government investment income, adjustment on grain transactions, and employee contributions to social insurance and government pension funds.

and also with greater uncertainty in monetary markets found it more difficult to get funds. Where much financing had been undertaken earlier with interest or principle payable at the holder's option in two or more currencies, the holder (wherever he was) would now ask payment in the highest currency, namely, United States dollars.[19]

Finally, we must note what effects changes in income dis-

[19] The price level effects of depreciation may well have been positive, however. See p. 114.

tribution may have had in the downswing. Wages, salaries, and supplementary labour income rose from 61.1 to 72.5 per cent of net national income from 1929 to 1933. Accrued net income of farm operators from farm production fell sharply from 8.5 to 3.0 per cent in the same period, investment income from 17.5 to 12.2 per cent, while the share of non-farm unincorporated business in the national income was stable. If we restrict ourselves to the effects on the average and the marginal propensity to consume, and assume that both propensities to consume labour income are higher than for investment income, the increased share of labour was a stabilizing factor. To the extent that the increased share of labour income was at the cost of agriculture, because of such factors as increased tariff protection to manufacturers, it is difficult to say what the net effects were on consumption.

There were other important reasons for the relative maintenance of consumer purchases. Transfer payments, including relief and the transfer portion of interest on the public debt, rose in absolute as well as relative terms in the downswing. Personal saving was negative from 1931 to 1933 inclusive. Dividends paid to residents were well maintained until 1932. The diversion from personal income in the form of personal direct taxes was constant, however. Finally, while purchases of durable goods, which can be most easily postponed, fell sharply, the declines in purchases of non-durables and particularly of services were more moderate. The durables content of consumer expenditures had probably risen in the late twenties as automobile sales rose, but the movements in the other types of consumer expenditures still dominated the total.

The decline in investment income reached its low point in 1932, a year before the low point for most of the components of GNE (including that for gross domestic investment). This point is worth investigating further because of the reliance of investment, in part, on the level of investment income. The volatile sector of investment income was corporation profits. Undistributed corporation profits actually became negative, as shown in Table 38. While corporation profits before taxes fell violently from 1929 to 1932, several of the charges against these profits maintained a remarkable stability. Income taxes were one-eleventh of corporation profits in 1929 and twice as large as corporation profits in 1932. As just noted, dividends to residents of Canada were well maintained until as late as 1932. Dividends to non-residents, which are not included in investment income, formed the largest charge against corporation profits; such dividends were well maintained until as late as 1933.[20]

As to the immediate factors behind the decline in corporation profits, it is interesting to consider the effects of changes in inventory book values on the change in profits. Changes in the prices of inventory stocks on hand at the beginning of a period will affect corporation profits, and also affect net income of unincorporated business. By means of an inventory valuation adjustment, one can measure that part of the change in inventory book values which is due to changes in prices of inventories on hand at the beginning of each period.[21] During the three years 1930-2, corporation profits and net income of non-farm unincorporated business fell by $776 million. Falling prices of inventories on hand apparently accounted for $473 million of this decline.

Government Policies in the Downswing

The government had to restrict gold outflows before the depression got under way.[22] While there were outflows of monetary gold (and a drawing down of external bank assets) late in the upswing, banks in Canada were able to maintain their reserves by borrowing Dominion notes under the terms of the Finance Act. In spite of a larger current deficit in 1930, the exchange rate did not depreciate — principally because of heavy net borrowing abroad through security issues, which were twice the level of the previous year. Canadian governments and corporations in 1930 were completing many projects

[20] The tendency to maintain dividends to the public in a downswing has been noted in other cycles. The maintenance of dividends for a time in this case may reflect in part the nature of the financing of the upswing. It has been estimated that 57 per cent of the share capital subscribed by the Canadian public in 1927-9 was for preferred shares, about 23 per cent for class A shares, and only 20 per cent for common shares. See K. G. H. Smails, "Corporation Finance and Company Law Reform," *Papers and Proceedings of the Canadian Political Science Association*, p. 156. The maintenance of dividends to non-residents may have been affected by the parent-subsidiary relationship, in that the subsidiary would not have to retain as much for future financing needs since it could secure funds later from the parent.

[21] In other words, the change in the book value of total inventories exclusive of the current value of the change in the stock of inventories in that year. The farm sector is excluded. Data derived from various tables in *National Accounts*. See also Table 21, and footnote 27, CHAP. IV.

[22] See Table 51 on the balance of payments.

undertaken earlier, and, as in previous years, had turned to the United States market for capital. While the current deficit continued on a smaller scale into 1931, the Canadian dollar continued to retain its parity with its trading partners until the devaluation of sterling in September 1931.

From September 1931 until the devaluation of the United States dollar in 1933 the Canadian dollar moved between sterling and the United States dollar, having appreciated in terms of sterling and depreciated in terms of the United States dollar. It was roughly half-way between these two currencies, thus effecting for a time something of a compromise to one dilemma which faced the Dominion government.

The policy alternatives facing the government in the downswing can be summarized as follows.[23] Monetary policy as known in some other countries simply did not exist. There was no central bank, no well-developed money market in which to conduct vast open-market operations or use the rediscount rate. Under the Finance Act the Department of Finance could advance Dominion notes to the banks on the deposit of approved securities. By adjusting the rediscount rate some control over borrowing would result, when banks wished to borrow. In the fall of 1932 an attempt was made to increase credit facilities. Through advances under the Finance Act, $35 million was added to bank reserves. The lending capacity of banks was raised, but current public loans of the banks continued to fall.

In terms of monetary policy, the immediate effective sphere of action which lay open to the government was in exchange rate policy. Here the issues were extremely complex, both before and after September 1931. A policy of depreciation is of doubtful value if considered solely as an instrument for (further) improving the trade balance, particularly in the unsettled circumstances of the downswing.[24] Such a policy can

23 For monetary policy and its limitations, see especially pp. 151-60 of the *Rowell-Sirois Report*, Book I: A. F. W. Plumptre, "Currency Management in Canada," *Proceedings of the Canadian Political Science Association*; and D. A. MacGibbon, "Inflation and Inflationism," *CJEPS*.

24 Thus Marcus finds that the domestic activity of Canada's main customers, rather than currency depreciation, was the main determinant of Canada's exports in various periods of the downswing. He adds, however, that currency depreciation tended to moderate internal deflationary pressures; removed the need for deflationary policies to protect the dollar; and moderated the competitive disadvantage Canada would have suffered with respect to depreciated currencies. See Marcus, *Canada and the International Business Cycle*, pp. 24-5 and CHAP. IV. See also pp. 118-21 herein.

also be regarded, however, as an attempt to moderate the fall in the level of domestic prices, or as a means of distributing the burdens of the downswing more evenly between the export and sheltered industries, or even as a more flexible alternative to increased tariffs. The difficulties in the way of any deliberate policy of depreciation were considerable; heavier import and debt costs would result;[25] any unorthodox monetary measures were regarded with suspicion by the financial community and large segments of the business community, not to mention the government;[26] and there was the likelihood of large capital outflows if confidence was seriously impaired, and also of deterioration in the current account to the extent that measures to retard the fall in income in Canada were successful while incomes abroad were still falling. On the other hand, with relatively fixed costs and falling export sales and prices, some important sectors of the economy (especially the Prairies) were in an impossible condition. Purchasing power was sharply reduced in these export industries and, in turn, purchases from domestic manufactures were reduced. It was argued that if the burdens of the downswing could be more equally distributed, some impetus

[25] The Canadian financial market was closely linked to those of New York and London. The first official estimates of non-resident ownership of funded debt of Canadian governments and corporations are for 1936. They show Dominion direct and guaranteed debt held by non-residents was 24 per cent of the total; provincial direct and guaranteed, 28 per cent; municipals, 25 per cent; all steam railway debt, 63 per cent; other corporations, 39 per cent; and all Canadian funded debt, 34 per cent. These proportions include bonded debt of foreign direct investments in Canada. The proportions would be somewhat higher at the beginning of the upswing. See D.B.S., *Canadian Balance of International Payments* (1939), p. 42. See also p. 50. About 55 per cent of Canada's bonded debt in the early thirties had an external payment feature of some kind. An important proportion of this was held in Canada, however; in this case depreciation, while still involving higher costs to the debtor, would not directly affect the Canadian exchange position. See W. T. G. Hackett, "Canada's Optional Payment Bonds," *CJEPS*.

[26] In describing the attempt in 1932 to increase bank reserves by $35 million, for example, the Prime Minister stated: "After having proved our ability to ride the storm, I feel that we are justified—to the very limited degree necessary in our case—in joining other countries in the adoption of monetary measures designed to encourage recovery. However, any broad action along this line is unnecessary and, as I have stated frequently on previous occasions, this country will not depart from the established principles of sound money." Canada, *Official Report of Debates, House of Commons*, 23-24 George V, 1933, pp. 927-8.

to revival might occur.[27] Furthermore, if import costs rose with depreciation, the tariff could be lowered and protection would be unchanged.

We shall not attempt to resolve this controversy, but a few points are worth noting. The alternatives in an open economy were more limited than those elsewhere. In the absence of instruments of control, monetary policy was broadly limited to the exchange rate, and even in this case the repercussions were complex. If efforts had been made to supply large credits at home at low rates, this would not have meant sufficient borrowers would have appeared. Clearly, monetary policy would have to be combined with government spending on a large scale to take effect. And for the important export industries only measures designed to increase export sales (including the retention of competitive costs) could be of lasting aid.

Depreciation as a policy depends partly on timing; after the United Kingdom left the gold standard, such a policy might have entailed less loss of confidence.[28] Policies designed to increase employment in Canada would also spill over into imports, although this effect would be limited by the higher tariffs already in existence and the exchange depreciation itself. Furthermore, public works would presumably be concentrated in fields with few import requirements, such as housing, in order to avoid problems in the balance of payments. Finally, although some of these problems would be severe in a downswing if Canada was out of step with her trading partners, there would be more scope in the upswing, when other countries undertook such policies and when current account surpluses existed to absorb some of the balance of payments effects. In an open economy, policy considerations involve not only avoiding getting out of step too much with other countries, but also taking advantage of developments elsewhere in timing one's own policies. Actually, comparatively little was done along these lines in the upswing. For one of the most serious obstacles

[27] Presumably the marginal propensity to consume of the depressed export areas, especially agriculture, was assumed to be greater than in eastern manufactures. This might have been the case if policies were designed to direct income to farmers rather than to creditors in manufacturing industries; it need not have been the case if they directed incomes to farmers from factory workers.

[28] See G. A. Elliott in his review of *Dominion Monetary Policy 1929-1934*, by F. A. Knox, *CJEPS*. Depreciation at that time would mitigate the deflationary effects of the appreciation of the Canadian dollar over sterling, which reduced Canadian dollar receipts from sterling sales.

to such policies was the fear of unorthodox monetary experiments, and particularly the damage which might result from any loss of confidence in the Canadian financial structure.

The main effort made by the government to offset deflationary forces was the use of the tariff.[29] In 1930-1 there was a sharp increase in protection. A partial retreat from this policy occurred in the extension of Imperial preferences in 1932, and more generally in the trade treaties with the United States and United Kingdom in the second half of the thirties.

The agricultural protectionism of the Smoot-Hawley tariff in 1930, duties on other Canadian products, and special United States duties on lumber and copper in 1932, struck severe blows at many Canadian industries. The Liberal government had already taken retaliatory action in 1930, but the newly elected Conservative government embarked on a frankly protectionist policy which emphasized not only retaliation but also the prevention of distress sales of United States and other merchandise in Canada and the maintenance of employment. The development of a favourable balance of trade and defence of the value of the Canadian dollar were also mentioned later.

A wide range of manufacturing industries was given sharply increased rates of duty, including the entire textiles and iron and steel schedules.[30] A number of agricultural products also received higher rates of duty. Administrative devices, and many more of the specific duties which bore heavily with falling prices, greatly enhanced the effect of rate increases. Arbitrary valuations were widely used, and the maximum dumping duty of 15 per cent ad valorem was raised to 50 per cent. A special excise tax was adopted for imports. Even many of the preferential rates were raised.

The effects were widespread. The major ones, for present purposes, were:

(1) The tariff accentuated the tendency to greater price rigidity in the manufacturing industries as compared to the industries producing primary goods. A larger share of the burden of the downswing was thrown on to the exposed regions, to be met, in part, by such expedients as contributions by the federal government to the CNR deficits and by relief transfers

[29] For tariff policy and its effects, see especially: McDiarmid, *Commercial Policy in the Canadian Economy*, CHAPS. XII-XVI; *Rowell-Sirois Report*, Appendix III, pp. 83-96; and Parkinson, *Memorandum on the Bases of Canadian Commercial Policy*, CHAPS. II-VI.

[30] McDiarmid, *Commercial Policy in the Canadian Economy*, pp. 272-7.

to provincial and municipal governments. A combination of factors affected income distribution by groups, of course. But it is worth noting that the share of national income received by farmers and workers in export industries fell from 23 per cent in 1929 to 12 per cent in 1932; that of workers in protected industries rose from 14 per cent to 15 per cent; and that of workers in service industries and others protected by natural factors rose from 29 per cent to 35 per cent.[31]

(2) The tariffs and other measures helped to preserve a greater share of the home market for protected industries. It has been estimated that the ratio of imports to gross value of production for manufactures was 25 per cent in 1928, 13 per cent in 1933, and only 14 per cent in 1936 (four years after the Imperial preferences of 1932, and one year after the trade treaty with the United States).[32] This does not necessarily mean that over-all output in Canada was higher than it would otherwise have been. To the extent that the tariff led to relatively higher and more rigid prices in the protected sector, some decrease in total sales must be regarded as an offset to any direct maintenance or gain in output and employment from the tariff.[33] Another offset would be loss of exports through retaliation and relatively higher costs. Finally, there is the loss from uneconomic allocation of resources, fostered by increased tariffs.

It seems clear that the tariff was able to secure a greater share of the domestic market for Canadian manufacturers, though a price had to be paid for this. It is also clear that the tariff was unable to prevent large decreases in output, employment, and investment in protected industries. The volume of manufacturing production fell by one-third from 1929 to 1933. Investment in manufacturing fell by 90 per cent from 1929 to 1933 and rose to only 37 per cent of the 1929 level in 1937.

31 The share of the last group would rise because of natural protection offered by cost of transportation, by strong growth in some cases, and by limited fluctuations in demand for necessities. The statistics are from the *Rowell-Sirois Report*, Book I, p. 149.

32 *Rowell-Sirois Report*, Appendix III, p. 94. The absolute size of the ratios does not necessarily measure the relative importance of imports and domestic output, but changes in the ratios should be significant. Part of the change would reflect changes in the composition of output and imports, related particularly to differing levels of those types of investment which have a high import content.

33 For an analysis of this point, see V. W. Bladen, "Tariff Policy and Employment in Depression," *CJEPS*.

Its proportion of total private investment was 29 per cent in 1926-9 and 19 per cent in 1934-7.[34] In one of the most heavily protected industries, textiles, the volume of output fell by only 10 per cent from 1929 to 1932. But in iron and steel products, which were also given a very large increase in protection, volume fell by 60 per cent. Where producers' or consumers' durables were involved, the tariff could not prevent violent fluctuations in output and investment.[35]

(3) Finally, the tariff changes did attract more subsidiaries and branches of foreign companies to Canada as well as lead to some extensions of existing subsidiaries and branches and to a somewhat larger Canadian content to their manufactures. The rate of entry of United States firms, and affiliations with Canadian companies, increased rapidly in 1930-4. It has been estimated that 26 per cent of all American-controlled or affiliated companies in 1934 had been established or acquired since 1930.[36] Although several factors were important, the most influential was undoubtedly the tariff increases.[37] Many of these companies, of course, just leased idle plant rather than set up new plant, but the effects of this on output and employment were important in several fields of manufacturing.

The tariff, while it gave protection to certain areas in Ontario and Quebec especially, could not be expected to solve the problems of the export industries. Indeed, it aggravated them. It was only as a result of the Ottawa Agreements of 1932, the broader trade treaties of the second half of the thirties, and (most important) the beginning of world recovery that these industries could begin to prosper.

Other efforts by the federal government were largely designed to meet the immediate needs of unemployment relief or to aid a few specific industries, rather than to undertake any large contra-cyclical policy. These measures will be considered later.[38] At this point, it is instructive to take an over-all look at

[34] The picture is not greatly changed if pulp and paper and non-ferrous metals are removed from manufacturing.

[35] See McDiarmid, *Commercial Policy in the Canadian Economy*, CHAP. XIV, for a study of the degree of success in maintaining output in several protected industries.

[36] Marshall, Southard, and Taylor, *Canadian-American Industry*, p. 21.

[37] *Ibid.*, p. 199.

[38] Wheat policy is dealt with on pp. 195-200. For government spending on relief works and direct relief, see p. 155. The comments which follow are mainly intended to give an over-all picture of all three levels of government together. For the pattern by levels of government, see Table 28 and D.B.S., *Government Transactions related to the National Accounts, 1926-1951*.

the government sector of the economy, as shown in Table 28. Expenditures by governments, net of transfers to other governments, actually rose in 1930 and 1931. Even at their lows in 1933, both federal and provincial-municipal expenditures were relatively close to the 1929 levels.[39] Judging from these figures alone, government expenditures exercised a comparatively stabilizing influence in the downswing, particularly in its early years. Since revenues fell in 1930 and 1931, while expenditures were rising, substantial deficits occurred in these years. Again, other things being equal, the effect would be stabilizing.[40] In 1932, expenditures fell faster than revenues, and in 1933 revenues rose as expenditures continued to fall; in both years, accordingly, the deficit fell. Thus, although the change in deficits was contra-cyclical in the early part of the decline, at the trough it was the reverse.

Government expenditures can be broken down into purchases of goods and services, transfer payments, and subsidies. The second of these rose sharply each year from 1929 to 1933, mainly because of larger payments for interest and relief. Expenditures on goods and services rose in 1930 and fell thereafter through 1933, mainly because of a decline of $142 million in purchases of goods and services from business from 1929 to 1933 – a drop of almost 50 per cent. Fully $100 million of this decline represented a drop in direct government investment, a drop accounted for equally by each of the three levels of government. This figure excludes government-owned enterprises, which are in the private sector of investment. Investment by these enterprises fell even more precipitously.[41] It is obvious that government expenditures as a contra-cyclical force suffered from some of the same problems which appeared in the busi-

[39] If transfers to other governments are included, federal expenditures rose from $340 million in 1929 to a peak of $387 million in 1931, then declined to $359 million in 1933.

[40] The net effect of government spending would take into account the net change in deficits. But allowance would have to be made also for types of taxes and types of expenditures, the effects on private investment of the sharp rise in taxes as a percentage of business income, and how the deficits were financed.

[41] Investment in durable assets between 1929 and 1933 fell as follows by sectors: business and institutions, by $788 million to a 1933 total of $141 million; housing, by $171 million to $76 million; direct government investment, by $100 million to $88 million (the decline was $145 million if the peak in 1930 is used); government-owned enterprises, by $132 million to $22 million. About $100 million of the decline in this last group was in federal government enterprises, and almost all of this was due to public steam railways.

ness sector, namely problems of maintaining investment in physical assets. With the completion of specific projects of various governments such as the Hudson Bay Railway and roads, and with the switch from works relief to direct relief in 1932, the government investment sector fell sharply.

Rising transfer payments for interest and relief offset part of the decline in government investment.[42] In contrast to other types of transfer payments, a large portion of the transfer content on the public debt is paid to financial institutions and might result (in the first instance) in a greater propensity to save.[43] Interest on the public debt as a percentage of national income rose from 5 per cent in 1929 to 11.5 per cent in 1933. The stimulating effect of government expenditures from this source might not have been as great as appear at first sight, therefore, unless offset by personal loans of banks and insurance companies. Furthermore, an important part of interest payments went to non-residents, with no effect on Canadian spending.

Thus investment by governments was increased in 1930 and was still at the 1929 level in 1931, but was cut sharply in the years 1932-3 when a revival was beginning. The deficits they incurred were the result of falling revenues while investment projects were being completed, relief and interest costs rose, and wage and salary payments were relatively slow in falling. Statements by officials make it clear such deficits were considered unfortunate necessities rather than deliberate policy. The business and financial community at large was critical of them.

Canada was fortunate in not running into banking difficulties of the type experienced elsewhere.[44] A number of factors account for the remarkable strength of the banking system. The banks in Canada were large branch banking systems, which were able to muster a great deal of both experience and

---

[42] Interest on public debt incurred to finance existing real assets is included in government expenditures on goods and services. The larger part of public interest was incurred for such "nonproductive" purposes as war or relief and is included in transfer payments.

[43] See D.B.S., *Government Transactions related to the National Accounts, 1926-1951,* p. 5.

[44] For the structure of the banking system and reasons for its strength, see Canada, *Report of the Royal Commission on Banking and Currency in Canada;* Bank of Nova Scotia, *Monthly Review,* March 1933; and Canadian Bank of Commerce, *Monthly Commercial Letter,* December 1932.

reserves in each bank. Uniform federal legislation and strict inspection, along with stiff requirements to start a bank, ensured that small and weaker banks could not be started or survive. The banking business was commercial, rather than land or industrial. Since, in practice, their liabilities were largely payable on demand, banks were not allowed to tie up their funds in longer term or non-liquid loans, including real estate loans. Their non-liquid investments were generally in the highest grades of securities, and the securities they helped underwrite were mainly government bonds and a few high-grade corporates. Furthermore, they effected an early and sharp liquidation of security loans after the stock market crash. Finally, they had recourse under the Finance Act to Dominion notes, on the pledge of suitable public securities. They could easily expand their cash balances, therefore, if loans rose or if they faced large withdrawals.[45]

It was noted earlier that the federal government did not undertake any large schemes to ameliorate the financial liquidation of the downswing. The discount rate on advances under the Finance Act was kept at 4.5 per cent until late in 1931. It was reduced then to 3 per cent, raised once more in the first half of 1932 to 3.5 per cent, and reduced again in May 1933 to 2.5 per cent.[46] No attempt was made to depreciate the Canadian dollar throughout the downswing – indeed, such a policy was regarded by the government as detrimental to Canada's credit abroad. In late 1932, however, a moderate attempt to increase the credit base was undertaken under the Finance Act, but, without new borrowings in excess of repayments, bank loans continued to fall.

The presence of a strong banking system did not mean, however, that Canada could avoid the repercussions of financial problems abroad. The financial problems of the United Kingdom led to the effects on the interest rate and exchange rate already noted, and gave à considerable shock to the international community. The depressing effects of banking difficulties in the United States will be mentioned shortly.

---

[45] They were not required at that time to keep any prescribed minimum cash reserves, but in practice kept about 10 per cent.

[46] Changes in this rate would not necessarily affect the interest rate structure in the sense in which this was true of countries with highly developed money markets. Nevertheless, from the point of view of contra-cyclical policy as now understood, it would be difficult to justify this pattern of rates.

TABLE 15

FLUCTUATIONS IN INDUSTRIAL PRODUCTION AND NATIONAL INCOME, SELECTED COUNTRIES, 1929-37 (1929 = 100)

Country	Industrial production 1932	1937	National income 1932	1937
Australia	—	—	76	116
Austria	61	103	83	78
Belgium	69	96	73(b)	95(b)
Canada A	58	100	—	—
B(a)	65	112	55	85
Chile	87	132	—	—
Czechoslovakia	64	96	84	89
Denmark(b)	91	136	88	124
Finland	83	156	81	139
France	77	83	84	102-122
Germany	58	116	59	97
Greece	101	151	98	152
Hungary	82	130	69	87
Italy	67	100	—	—
Japan	98	171	84	139
Netherlands	84	103	75	79
New Zealand	109	126	—	—
Norway	93	130	—	—
Poland	63	109	—	—
Roumania	89	132	—	—
Sweden	89	149	83	125
Union of South Africa	—	167(c)	91	146
United Kingdom	83	124	85	111
United States(d)	53	103	48	84
U.S.S.R.	183	424	—	—
World, excluding U.S.S.R.	64	104	—	—

SOURCES: Industrial production indexes are from League of Nations, *World Production and Prices, 1938-40*, p. 39. National income indexes derived from United Nations, *Statistics of National Income and Expenditure*, Appendix Table A.

(a) The B series for industrial production in Canada excludes building and electric power; the former has a weight of 16 in the A series. A few of the older series for industrial production include a small building component.

(b) 1930 = 100.

(c) 1936.

(d) National income data are those of the United States Department of Commerce. The revised index for industrial production is used. The unrevised figures, 54 and 92, entered the world index.

International Comparisons of the Downswing

Comparisons of industrial production by countries suffer from the differing coverage of the indexes. The Canadian index, for example, includes construction with a weight of 16, a factor which depressed the index considerably in the downswing. Data on national income are more inclusive, but concepts and methods of computation differ widely here too, and fewer countries possess series for earlier years. There are differing peaks and troughs by countries, moreover; if allowance were made for this, the statements below would be modified somewhat.

The broad picture is clear enough, however. From 1929 to 1932, industrial production declined by 35 per cent in Canada (measured by an index which excludes construction and electric power). Only five of the twenty-one other countries shown in Table 15 experienced a more severe decline in industrial production between these years, namely Austria, Germany, Czechoslovakia, Poland, and the United States. Although the decline in Canada appears to have been about the same as that for the "world" as a whole (excluding the U.S.S.R.), it should be noted that the severity of the decline in the United States would have a large effect on the total index because of the weight of the United States in total industrial production. The fact is that, judging from industrial production, a large number of countries felt the effects of the downswing more moderately than did Canada.

Data on national income accentuated this conclusion. In the seventeen countries shown, only the United States experienced a more severe decline from 1929 to 1932. A comparison of national incomes shows a relatively more depressed picture for Canada than does a comparison of indexes of industrial production, primarily because the large and severely depressed agricultural and construction industries are included in the former measure.

Two questions are particularly relevant for our analysis. First, why was the Canadian downswing so severe compared to those of other countries? A complete answer cannot be given short of studying carefully the fluctuations in other countries. In a later chapter, however, when the reasons for the severity of the collapse and the incompleteness of the recovery of Canada are summarized, some of the possible answers to this question will be brought out. Secondly, how did the downswing in Canada compare with those in the two countries which most directly affect it? In particular, the fairly similar declines in aggregative series for Canada and the United States, and the predominant role that country had attained in Canada's foreign economic transactions, suggest a closer comparison of their experience is warranted.

TABLE 16

COMPARATIVE INDEXES FOR CANADA, THE UNITED STATES, AND THE UNITED KINGDOM, 1933 AND 1937.
(1929 = 100)

Index	Canada 1933	1937	U.S.A. 1933	1937	U.K. 1933	1937
GNP	58	87	54	87	—	—
GNP, constant dollars	71	98	72	102	—	—
National income	51	85	45	84	89	111
Industrial production	71(a)	112(a)	63	103	88	124
Minerals	90	154	71	104	79	94
Manufacturing	68	105	62	103	90	127
Construction expenditures	21	50	15	47	115(b)	152(b)
Wholesale prices	70	89	69	91	63	80

SOURCES: Data on GNP, national income, and construction expenditures for Canada were derived from *National Accounts,* Tables 2 and 3; those for the United States from U.S., Department of Commerce, *National Income: A Supplement to the Survey of Current Business,* pp. 146, 150 and 158. U.K. national income is from A. R. Prest, "National Income of the United Kingdom, 1870-1946," *Economic Journal.* Industrial production is from League of Nations, *World Production and Prices, 1938-39,* p. 39, and the components are from various issues of the *Statistical Year Book*: the U.S. index is the revised index.

(a) To ensure greater comparability, the index of industrial production for Canada is shown exclusive of construction and electricity.

(b) Represents value of building permits.

The statistical picture present in Table 16 indicates the

United Kingdom experienced a much more moderate decline than did Canada and the United States. The downswing in Canada was only a little less severe than that in the United States.[47]

The relative mildness of depression in the United Kingdom can be linked largely to the more moderate pace of the preceding upswing and the relatively small decline in construction.[48] The United Kingdom did not experience violent fluctuations of investment to the extent that Canada did. Some investment demand was carried over into the thirties; this was particularly true in housing which, in addition, received subsidies and other government aid. Special problems of adjustment faced several important industries, such as coal, but output in many industries was only moderately interrupted.[49] This does not mean the United Kingdom did not suffer from the downswing. There was a considerable amount of unemployment before the thirties, reflecting mainly the stagnation of her export industries; even a moderate decline in such circumstances would create great hardship. Her exports were reduced by half in the downswing from levels which had been none too high.

If one looks at the four main sectors of GNE, only on government account was the decline in the United States more moderate than that in Canada. Since the components of GNE occupied different proportions of the 1929 total in the two countries, however, one must also ask what proportion of the over-all decline in GNE was contributed by each component. A striking difference between the downswings in the two countries, as shown in Table 17, was that gross domestic investment contributed much more to the decline in GNE in Canada than it did in the United States. (This difference was due to investment in non-residential construction and producers' durables; the percentage decline in residential construction after 1929 was far greater in the United States than in Canada, and the difference is accentuated if the 1925-6 peak for such construction in the United States is used.) In an earlier chapter it was noted that gross domestic investment, which is the most volatile major component of GNE, formed a far larger proportion

---

[47] The same conclusion was reached by Malach, *International Cycles*, pp. 34 and 91.

[48] For an analysis of the downswing in the United Kingdom, see particularly Schumpeter, *Business Cycles*, pp. 954-71. See also Lewis, *Economic Survey*, CHAP. V.

[49] Schumpeter, *Business Cycles*, p. 963.

of GNE in Canada than in the United States in the last half of the twenties. In considering the extent to which the declines in investment in the two countries affected income and employment, however, one point must be kept in mind. Canada imports a much larger proportion of the supply of commodities available for domestic use than does the United States. A large part of the decline in Canadian investment in machinery and equipment in particular would directly affect foreign (mainly United States) rather than Canadian income and employment. No precise measure can be given of the effects on domestic income and employment. If, however, the direct import content of Canadian expenditures for machinery and equipment is assumed to be 35 per cent, and that for construction 10 per cent, it still appears that the percentage contribution of such investment to the decline in domestic output was considerably greater for Canada than for the United States.[50]

The government sector also made a greater contribution to over-all decline in Canada than in the United States.[51] It was noted earlier that the decline in investment by Canadian governments was particularly large. The decline in consumer expenditures was greater in the United States, however, in part because of the greater role of durables in total consumer expenditures in that country. The decline in expenditures on consumer durables from 1929 to 1933 accounted for 12 per cent and 9 per cent of the total decline in GNE in the United States and Canada respectively.[52]

One point which deserves comment is the relative role of international transactions in the downswing. The data as presented here might suggest Canada fared better than the United States in this respect. Canada had large deficits in her current international transactions in 1929 and 1930, but these deficits had disappeared by 1933; there appears, therefore, to have been an offset of fully 12 per cent to the decline in the other compo-

[50] This conclusion would be strengthened if some (presumably small) allowance for the direct import content of United States investment was also made. For the direct import content of certain types of Canadian expenditures in 1929, see p. 8. Presumably the proportions would be somewhat smaller in the downswing, as a result of higher tariffs.

[51] Government enterprises are treated differently in the two sets of accounts, but the statement is not invalidated by this. See Table 18, footnote (c).

[52] Such durables probably have a large import content in Canada, so that the effects of the decline on domestic income would be somewhat less in Canada than is implied by these ratios. See also footnote 109 in chapter II.

TABLE 17

COMPARISON OF THE DECLINE IN GROSS NATIONAL EXPENDITURE, CANADA AND THE UNITED STATES, 1929-33(*a*)

Component	1933 as a percentage of 1929		Percentage contribution to decline in GNE	
	Canada	U.S.A.	Canada	U.S.A.
Consumer expenditure	65.7	58.8	58.3	67.7
Domestic investment	11.3	8.3	47.2	30.2
Residential construction(*b*)	30.8	11	6.6	5.2
Non-residential construction	16.3	17	15.6	8.7
Machinery and equipment	14.1	27.7	19.6	9.7
Inventories	− 134.8	− 103.6	6.0	1.0
Government expenditures	77.1(*c*)	93.9	6.0	1.0
Foreign investment	(*d*)	19.5	+ 12.0	1.3
Exports of goods and services	50.6(*e*)	38.9	31.2	9.9
Imports of goods and services	42.6	37.2	+ 43.2	+ 8.5
Gross National Expenditure	57.6	53.7	100.0	100.0

SOURCES: Derived mainly from data appearing in the official *National Accounts* publications noted in the previous table. The United States export and import series are from U.S., Department of Commerce, *The United States in the World Economy*. United States residential construction is from Gordon, *Business Fluctuations*, p. 374. The data are the current dollar series for both countries. Some rounding has been necessary, particularly in the construction components of GNE for the United States.

(*a*) There are a number of conceptual differences in the two sets of accounts. Inventories in the Canadian data represent changes in book values, except in agriculture, while United States data show the value of the physical change. See also Table 18, footnote (*c*). For these and other differences, see the sources mentioned above.

(*b*) It should be noted that the peak for residential non-farm construction in the United States was 1925-6. The relevant data for 1926, 1929, and 1933, in billions of dollars, are 4.5, 2.8, and 0.3.

(*c*) 1933 was 69 per cent of 1930.

(*d*) From a substantial deficit to balance. The corresponding figure for the United States indicates a sharp reduction in her current international surplus.

(*e*) 1932 was 45 per cent of 1928.

nents of GNE. But to stop at the current balance would be extremely misleading, for the levels of total current receipts and payments are very relevant to discussions of changes in output and employment. The extent of decline in such transactions was greater for the United States than for Canada, but the place of such transactions in the two countries is quite different. Exports of goods and services amounted to 27 per cent of GNE in Canada in 1929, and about 30 per cent in 1926-8; imports of goods and services amounted to about 30 per cent of GNE throughout the four years. Exports and imports of goods and services in the United States were only 7 per cent and 6 per cent respectively of GNE in 1929. The decline in international transactions had an impact on Canada which could hardly be duplicated in the United States. While Canada's current account deficits had disappeared by 1933, the severe effects on output and employment continued as long as the over-all level of transactions remained low.

The two major points which stand out in a comparison with the United States, accordingly, are the greater contribution of business investment in construction and durables to the decline in Canada, and the differing impact of the falling level of international transactions. If one turns to activity by industry, some further points arise. In seven of the eleven groups shown in Table 18, and in total, there were smaller decreases in Canada than in the United States, although some of the changes were not very different. The different importance of some of the industries in the two countries must also be kept in mind. National income originating in agriculture fell more sharply in Canada than in the United States. Short wheat crops and depressed wheat prices in particular, while not unimportant to the United States economy, were of far greater relative importance to Canada.[53] So, indeed, was the severe collapse of international prices of agricultural and raw material products generally in 1930 and later. Canada's mining industries, nevertheless, fared better than those of the United States, particularly because of the increase in the output of gold in the downswing. The smaller decline in income originating in manufacturing, as

[53] The greater importance of this industry in Canada is not adequately brought out in Table 18 because of the short Canadian wheat crop in 1929. See footnote (a) of that table. Canada's wheat crops were roughly half as large as those of the United States in the last half of the twenties, while GNE in Canada in 1929 was only 6 per cent of GNE in the United States.

compared to the United States, was related in part to the processing of metals.[54]

Finally, one should note the quite different role of international income transfers in the two countries. Net payments of interest and dividends abroad by Canada were 5.4 per cent of national income in 1929 and, with the more rapid decline of national income than of such payments, fully 9.2 per cent of national income in 1933. Net receipts of such income from abroad by the United States were only 0.7 per cent of national income in both years. The significance to Canada of her large foreign-pay debt was noted earlier in this chapter. Dividends were maintained for a time in the downswing in both countries. In the United States, this had an anti-cyclical effect in the early stages of the downswing since it supported disposable income and therefore tended to maintain consumer expenditures.[55] In Canada, however, much of this effect was absent since such a large proportion of dividends was paid abroad.[56]

It is difficult to genaralize about two countries which have differing economic structures, even when the economic relations between them are close. The following broad observations may be warranted, however. The cyclical downswing in United States and world industrial output occurred at approximately the same time as over-production appeared in a number of world primary products. While both Canada and the United States were affected by the collapse of prices of primary products, Canada was more vulnerable.[57] A larger sector of the Canadian economy was engaged in the production and processing of agricultural and raw material products than in the United States.[58] A much larger portion of Canada's primary

---

[54] Detail of income originating in manufacturing has not been published for Canada. Related indicators show, however, that the Canadian non-ferrous smelting industry rose from the tenth largest manufacturing industry to third largest, between 1929 and 1933, in terms of gross value of production. For comments on durable goods in manufacturing, see the text which follows.

[55] See Schumpeter, *Business Cycles*, p. 952.

[56] In 1926-30, 57 per cent of Canadian dividend payments were to non-residents. See D.B.S., *Canada's International Investment Position, 1926-1954*, p. 41. See also p. 50.

[57] The special case of gold has already been noted.

[58] See Table 18 and note particularly footnote (*a*) of that table. The manufacturing sector in Canada includes, as already noted, a large segment engaged in processing primary products. Important parts of the various service industries, such as transportation, are engaged in providing services for primary industries.

TABLE 18

NATIONAL INCOME BY INDUSTRY,
CANADA AND THE UNITED STATES, 1929-37(*a*)

Industry	1932-3 low as a percentage of 1929		1937 as a percentage of 1929		Percentage of total in 1929	
	Canada	U.S.A.	Canada	U.S.A.	Canada	U.S.A.
Agriculture	32.2	38.6(*b*)	71.8	90.6	12.1	9.1
Forestry, fishing, trapping	32.1(*b*)	31.5(*b*)	93.4	58.7	2.2	0.1
Mining	47.6(*b*)	31.6	156.1	92.6	3.9	2.4
Manufacturing	46.7(*b*)	32.7(*b*)	92.7	87.7	24.5	25.2
Construction	23.8	19.9	50.7	54.6	6.1	4.2
Transportation, communication and public utilities	56.8	52.5	78.1	76.7	12.8	10.8
Wholesale and retail trade	56.2	41.1	91.1	91.2	13.2	15.0
Finance, insurance and real estate	66.9	43.4	76.8	60.6	9.9	15.0
Services	52.6	53.6	68.4	79.2	12.7	11.6
Government(*c*)	96.4	101.1(*b*)	106.5	152.4	8.0	5.9
Non-residents(*d*)	86.6	45.6	86.6	23.0	− 5.4	0.7
TOTAL	51.2	45.3	84.8	84.3	100.0	100.0

SOURCE: Derived from data appearing in the official National Accounts publications noted in Table 16, pp. 50-1 for Canada and p. 158 for the United States.

(*a*) The results would vary somewhat if the actual peaks were used, where they differed from 1929. The most important variation would be in agriculture. Income originating in Canadian agriculture in 1933 as a percentage of 1928 was only 22.6 per cent, and as a percentage of 1926-8 only 23.4 per cent; 1937 as a percentage of 1926-8 was 52.1 per cent. Income originating in Canadian agriculture from 1926-8 as a percentage of total national income in 1926-8 was 17.9 per cent.

(*b*) Low point in 1932.

(*c*) Income originating in government business enterprises is distributed by industrial groups in the business sector in Canadian data, but included with government in the United States data. The figures shown for the United States are not greatly changed, however, if government business enterprises are excluded from the government sector.

(*d*) The figures for Canada denote decreases in negative items.

output, furthermore, was exported. These industries were affected not only by the fluctuations in domestic and foreign industrial production and the over-production of a number of primary products, but also by substantial restrictions on foreign trade. On the other hand, United States manufacturing output involves a greater proportion of finished durable products, which were very severely affected in the downswing. In Canada, much of the decline in consumers' and producers' durables directly affected imports rather than domestic output.[59] Even this last point, however, must be considered in the context of the rate of investment in each country just before the downswing. Both countries were investing heavily in the last half of the twenties, and both had a large stock of relatively new capital when the downswing began. Investment as a proportion of GNE was greater in Canada than in the United States, however, and it would appear that the decline in durable business investment contributed more to the over-all decline in Canada than in the United States. The effects of heavy investment in the twenties were even more significant in retarding the upswing.[60]

Conclusions on the Downswing

The outstanding developments in the international downswing were the severity of the United States decline and the collapse of world trade and finance. The extent of the Canadian decline was related in part to the severity and length of the international downswing. The collapse of exports started a cumulative downswing via the multiplier-accelerator process. Because of the growing deterioration of the international economic situation and the heavy exploitation of existing investment opportunities, the expected profitability of long-term investment was also severely reduced and autonomous investment collapsed.

The downswing was accentuated by the rigidity of a num-

59 Statistical comparisons are difficult to make, but it appears that in 1929 about 35 per cent of income originating in manufacturing in the United States was in iron and steel, machinery, and transportation equipment (including automobiles). In the same year, roughly 20-25 per cent of gross and net value of manufacturing output in Canada was in the same industries.

60 The different monetary experiences of the two countries should be noted. Bank failures in the United States, which accentuated her downswing, had no parallel in Canada. Canada did not escape the repercussions of the bank failures, however, as will be noted in the next chapter.

ber of costs and the uneven nature of the decline. Some of these costs, such as the interest on debt held abroad and the deterioration of the terms of trade, involved relative shifts in income between Canada and other countries. Others, such as higher tariffs, sticky wage rates, and relatively rigid prices of manufactures, also involved considerable shifts in income within the country. The severity of the downswing was also partly determined by the extent of monetary deflation, involving not only the usual desire for liquidity in response to sharply falling prices, but also the speculative excesses and over-indebtedness of the previous upswing, and some of the effects of the sterling crisis of 1931.

Government monetary policy was conspicuous by its virtual absence, reflecting the lack of instruments of control, the varying needs of different parts of the economy, and a desire to avoid experimentation in view of the large foreign debt. Tariff action was rapid and drastic, but it tended to throw more of the burden of the downswing on export industries, and it could not prevent large decreases in sales of protected durables. Government spending was more stable than other components of expenditure, but it cannot be called contra-cyclical since both over-all spending and deficits fell as the depression continued.

A full explanation for the relative severity of the Canadian decline has not been attempted. Three broad sets of factors were noted above, however, which are relevant in this regard. First, the decline in the United States was exceptionally severe. Few, if any, countries have such close economic ties with the United States as does Canada. Secondly, the nature of the international collapse, with the sharp decline in primary prices and the restriction of world trade, struck particularly hard at a country in which per capita foreign trade was so high and primary exports bulked so large. Finally, the depression began at a time when very substantial additions had just been made to the stock of capital, and a considerable debt to non-residents incurred.

CHAPTER FOUR

The Beginning of Recovery, 1932-3

Gross national expenditure reached its lowest point in 1933. The decline was slower in 1932, however, and a large number of production series show a low point in 1932 or even earlier. Although the words "lower turning point" will be used in this connection, it is well to keep in mind that there was no specific time when all series turned upward.

In this chapter the sources of expansionary pressures will be evaluated. Annual data are clearly not suitable for this type of analysis, for they hide significant changes in the direction of activity within a given period. Monthly data are subject to large fluctuations owing to inadequacies in the statistics or to the technique used to remove seasonal forces. Although they do not permit as precise measurement, quarterly data indicate the broad movements in which we are interested and are less subject to errors in interpretation arising from inadequacies in the statistical data.[1] Except in a few cases where a seasonal pattern is not evident, the data are adjusted for seasonal movements.

The most comprehensive indicator of monthly economic activity, the index of the physical volume of production, reached its lowest point in the first quarter of 1933.[2] There followed two quarters of rapid increase, and a levelling of the index in the fourth quarter of 1933. Since the fall in economic activity slowed down noticeably in mid-1932, it appears in some series that there were two lower turning points. There was a fairly general decrease in activity in Canada toward the end of 1932, however, and a sharp decrease in the opening months of 1933 carried the index of physical production to its lowest point. The first quarter of 1933 is taken as the lower

[1] It is true, nevertheless, that more precise analysis requires seasonally adjusted monthly data. For this reason, some of the major monthly series are used below, particularly around the turning point.

[2] The components of this index are industrial production and distribution. The former includes mineral production, manufacturing, construction, and electric power. The latter includes trade employment and carloadings in particular. Agricultural production is not directly included in the index. See Table 52 for quarterly series in 1932-3.

turning point, and the timing of the various series is considered with respect to this quarter. In setting forth the order of recovery, a certain amount of judgment must be exercised; not only was there a broad range of time in which the reversal occurred among the various series, but also within some series the movements became very slight for some time before the upswing actually got under way.

Which industries can be regarded as giving a stimulus at the lower turning point? At this point only data on production

PRODUCTION AND OTHER SERIES AT THE LOWER TURNING POINT

Index	Lowest quarter in downswing
Leading the upswing	
Government bond prices and yields(a)	I, 1932
Stock prices(a)	II, 1932 (or I,1933)
Mining production	III, 1932
Forestry production	III, 1932 (level till II, 1933)
Electric power	IV, 1932
Export value, excluding gold	IV, 1932
Lowest point in first quarter of 1933	
Physical volume of business	
Manufacturing	
Distribution	
Wholesale prices	
Demand deposits	
Export volume	
Import volume	
Retail sales, department and chain stores	
Lagging behind other series	
Construction	II, 1933
Employment in industry (excluding agriculture)	II, 1933
Notice deposits	III, 1932 or IV, 1933 and I, 1934
Current loans(b)	III, 1936 but level for 3 quarters after I, 1933

SOURCE: Derived from various issues of D.B.S., *Monthly Review of Business Statistics.*

(a) Not adjusted for seasonal.

(b) Longer-term factors played a role in the continued decline shown here. See Edward Marcus, *Canada and the International Business Cycle, 1927-1939*, p. 131.

and employment will be used, but once the developments leading to the upswing have been noted data on prices will be introduced. It should be kept in mind that the low point in production (excluding agriculture) was the first quarter of 1933, while that for employment in manufacturing was the second quarter of 1933.

LOW POINTS IN EMPLOYMENT AND PRODUCTION, 1932-3(a)
(Adjusted for seasonal)

Employment data

Consumers' goods industries		Producers' goods	
Durables		Materials	
Furniture	II/33	Rough dress	
Electrical appartus	II/33	lumber(b)	II/33
Automobiles	IV/32	Pulp and paper	II/33
Other		Clay, glass, stone	II/33
Textile products	I/33	Logging	IV/32
Hosiery & knit goods	II/33	Mining	I-II/33
Retail trade	I-II/33	Equipment	
Leather & products	IV/32	Iron and steel	I-II/33
Service industries		Crude and rolled	II/33
Hotel and		Machinery	II/33
restaurants	IV/32-I/33	Agricultural	
Railways	IV/33	implements	IV/32
Trade	II/33	Construction(c)	III/33
		Building	II/33
		Highway	III/32 and III/33
		Railway	III/32

Production data

Consumers' durables and nondurables		Producers' materials and equipment	
Automobiles	IV/32	Nickel	III/32
Boots and shoes	IV/32-I/33	Coal	II/33
Textiles	I/33	Newsprint	I/33
Slaughterings	(d)	Planks and boards	
Foodstuffs and flour	I/33	exports	III/32
		Iron and steel imports	I/33
		Iron and products	I/33

SOURCE: Derived from various issues of D.B.S., *Monthly Review of Business Statistics.*

(a) Where successive quarters given, index was level in the two quarters.

(b) Level before this.

(c) Rose in I/33 because of highway building.

(d) Level in 1932.

Among the consumer durable goods, automobiles showed a distinct lead in both production and employment. The lowest point in automobile production was actually in the fourth quarter of 1931, but the subsequent increase immediately thereafter was lost through 1932. The turning point for automobile sales was due to export sales, which rose in the last half of 1932 and, more rapidly, in 1933.[3] In spite of this lead, automobile production was only 40 per cent of the 1926 level by the third quarter of 1933.

The textile industry also showed distinct signs of recovery in 1932. Although it shared in the general decline in production in the first quarter of 1933, its recovery in the next three quarters carried production to 132 per cent of the 1926 level. The low in textile employment, furthermore, occurred one quarter before that in manufacturing generally. The substantial increase in protection for this industry in 1930-1, rapid growth in some of the new lines such as rayons, and the relative stability of sales characteristic of some non-durable consumer goods, all helped to maintain and increase output. Production of boots and shoes levelled out after the fourth quarter of 1932 and registered a strong recovery in the second and third quarters of 1933. Inspected slaughterings showed stability of production at a high level all through 1932 and a good recovery beginning in the first quarter of 1933. Production of foodstuffs also showed a relatively good recovery after the first quarter of 1933, partly because of exports.

Some producers' materials led the recovery. This was probably due in part to the placing of orders in anticipation of construction and production activity, but to a large extent it represented recovery in exports. In volume terms, exports of nickel and of planks and boards reached a low as early as the third quarter of 1932. Most producers' goods and materials, except these two and agricultural machinery, reached their low point of production in the first quarter of 1933, and of employment in the second quarter of 1933; that is, they did not lead the recovery, but conformed to (and determined) the over-all pattern. Both railway and highway construction showed leads in employment, but in the latter it was not sustained.

On the whole, it was the industries producing consumers'

[3] Domestic consumption is not available on a monthly basis. On an annual basis, however, domestic consumption of automobiles fell in both 1932 and 1933, while exports levelled out in 1932 and rose in 1933. See Table 46.

goods which led at the lower turning point.[4] Turning points for industries cannot be set too dogmatically because of very short-term irregular fluctuations. The data on employment and production, however, combined with a careful reading of the period, suggest some industries producing consumers' goods showed strong signs of recovery in 1932, and (after a temporary relapse early in 1933) recovered rapidly for a period. The percentage increases in some of the industries producing producers' materials and equipment were much greater than those in the consumers' goods industries in 1933, but production in the former had reached abysmally low levels or even ceased altogether for a short period. The industries producing consumers' goods were a sustaining force in the depression, relatively speaking. Once the recovery was under way, revival in the producers' goods sector was extremely important for the recovery because it was here that so much of the preceding depression had occurred.

Resistance to Deflation in Mid-1932

It is necessary to look at 1932 fairly closely for several reasons. First, the slowing down of the rate of decrease needs some explanation since it was the first really distinct sign of the end of the downswing. Secondly, some of the forces in the turning point in early 1933 will be clearer. Actually, there was no large increase in economic activity throughout the world in 1932. There was some improvement after the summer in several countries, however, and a marked resistance for a time to deflationary forces, in contrast to the fairly regular decreases before then.

As Table 52 indicates, the physical volume of production in Canada fell from the first to the second quarter of 1932, but this drop was almost wholly attributable to the decline in construction. The deceleration of the downswing was most directly linked with manufacturing activity in the second and third quarters. The stability in mid-1932 was due to production of consumers' goods rather than producers' goods. The rise in agricultural marketings after the first quarter of 1932 was also important. Mining supplied some support in the second quarter

4 See D.B.S., *Monthly Review of Business Statistics* (August 1933), pp. 6 and 10. According to the D.B.S. indexes, the low in consumers' goods production was February 1933, while that of producers' goods was April 1933.

but not in the third, while the sharp fall in the level of construction after the first quarter of 1932 worked against recovery.

There were several encouraging factors in 1932, the more important of which can be noted briefly.

(1) Growing resistance to depression appeared in many countries in mid-1932, as the series in Table 19 indicate. Attempts in the United States to ease the financial picture, though not successful, were a step in the right direction. Some easing of the banking and credit situation in the United States was a prerequisite for the return of confidence.

One of the interesting points about the series in Table 19 is the relatively greater resistance to depressive forces in Canada than in the United States in the first half of 1932, particularly if allowance is made in the Canadian index for a drop of 60 per cent in construction activity in the second quarter.[5] One reason for this may well have been the greater resistance to price deflation in Canada after the Canadian dollar depreciated with respect to United States currency in September 1931. Wholesale prices in the United States fell by 13 per cent from mid-1931 to mid-1932; those in Canada dropped only 7 per cent, falling slowly after the third quarter of 1931, but remaining stable from the second to the third quarter of 1932. In September 1931, the United States dollar sold for $1.04 Canadian; in December for $1.21; and in the second quarter of 1932 a level of $1.13 was attained, and approximately maintained for the rest of 1932. Some of the deflationary pressure from abroad was thus checked.[6] There may have been other factors in the slowing down of the price decreases – for example, short-term changes in the rate of inventory liquidation in Canada – but lack of suitable data makes it impossible to check them.

(2) In the previous crop year, beginning on August 1, 1931, Canadian wheat production had been extremely low because of a very low yield compared to the twenties (though average seeded acreage was much higher than in the twenties). With an average farm price of only 38 cents per bushel, the farm value amounted to $124 million – well below the $205 million in the previous crop year and $317-$488 million in the previous five years.[7] Sales prospects seemed brighter in mid-1932, since

[5] See footnote (a) to Table 19. On the other hand, the United States recovery seems to have been somewhat better in the second half of the year.

[6] See Bank of Nova Scotia, *Monthly Review*, September 1932.

[7] Cash income from wheat was only $95 million in 1931, compared to $334-$451 million in 1926-9.

it was expected that the United States winter crop would be low
and that other exporters would have small supplies for export
in the second half of 1932. In the last half of 1932, in fact,
Canadian wheat exports were a much higher proportion than
usual of world exports. The actual yield and acreage increased
appreciably over the previous crop year, offsetting a further
decline to 35 cents in average farm price and raising farm
value to $155 million. Cash income from wheat rose by one-
quarter to $120 million.

(3) The impending Imperial Economic Conference at Ottawa was another cause for optimism in a number of Canadian
industries. The preferences given to Canada in the United
Kingdom tariff of September 1931 were to extend for one year

TABLE 19

INDUSTRIAL ACTIVITY IN SELECTED COUNTRIES, 1932-3(a)
(1925-9 = 100)

Country	1932				1933			
	I	II	III	IV	I	II	III	IV
Germany(b)	67	66	64	67	69	73	77	79
France(b)	83	77	76	79	84	89	91	88
United Kingdom Board of Trade(c)	90	89	82	90	89	91	91	99
London and Cambridge	92	84	79	88	89	90	89	99
Japan	106	106	116	124	123	128	135	144
Canada(b)	73	68	68	65	57	67	81	79
United States(b)	63	55	56	60	57	72	84	68
U.S. building activity	22	20	18	15	11	23	21	20
World (excluding U.S.S.R.)(b)	72	67	66	70	69	79	86	79

SOURCE: League of Nations, *World Production and Prices, 1925-
33*. Revised U.S. index (base 1947-9) is 34, 30, 29, 32, 30, 37, 44, 38.

(a) In comparing series, it must be kept in mind that indexes for
Canada, France, and Germany include building, that for the United
States does not. The United Kingdom Board of Trade index includes
about 30 per cent of building construction. The United States building index consists of contracts awarded in 37 states for floor space
for residential buildings (F. W. Dodge Corporation).

(b) Adjusted for seasonal.

(c) Base 1924, 1927-9 = 100.

only, unless the Ottawa Conference continued them. Many Canadian industries in 1932 were preparing to take advantage of the existing preferences and of the ones expected from the Ottawa Conference.

(4) There were a number of readjustments taking place within Canada to facilitate recovery. The long process of deflation eliminated some of the excesses of the previous boom by necessitating reorganizations, which involved write-downs of capitalization or a better balance of bonded and equity capitalization. Commercial failures had eliminated many weak firms. The turning point in commercial failures was before that of many annual series: they reached a peak in numbers in 1932, and the liabilities involved were also at a peak before 1933. Both numbers and liabilities involved fell sharply in 1933.[8] Attempts to work off inventory and repay loans, while immediately depressing, served to put many firms in a liquid position and enabled them to participate quickly in any revival.[9] Under the impetus of falling sales and income, and in some industries of severe competition by price or otherwise, high-cost equipment and plants were discarded or shut down in order to reduce costs.[10] Productivity appears to have risen after the downswing had been under way for a time.[11]

Consumer expenditure fell more sharply in 1932 than in 1931, value decreasing 15 per cent and volume 7 per cent. Value and volume continued to fall in 1933, but the rate of fall slowed down to 7 and 3 per cent respectively. The rate of decline in the largest segment of expenditures, consumers' non-durable goods, did not increase in 1932, however, and in 1933 the non-durable, durable, and service groups all showed much slower rates of fall. The monthly index of retail sales value for chain and department stores (adjusted for seasonal) declined

[8] In terms of liabilities involved, somewhat different peaks appear in different series. But all show a high level in 1930-2 and a sharp drop in 1933. See *C.Y.B.*, 1936, pp. 967-72, for estimates from Dun's Bulletin and those compiled under the Bankruptcy and Winding Up Acts.

[9] With respect to the level of inventories, the scanty evidence is not very conclusive. One does not get the impression from annual data, however, that there was much over-all success in Canada in reducing inventories as a ratio of sales. See Tables 21-23.

[10] The newsprint industry, for example, was attempting to lower unit costs by closing down high-cost mills and, to achieve liquidity, was converting inventories into cash by restricting wood-cutting operations. See the *Financial Post*, January 16, 1932, and October 1, 1932.

[11] G. D. Sutton, "Productivity in Canada," *CJEPS*.

through 1932 and in the first quarter of 1933; it rose in May, but was fairly stable for the rest of 1933. The evidence does not suggest any strong independent movement in total consumption to start the recovery.[12]

One other factor can be mentioned here briefly.[13] Expenditures for repair and maintenance of equipment and plant cannot be postponed indefinitely, particularly if grave uncertainty about the outlook for profits persuades business men to keep existing equipment going as long as possible. The low point for both repair and maintenance and investment was in 1933; but, in a number of industries, expenditures for repair and maintenance reached a low point before gross domestic investment; the decline in the former in 1933 was quite moderate, compared to that in the latter; and total expenditures for repair and maintenance actually exceeded investment in 1933.

There were, however, a number of factors still definitely retarding recovery in 1932. Although a number of countries continued the recoveries begun in mid-1932, economic activity in the United States experienced further setbacks toward the end of 1932 and early in 1933. These renewed declines were associated particularly with a new wave of bank failures in that country. While yields rose in 1932, the continued low price of wheat moderated the recovery in farm income. The new United States tariffs on lumber and copper in 1932 struck further at two important segments of the Canadian economy. The low level of investment in Canada was a serious problem. Construction activity had been decreasing rapidly through 1931 but just collapsed after the first quarter of 1932 and continued to be extremely low for several quarters thereafter – thus nipping the recovery in the bud. This had widespread effects, on lumber and iron and steel output, for example, and partly explains why these and other supplying industries were so depressed in the initial recovery period early in 1933.

12 This need not contradict the view expressed earlier that production of certain types of consumers' goods reached a low point before the first quarter of 1933. In some industries, such as automobiles and meats, greater export markets were in prospect. In others, such as foods and some types of clothing, one might expect an early recovery in sales (or at least stability) because of their non-durable nature. In both types, production for inventory could occur in the expectation of greater sales, especially once the price declines stopped and where inventories had been reduced. The suggestion above is that *total* consumer expenditures helped by falling less than other spending, and by slowing down its rate of fall, but did not lead in the upswing.

13 See the section on investment, p. 110.

In summary, the depression continued in 1932 in Canada, but some resistance to it developed in the second and third quarters. Export value and volume levelled out for a time. The decline in wholesale prices continued but at a slower rate, and a moderate rise occurred for a few months. Several branches of production, particularly consumers' goods, levelled out or rose for a time. The recovery could not get under way in Canada, however, because of the setback to recovery in the United States and the collapse of construction in Canada. It was not until early in 1933 that the Canadian recovery really got under way.

Reversal of the Downswing in 1933

We shall look first at the "external" forces of recovery in terms of the role of recoveries abroad and the effects of policies abroad. These external forces were the trigger in Canadian recovery at the lower turning point. The halting response of some parts of the Canadian economy to greater export and domestic sales was in some respects the most serious drag on recovery.

The world economic depression reached its lowest point in the middle of 1932.[14] Industrial activity, which had fallen by 37 per cent between 1929 and 1932, rose by 14 per cent in 1933 (excluding the U.S.S.R.). Industrial unemployment in the world reached its maximum in the third quarter of 1932. The quantum of world trade which had fallen to 75 per cent of 1929 by 1932 remained at that level in 1933.

In spite of a setback in the United States in the first quarter of 1933 and after July 1933, countries such as the United Kingdom, Germany, Japan, and France experienced a fairly steady recovery from about mid-1932 through 1933. In some countries recoveries were slowed down in the first quarter of 1933, and France was not able to sustain her recovery through 1933. In the United Kingdom there was a modest improvement in 1932 as compared to 1931, due in some measure to the abandonment of gold. This step eased the deflationary pressure on prices in the sterling group of countries, whereas gold bloc countries such as France, which did not devalue until much

---

[14] For comments and data on the world economic situation and individual countries, see the following publications of the League of Nations: *Statistical Year Book, World Production and Prices, Review of World Trade* and *World Economic Survey.*

later in the thirties, found themselves subjected to deflationary pressures on a number of occasions. On the one hand, many countries did not have the short but spectacular recoveries which occurred in the United States and Canada after the first quarter of 1933; on the other, for many of them recovery began from a higher level than it did in the United States and Canada and was less erratic.

Canadian exports to the United Kingdom were rising well before the events of March 1933 in the United States and finally reversed Canada's downswing.[15] Total exports to the United Kingdom rose in 1932 as a whole while those to the United States and other countries continued to fall. After July 1932 exports to the United Kingdom began to persistently exceed the levels of the same months one year earlier.[16] This pattern did not appear with exports to other Commonwealth countries until May 1933; with the United States, until July 1933; and with other non-Commonwealth countries, until August 1933. It is difficult to disentangle the effects of the various forces affecting exports in the period just before the low point in Canadian industrial production in February 1933. The earlier recovery in the United Kingdom, firm preferences, and improved overseas wheat sales contrast with a continued decline in the United States and the new tariffs imposed by that country. It is significant, however, that from October 1932 to the low point of the index of physical volume of business in February-1933, exports to the United Kingdom were 34 per cent of the total Canadian exports, compared with 26 per cent in the same period one year earlier. If wheat is excluded from the totals, exports to the United Kingdom made up 33 per cent of total exports in the five months ending February 1933 and 27 per cent in the five months ending February 1932. While exports to the United States had been 38 per cent of total

15. The precise turning point in total exports cannot be ascertained by the data given in this paragraph. The export values given in Table 52 reached a low in the fourth quarter of 1932, one quarter before the low in general business activity. Malach, using a deseasonalized monthly series for merchandise exports adjusted for balance of payments purposes, places the trough in such exports in December 1932. See Malach, *International Cycles*, pp. 40-3, and 133.

16. The monthly export data include some wheat to the United Kingdom which should properly be assigned to other countries. Excluding wheat entirely, exports to the United Kingdom in the last half of 1932 were moderately below those of the last half of 1931, and moderately above those of the first half of 1932 in the first half of 1933.

Canadian exports in the second half of 1931, they were only 26 per cent of the total in the second half of 1932.

As for imports, those from the United Kingdom began to exceed the levels of one year earlier in the second quarter of 1933, while those from the United States did not begin to do so until the fourth quarter of 1933. Of course, this was partly due to the slow revival of investment in Canada and the effects on investment imports from the United States, but it was probably due to preferences as well. As a result of these changes in exports and imports, the merchandise trade surplus was enlarged in 1932 and again in 1933, and by 1933 the current account was in balance. The trade deficit with the United States was gradually reduced as imports continued to fall in 1933 while exports rose, and a rise in exports faster than that in import raised the surplus with the United Kingdom.

It is interesting to note that exports to the United Kingdom (with and without wheat) were tending to rise in the second half of 1932 in spite of a rapid rise in the value of the Canadian dollar in terms of sterling. Moreover, exports to the United States were falling off in this period in spite of a discount of about 13 per cent on the Canadian dollar in terms of the United States dollar. It seems clear that other factors were predominating, particularly the different cyclical experience of Canada's two main customers in this period. Once the recovery in the United States really got under way, after the first quarter of 1933, the gradual return of the Canadian dollar to parity with the United States dollar did not prevent an increase in exports to the United States (or a further decrease in imports from the United States in 1933 as a whole).

As noted earlier, after April 1932 economic activity in Canada approximately maintained a plateau until November.[17]

---

[17] It will be noted that the low in Canadian industrial production before the small and brief increase of 1932 was in April, while in the United States it was in July. The Canadian index of industrial production includes construction; but if one considers only Canadian and United States manufacturing, the low points before the brief levelling of 1932 were still the same as those for industrial production. The lows in 1933 were February for Canada and March for the United States, when industrial production or manufacturing are considered. This is surprising in view of the fact that many Canadian series are export series, and particularly raw materials; they should then tend to follow United States production series. Moses Abramovitz has indicated that stocks of raw materials, and particularly import stocks, typically lag behind production in the United States. See his *Inventories and Business Cycles*, CHAPS. IX and X. The explanation

Thus Canada was receptive to a favourable stimulus. Such a stimulus did come in the form of continued recovery overseas, but this was swamped by other forces for a time. After June 1932 a number of industries were having difficulty in maintaining production, since larger domestic sales had not materialized and many exports were still falling. Production decreased slowly and irregularly during the last half of the year. In December, January, and February, however, the index of physical volume of production fell by 12 per cent. One factor in this was the decline once more of construction toward the end of 1932. In addition, the increasing seriousness of the banking crisis in the United States was beginning to show more sharply in United States production. Industrial production in the United States, which had risen in the fourth quarter of 1932, now fell once more and particularly in March.

It is possible that some of the natural adjustments to depression, coupled with rising overseas exports, would have brought a moderate recovery in Canada eventually. The spark which set off the spurt in activity, however, was much more spectacular. The banking difficulties in the United States had come to a head, and the new administration was expected to take action on a number of fronts. The depression had revealed serious weaknesses in the United States banking system, which greatly accentuated the impact of the depression both in the United States and elsewhere. Bank suspensions in the United States before the depression had ranged from 367 in 1922 to 976 in 1926. In 1930 they rose to 1,352, and in 1931 the crisis in sterling and withdrawals of short-term balances from the United States, along with internal drains of currency, raised the number to 2,294. Loans to banks by the Reconstruction Finance Corporation, and the Glass-Steagall Act,[18] eased the banking situation somewhat in 1932, but late in 1932 it deteriorated again, and in March 1933 the system collapsed. On March 5 the President ordered all banks closed for four days

probably lies in the fact that exports overseas were more buoyant than exports to the United States in both years, while the banking crisis in the United States in February and March dragged United States production to a very low point. Purchases on contract may also form part of the explanation, since these would tend to maintain exports for a time when United States production fell.

[18] This Act permitted the use of formerly ineligible paper as backing for advances from the federal reserve banks. Furthermore, government bonds could be used in place of commercial paper, or of gold above a 40 per cent minimum, to back federal reserve notes.

and put an embargo on gold withdrawals or exports. The crisis itself was over fairly quickly, for currency payments were generally resumed by March 15. On April 19 an indefinite embargo was put on gold exports.

Events in March and April had led to widespread expectations in the United States and Canada that strong steps would be taken to raise prices. These expectations were not disappointed, for in April the United States embarked on a bold and controversial experiment in recovery. The President was given powers to attempt to raise prices by Federal Reserve purchases of government securities, by issue of Treasury notes to meet maturing debt, and if necessary by reducing the gold content of the dollar. In October a gold purchase programme was begun in order to depreciate the dollar, and in January 1934 the dollar was devalued and gold nationalized. Large-scale spending on public works was undertaken, and codes were to be set up for industry under the National Recovery Act.

TABLE 20

SELECTED UNITED STATES SERIES IN 1933
(1926 = 100)

Series	March	July	December
Industrial production	56.9	90.2	72.6
Manufacturing production	54.0	90.0	72.0
Wholesale prices (Bureau of Labor)	60.2	68.9	70.8
Common stock prices	43.2	80.4	70.4
United States dollar in Canadian funds	1.199	1.058	.995

The sharpness and brevity of the "Roosevelt boom" are clear from Table 20. The effect in Canada was bound to be marked, given the close trading, financial and corporate connections between the two countries. Speculative buying appeared because of the expected transmission of higher commodity prices to Canada via higher import and export prices, and because of some expected inventory build-up. The depreciation of the United States dollar set off by the events of March and April, and the appreciation of sterling in terms of Canadian currency, had a number of effects on Canada. The price of gold rose sharply in 1933, to the benefit of Canadian and other gold producers. With the recovery in the United States finally under way, exports to that country could rise.

The available data suggest that the low point in general business activity in Canada was in the first quarter of 1933, probably in March, and was preceded by that in exports.[19] The early phase of the recovery can be traced by four composite indexes. The indexes of physical volume of production, industrial production and wholesale prices all reached their lowest points in February 1933, with the index levels at 67.0, 60.9 and 63.6 respectively.[20] Industrial employment continued to fall slowly, however, to a low of 78.7 in June. The physical volume of production and industrial production rose to peaks of 90.8 and 90.2 respectively in September, then declined somewhat in the fourth quarter; about half of the improvement occurred in May and June, immediately after the developments in United States banking and monetary policy in mid-March and April. Wholesale prices weakened slightly after rising to 70.5 in July and were level at about 69 for the rest of the year. Employment in industry, on the other hand, recovered steadily after June 1933 and did not feel the effects of easing production until 1934.

All of the components of the index of production shared in the increase – it was a general upward movement. The manufacturing industries exhibited the strongest advance from the first quarter, an advance of about 50 per cent, with some industries producing consumers' goods (such as foodstuffs, textiles, and boots and shoes) showing particularly strong increases. In percentage terms, iron and steel manufactures rose more than most groups, but since in March, April, and May there was no production of pig iron in Canada at all and little steel production, the percentage changes do not mean very much. In fact,

[19] See Table 52 for quarterly data. For more precise monthly timing, see the reference to Malach in footnote 15 of this chapter. Malach places the trough of the Canadian business cycle in March 1933 (the same month as in the United States) since the medians of all four sets of series he uses fall in this month.

[20] The February low for industrial production in Canada involved some special factors. Steel production had been running from 40 to 50 per cent of the 1926 level in the last months of 1932, rose to 66 per cent in January, but fell to 20 per cent in February and about 15 per cent in the next two months. Production of pig iron ceased altogether in mid-February and did not resume until the end of July when stocks were depleted. One reason for the collapse of steel and pig iron production was simply that rail orders were completed and none were in view. See the *Financial Post*, March 25 and July 29, 1933, and p. 211 of this text.

in the 1933 recovery there was no real recovery in some components of the iron and steel group or in construction until June or July, and the level of operations was very low even when the series were at their highest.[21]

As might be expected from the nature of pricing in these fields, prices of raw or partly manufactured goods responded far more to the above forces than did those of fully or chiefly manufactured goods. Between February and July, the price index of the former rose from 50.8 to 63.0, that of the latter from 66.9 to only 72.4.[22] Prices of vegetable products, especially of grains, and of non-ferrous metal products rose particularly sharply. Quite apart from the over-all psychological effects of a rising price level, therefore, some part of the price maladjustments of the downswing were being corrected.[23] In the international sector, the terms of trade had deteriorated from 101 in 1929 to 85.9 in 1932; they improved to 85.5 in 1933.

What were the factors responsible for the rise in prices? The effects on Canada of actual or prospective inflationary measures in the United States have already been noted. It was widely believed that recovery was finally under way, and this belief was bolstered by the knowledge that strong measures were being (or were to be) undertaken in the United States and several European countries. The desire to buy at low prices was bound to increase purchases, especially where inventories had been successfully reduced. The decrease of world stocks of raw materials after the autumn of 1932, in response to industrial recovery in a number of countries and some successful attempts to control output, eased the downward pressure on prices. Exports of Canadian base metals to overseas countries were rising quite sharply, and prices of many non-ferrous metals rose as early as February. The rise in wheat prices from the end of December, due in part to crop damage in North

21 "While the industries concerned with both producers' and consumers' goods recovered in 1933, the advance in consumers' goods commenced earlier and was relatively greater than in producers' goods. . . . While the percentage gain (in production of producers' goods) was nearly as great as in consumers' goods, the level of operations was relatively much lower, a condition which has obtained for three years." D.B.S., *Monthly Review of Business Statistics*, January 1934, pp. 6-7, and August 1934, p. 10.
22 Index base is 1926 throughout, unless otherwise noted.
23 Part of this correction was lost by December.

America, helped to stabilize wholesale prices in the opening months of 1933.[24]

With substantial changes in world economic activity and prices under way, it was unlikely that movements in the exchange rate in this period would play the predominant role in Canadian price changes. Nevertheless, two points are worth noting. After the United Kingdom left the gold standard and the Canadian dollar depreciated in terms of the United States dollar, prices in Canada had fallen more slowly than those in the United States. When the United States also went off the gold standard early in 1933, and the Canadian dollar appreciated in terms of the United States dollar, prices in the United States rose faster than those in Canada. At the same time, the Canadian dollar depreciated with respect to sterling, tending to remove thereby some of the downward pressure on domestic prices occasioned earlier by appreciation with respect to sterling.

Canadian prices rose, therefore, because of the effects of such external factors as the actual and proposed measures in the United States and recovery overseas. What was the role of internal spending and inventory change within Canada in this respect, and in the 1933 upswing generally?

Comprehensive measures of domestic sales based on periods shorter than a year are not available, but the available data do not suggest any substantial rise in domestic sales within the year. Unadjusted retail sales did not reach the levels of one year earlier until September 1933 and were close to the late 1932 levels for the rest of the year. This comparison with unadjusted data may be vitiated, of course, since the trend of sales changed within the period. The seasonally adjusted index of sales of department and chain stores reached a low point in the first quarter, but rose very little through the year.[25] Each of the groups included in the annual retail sales index fell from 1932 to 1933. Consumer, government, and investment expenditures, as shown in the National Accounts, all declined in 1933 as a whole, though the rate of decline slowed down considerably for consumer expenditures.[26] Adjusted merchandise exports rose from $492 to $532 million. Because of price in-

---

[24] See the Canadian Bank of Commerce, *Monthly Commercial Letter* for July 1933 for an analysis of the reasons for price increases, and also D.B.S., *Monthly Review of Business Statistics* for March 1933 for world stocks of primary products.

[25] *C.Y.B.*, 1937, p. 622.

[26] Some part of these decreases in National Accounts' components was embodied actually in the decrease in imports in 1933.

Table 21

INVENTORY INVESTMENT, 1928-37
(Millions of dollars)

Item	1928	1929	1930	1931	1932	1933	1934	1935	1936	1937
Change in inventory values	157	61	−154	−290	−216	−82	70	47	−50	94
Inventory valuation adjustment	3	−12	193	175	105	−19	−40	−18	−34	−86
Value of physical change – Total	160	49	39	−115	−111	−101	30	29	−84	8
Agriculture (including grain in commercial channels)	35	−95	−2	−52	21	−23	12	—	−153	−104
Excluding agriculture	125	144	41	−63	−132	−78	18	29	69	112
Change in inventories in 1935-9 constant dollars										
Total	158	48	126	−159	−80	−125	24	48	−184	−74
Agriculture	56	−84	96	−95	63	−46	4	15	−113	35
Excluding agriculture	102	132	30	−64	−143	−79	20	33	71	109

SOURCE: Derived from the *National Accounts*. The unpublished constant dollar series for agriculture was supplied by courtesy of the National Income Section, Dominion Bureau of Statistics.

creases, non-monetary gold available for export rose from $70 to $82 million. Almost every important export except newsprint rose in value from 1932 to 1933, and the volume of exports was almost 10 per cent higher. Such facts would suggest that most of the increase in sales within the year and for the year as a whole was in the export sector.

Turning to inventory investment, Table 21 indicates clearly that the non-agricultural sector of the economy was unable to reduce its physical stocks until 1931.[27] In other words, production (including imports) must have run ahead of sales (excluding inventory change) for some time after the downswing began. In addition, a large build-up of agricultural inventories occurred in 1930. Inventory values fell sharply, however, since price decreases affected the whole stock of inventories on hand. In each of the three years after 1930 the non-agricultural sector was able to reduce its physical stocks of inventories, indicating that production had been cut back more than sales. The agricultural sector was able to reduce its physical stock of inventories in 1931 because of crop failure, built them up again in 1932, and reduced them once more in the next year. The above evidence suggests that the physical stock of inventories at the end of 1932 must have been only moderately below the total at the beginning of the downswing.[28] Considering the sharp decline in sales volume, the ratio of inventory to sales in physical terms must have been much higher both for agriculture and non-agricultural business. It will be noted also that in both 1931 and 1932 the change in inventory book values in the non-agricultural sector exceeded the value of the physical change, indicating further pressure on profits by changes in the prices of inventories on hand at the beginning of each period.

[27] Data on inventories are particularly scanty, and only a few scattered industry series are available on a monthly basis. Certain figures can be put together from the National Accounts on an annual basis. Except for agriculture (including grain in commercial channels) all the data are in terms of changes in book values. Except for agriculture, in other words, the series show not only the value of the physical change in inventories but also the change in the book value of the whole stock of inventories because of price changes. An estimate of value of physical change can be made by applying the inventory valuation adjustment of the National Accounts. This procedure removes changes in book value due to the effects of price movements on the stock of inventories at the beginning of each period. Changes in the physical stock of inventories are also available. Only book values are available for most industry groups.

[28] See Table 40 for the higher carryover of wheat in particular.

Table 22

RATIO OF STOCKS TO PRODUCTION IN THE MANUFACTURING
INDUSTRIES OF CANADA, 1929-37
(Millions of dollars)

| | Production | | Stocks(a) | Ratio of stocks to | |
	Gross	Net		Gross	Net
1929	3,883	1,755	868	22.4	49.4
1930	3,280	1,523	849	25.9	55.7
1931	2,555	1,252	710	27.8	56.7
1932	1,980	956	600	30.3	62.8
1933	1,954	920	573	29.3	62.3
1934	2,394	1,087	599	25.0	55.1
1935	2,654	1,153	611	23.0	52.9
1936	3,002	1,290	652	21.7	51.1
1937	3,625	1,509	757	20.9	50.2

SOURCE: D.B.S., *Census of Manufactures.*
(a) Materials on hand, stocks in process, and finished products
on hand. A breakdown between the first two items and the last one
is not available before 1931. Data on stocks are book values.

The extent to which manufacturers were actually able to
reduce stocks in some meaningful sense of the term, for example as a ratio of production, is indicated in Tables 22 and 23.
This comparison suggests that they were unsuccessful until
1933, since production was not cut back enough in relation to
sales to prevent the ratio of stocks to production from rising
steadily until then. In that year a number of industries increased
their exports, and domestic consumption fell at a much slower
rate than earlier. Thus it would appear that the manufacturing
industries were not, in effect, able to reduce inventory ratios
on a general basis until the upswing came.[29] Care must be used

[29] An attempt was made to show inventories as a ratio of sales
rather than production. To make this comparison, domestic sales
plus exports for manufacturers were estimated by adding imports
to production and adjusting this by the change in manufacturing
inventories. See p. 454 of the *C.Y.B.*, 1934-35. A number of
serious classification, valuation, and timing problems are involved in this method, so that it has not been used above. The
results for the manufacturing industries, however, were broadly
the same as those suggested by the ratio to production measure,
that is, inventories rose as a ratio of sales in the downswing.
It should be noted that this behaviour appears to be typical
in downswings; the stock-sales ratio usually rises until perhaps
shortly before the turn. See Abramovitz, *Inventories and Business
Cycles*, CHAP. VI.

in interpreting such tables, because of problems in valuation and classification. In particular, to the extent that stocks were not promptly written down in value, a comparison with production at current cost would overstate the ratio of stocks to production in a period of declining prices. The broad results should be meaningful, however.

Table 23

PERCENTAGE RELATION OF BOOK VALUE OF MANUFACTURING STOCKS TO GROSS VALUE OF OUTPUT BY INDUSTRY, 1929-34

Industry group	1929	1932	1933	1934
Vegetable porducts	20.9	30.6	31.9	29.1
Animal products	14.0	16.0	16.2	14.4
Textile products	23.2	23.4	22.0	21.6
Wood and paper products	26.0	34.2	26.0	22.3
Iron and its products	22.7	49.1	48.5	33.7
Non-ferrous metals	21.5	36.8	33.9	24.5
Non-metallic minerals	24.8	32.4	30.3	26.9
Chemicals	23.7	31.5	31.1	27.8
Miscellaneous products	29.1	30.3	32.1	30.5
Total(a)	22.2	30.0	29.1	24.9

SOURCE: D.B.S., *Census of Manufactures.*
(a) Ratios differ slightly from preceding table because of rounding.

In 1933 a number of manufacturing industries were able to reduce the ratio of stocks to output and to sales. Two sets of forces would have opposite effects on stocks in 1933. Some firms would be anxious to reduce inventories relative to sales in order to have a more desirable ratio of stocks to sales, to avoid losses through any renewal of price decreases, or to achieve a more liquid position. On the other hand, those firms which had reduced inventories by 1933, or were now firmly convinced the upswing was under way, would tend to build up inventory while prices were still low. It is possible that inventories were reduced relative to sales in some industries for part of 1932 and built up for part of 1933; this would be quite consistent with the annual data.[30] Over-all, however, inventory

---

[30] Industry comments in the *Financial Post* suggest there were increases in stocks in a number of industries in 1933 in the expectation of price increases. See also Bank of Nova Scotia, *Monthly Review,* August 1933, for a view that stocks had been reduced earlier and were raised once more in 1933.

accumulation by manufacturers during 1933 does not appear to have been a significant stimulus. It is important to note from Table 21, nevertheless, that the pressure on GNE from liquidation of non-agricultural inventories as a whole was much less in 1933 than in the previous year, and that inventory price losses had ceased.

It was noted above that consumer demand lagged behind exports. But investment demand for producers' materials and equipment lagged even more, as evidenced, for example, by the lead in the index of consumers' goods production over producers' goods.[31] While a number of producers' materials, such as some metals, received an export stimulus, the very low level of construction adversely affected a whole range of supplying industries. From February through June of 1933 the monthly index of construction was virtually stable at about 20 per cent or less of its 1926 level, compared to 43.1 in 1932 as a whole and 91.2 in 1931. Construction responded thereafter to recovery and rose to an index level of 40.5 in the fourth quarter. One reason for the collapse of construction in 1932 and its failure to revive in part of 1933 was the decline in government construction. In the spring of 1932 the various governments largely abandoned the programme of relief works and restricted themselves to direct relief, in accordance with a decision made at the Dominion-Provincial Conference of April.[32]

The recovery began to slacken after September 1933 because of several temporary deterrents. The slight relapse in recovery in the United States after July in itself would limit the extent of recovery in Canada, especially when the recovery was so young and domestic recovery policy so limited. After June, wheat exports began to run well below those in 1932, and the Canadian price fell off after July. Net farm income fell again in 1933 as a whole in spite of higher average prices for farm products. Another depressing factor was the failure of the World Economic Conference. Agreement could not be reached on monetary policy, the gold bloc holding to a stable monetary standard and the United States in particular desiring inflationary moves. The tariff truce achieved at the Conference was abrogated shortly afterwards as many countries withdrew

[31] Annual data in constant dollars show consumption fell 3 per cent in 1933, investment in durable assets 32 per cent. See also footnote 4 of this chapter.

[32] Relief works expenditures by all governments fell from $64 million in 1931 to $43 million in 1932, then to only $17 million in 1933. Total relief expenditures by all governments were $95-98 million in these years. *P.P.I.*, p. 208.

from it. Finally, some components of domestic demand do not appear to have reacted strongly in 1933, a factor which would limit the increases in output which were under way.

Investment and the Beginning of Recovery[33]

A serious limitation on the extent of the over-all recovery in its initial stage (and in the upswing), was the great degree of excess capacity. This meant that new investment would hardly react strongly in response to rising sales or, in other words, that any acceleration effect from greater consumption and exports would be relatively small. Existing plant would be worked to the maximum, furthermore, as a result of the pessimistic outlook engendered by developments in the downswing and by uncertainty about the duration and degree of recovery. There is direct evidence in the National Accounts that the stock of capital may not even have been maintained in these years, for depreciation greatly exceeded durable private investment. Once the recovery was definitely under way, however, such deferred replacement could be expected to stimulate recovery.

Estimates of total excess capacity are not available, but some revealing industry estimates exist.[34] In the newsprint industry, for example, the percentage of capacity utilized was only 63 per cent in 1931, 51 per cent in 1932, and 55 per cent in 1933. In 1926 the corresponding figure was 86 per cent, and from 1927 to 1929 about 74 per cent.[35] A few of the firms in this industry were operating at a much higher proportion of capacity in the early thirties than is indicated by the above ratios, and the rest were at levels well below the above ratios. Only 10 per cent of rated steel capacity was in operation in 1932.[36] The automobile industry operated at 16 per cent of its capacity in 1932, as contrasted with 66 per cent in its best production year of 1929.[37] Plants for railway rolling stock and the foundries producing castings for them were operating at less

[33] Adequate monthly series on durable investment are not available. Some series related to construction and to producers' durables were noted earlier. The annual estimates used here should be interpreted cautiously, since they are probably better indicators of trends than of short-term changes.

[34] It should be noted that in some industries the concept of excess capacity is vague. A closed mine, for example, may or may not be treated as excess capacity. See also p. 188.

[35] See Table 42.

[36] *Financial Post*, July 8, 1933.

[37] *C.Y.B.*, 1934-35, p. 460.

than 25 per cent of capacity at the end of 1931.[38] A survey early in 1932 showed operating ratios, as a proportion of normal capacity, ranging from 35 per cent in industries producing machinery to 76 per cent in textiles.[39] For many industries, and particularly for those heavily capitalized such as newsprint, the need was for greater operations, scaling down of excessive and rigid capitalization, and elimination or closing of high-cost plant, to the point where current and prospective levels of business could carry the debt charges and either show some profit or reduce losses.

Another important factor in the lag of investment was the fact that much of the investment undertaken in the last year or so of the boom could not be cut suddenly. Many of the projects required several years for completion and could be abandoned only at a large loss. The electric power industry found itself with several large undertakings at the end of the twenties which were not completed until three or more years after 1929.[40] The mining industry had also undertaken expansion in the late twenties, some of which was not completed until a year or more after the depression struck. The important point is that, once completed, there would be a lag in the upswing, so that it was not until 1934 or later that investment in some groups began to rise.[41] Such large projects require a great deal of time for completion, and also considerable planning and favourable prospects over a very long period before they are undertaken on any scale once more.

Both private and public investment in durable assets reached a low point in 1933, in both current and constant dollars, according to annual data. Judging from changes in absolute terms, the large utilities group was slower to react to the depression. The largest absolute fall in 1930 and 1931 was in the manufacturing group, with primary industries also showing a large fall in 1931. In 1932 the absolute decrease in these two groups slowed up, partly because of the low levels to which investment had already fallen and possibly also because in mid-1932 some improvement in economic activity seemed likely. In 1932, however, investment in utilities dropped sharply, with particularly large absolute and relative decreases in steam railways and central electric stations, while housing

[38] *Financial Post,* January 23, 1932.
[39] Canadian Bank of Commerce, *Monthly Commercial Letter,* March 1932.
[40] *Financial Post,* June 25, 1932.
[41] Footnote 35, CHAP. VII, is of interest in this context.

and institutions also showed larger absolute decreases in this year. In effect, in the first two years of the downswing the drop in investment was delayed, both because some large projects were completed and because government expenditures on relief works were undertaken. In 1932 these projects had been completed, and governments were curtailing expenditures on relief works. In 1933, for example, no new water-power developments were initiated, though some projects were completed.

In 1933 the rate of decrease in investment in durable assets slowed somewhat to 33 per cent, as compared with 44 per cent in the previous year. A number of primary and secondary industries reached a low point in 1932, but their combined increase in 1933 was slight and was more than offset by decreases elsewhere. As was noted above, however, a distinct revival in economic activity occurred after the first quarter of 1933. The curve of new investment, if available on a monthly basis, would likely show a decrease through 1932 and at least the first quarter of 1933, but a revival in mid-1933. This revival, however, would not compensate fully for the previous year's decrease, thus leading to a drop in the 1933 annual data compared to 1932.[42]

The crucial point to note is that the increases in investment in 1933 did not occur in the larger industries. In what had been the really large areas of investment in the late twenties, namely, agriculture, manufactures, utilities, housing, and investment by government departments, investment continued to fall in 1933 as a whole compared to 1932 as a whole. The manufacturing industries shown above as "leaders" rose by $8 million in 1933, but other manufactures fell by about $50 million. While investment by private electric railways was stable in 1933, that by other private utilities fell by $30 million. Investment in publicly owned utilities fared no better, with no category showing an increase in 1933. Even when total investment rose in 1934, there was a conspicuous lack of any large impetus from the major groups of manufacturing and utilities. Investment by federal and municipal government departments also showed little change in 1934. Direct government investment was more stable than either business investment or that by government-

[42] The quarterly index of construction volume fell in both the first and second quarter of 1933 but rose in the next two quarters. See Table 52. The deseasonalized index of volume of iron and steel imports (including both consumers' and producers' durables) was as follows for the quarters of 1932 and 1933: 43.4, 35.1, 28.5, 33.1, 24.7, 26.0, 35.9, 41.4.

Table 24

ABSOLUTE CHANGE IN NEW INVESTMENT IN DURABLE ASSETS
BY SIGNIFICANT GROUPS, 1931-4
(Millions of dollars)

Group	1931-2	1932-3	1933-4	Total investment in 1931
Primary industries	− 30	− 9	+ 21	76
Manufacturing	− 74	− 41	+ 8	157
Utilities	− 126	− 40	+ 7	221
Private utilities only	− 65	− 29	+ 10	128
Trade, finance and commercial services	− 18	− 7	+ 9	48
Business	− 248	− 97	+ 45	502
Housing	− 72	− 20	+ 22	168
Institutions	− 20	− 17	− 2	52
Government departments	− 50	− 30	+ 24	159
Other than business	− 142	− 67	+ 44	379
Total	− 390	− 164	+ 89	881

SOURCES *P.P.I.*, p. 150. The leads and lags shown below were
also derived from this publication.

The following industries show leads and lags in investment
around the 1933 turning point.

Industries reaching a Low Point for New Investment

Before 1933	*After 1933*
Primary fishing, woods, mining	
In manufacturing	In manufacturing
Rubber, leather, tobacco	Clothing
Textiles	Printed and publishing
Wood products	
Transportation equipment (level 1932-3)	
Chemical products	
	Publicly owned utilities except steam railways
	Private telephone companies
Commercial services	
	Finance
	Institutions
	Municipal enterprises and institutions

owned enterprises, but did not lead at the turning point.[43]

Finally, it will be noted from Table 25 that the fall in engineering construction was fairly slow at first as major projects were completed; government engineering construction actually rose in 1930. The largest absolute and relative declines in engineering construction came in 1932, just when some resistance to the downswing was appearing in other sectors of the economy.

Table 25

ENGINEERING CONSTRUCTION, 1929-37
(Millions of dollars)

| | Private | | Government departments | |
	Total	Change	Total	Change
1929	198		110	
1930	186	− 12	138	+ 28
1931	141	− 45	115	− 23
1932	64	− 77	79	− 36
1933	38	− 26	57	− 22
1934	41	+ 3	77	+ 20
1935	62	+ 21	87	+ 10
1936	64	+ 2	79	− 8
1937	70	+ 6	131	+ 52

SOURCE: *P.P.I.*, pp. 149 and 151.

The downward swing of private engineering construction was clearly more violent than that of government engineering construction, and the revival in 1934 in the former was very weak. The completion of projects in the downswing, combined with the extensive planning and very favourable long-term outlook necessary for such large projects, helps account for the slow recovery of total investment in the first few years of the upswing. There was actually very little recovery in private engineering construction until the increase of 1935, and not much change in the next two years, while as late as 1936 government construction was still well below the levels in the first few years of the downswing.

In summary, the low point in Canadian economic activity was in the first quarter of 1933. The spurt in prices and output for the next two quarters mainly reflected the response of the

43 See footnote 41, CHAP. III, for the relevant data.

economy to external developments. Two of these were particularly important. Exports to overseas countries rose, and export prospects improved, as a result of recovery in the United Kingdom and in other overseas countries, better wheat sales for a time and the Ottawa Agreements. The early rise in exports to the United Kingdom was particularly notable. The other and more important factor was the brief but strong burst of activity in the United States after the first quarter of 1933. The impact of this on Canada was due partly to increases in current exports, and partly to such factors as the expected increases in exports and the general price level, speculative buying in Canada and elsewhere, the rise in Canadian security prices, and the higher price of gold.

The domestic determinants of final demand were not very strong in 1933. Consumer, government, and investment expenditures all declined for the year as a whole, although some increases probably occurred for part of 1933. Although not a dynamic factor in the 1933 recovery, consumer expenditures did tend to place a broad limit to the downswing. In both 1932 and 1933, for example, they exceeded disposable income, that is, personal saving was negative. The completion of private and public projects maintained investment in durable assets for a time in the downswing. The lag in such investment at the lower turning point and the weak increases in 1934, however, limited the extent of the recovery in its initial stages.[44]

[44] As noted at the beginning of this chapter, it seemed best to rely mainly on quarterly data for our purposes when this study was made. Recently, however, some of the inadequacies in the data have been corrected, particularly through an improved technique for removing seasonal movements from the monthly series. See the paper by Edward J. Chambers, "Canadian Business Cycles since 1919: A Progress Report," presented at the annual meeting of the Canadian Political Science Association in Ottawa, June 1957. Chambers suggests a cyclical peak for Canada in April 1929, with the peak in total exports nine months earlier but that in non-agricultural exports coinciding with that of the business cycle. He tentatively places the cyclical trough for Canada in March 1933, with the trough in total exports one month later and that in non-agricultural exports one month earlier. These findings agree fairly well with those noted in this study, except that the lead in exports at the trough is less clear-cut than that suggested here. See pp. 70, 119-20, and 123, in this text, and the accompanying footnotes.

CHAPTER FIVE

The Recovery from 1933 to 1937

The recovery of the Canadian economy in the thirties was incomplete. By 1937 GNE had attained the 1926 level, but was still 13 per cent below that of 1929. The recovery appears even weaker if it is put in the perspective of a 10 per cent increase in population from 1929 to 1937. In 1937 some 10 per cent of the civilian labour force was still without jobs and seeking work.

The International Background of the Upswing[1]

The recovery of world economic activity from 1932 to 1937 was also incomplete. After five years of recovery there were still large numbers of unemployed in a number of countries. In 1937, in spite of more rapid recovery generally since 1935, the volume of world manufacturing and industrial production (both excluding the U.S.S.R.) were only 4 per cent over the 1929 level. As will be noted later, the extent of recovery varied considerably by countries. The volume of world trade in foodstuffs, in raw materials, and in manufactures recovered more slowly than world production of such products in the upswing, in relation to both 1932 and 1929. The general recovery picture would be worse if one were to take account of increases in population and productivity since 1929. Wholesale prices in a large number of countries remained well below 1929 levels, in spite of the more rapid increases in 1937, and prices of commodities entering world trade were only at half the 1929 level by 1937. With a substantial degree of unemployment still existing, a brief but sharp downswing occurred late in 1937, mainly in the United States.

The forces leading to and extending the world recovery

[1] The international aspects of the upswing are dealt with particularly well by Lewis, *Economic Survey, 1919-1939*, CHAP. IV. For longer trends particularly, see CHAPS. XII and XIII of that publication. See also Department of Commerce, *United States in the World Economy* and the publications of the League of Nations, particularly *International Currency Experience* and the various issues of *Review of World Trade* and *World Production and Prices*.

were varied. To an important extent, they reflect the natural reaction of various economies to a downswing: the need for replacement of durables accumulates; technological change continues and is applied particularly when costs are not expected to shrink further; the stronger trends in relatively new industries, such as the application of electric power, reassert themselves; the economic fabric is strengthened by the demise of weaker firms; and so on. But there were other important factors in the recovery, chief of which was government action to expedite it. Such action was not entirely positive in its effects. Restrictions on international trade, which often accompanied inflationary policies, offset the stimulating effects of the latter on other countries. Government policies unduly raised some costs. In the United States a great deal of antipathy developed between government and the business community, with some restrictive effects on investment. Nevertheless, government intervention of various types was an important factor designed both to effect reforms in the economy and expedite recovery. A number of obstacles to recovery were removed. Easy money policies were generally followed. Public spending was undertaken on a large scale in a number of countries, both to speed recovery and, especially toward the end of this period, for armaments.

Given these efforts and the endogenous forces leading to recovery, the question arises as to why the recovery was incomplete. Obviously, generalization about a situation which varied from country to country is difficult, but a few of the more important reasons are noted below, and the recovery in Canada's main markets is considered in more detail later.

The relatively slow revival of output of capital goods was an important brake on recovery. World manufacturing output of consumption goods (excluding the U.S.S.R.) was 80 per cent of the 1929 level in 1932; this percentage increased steadily to levels of 90 and 94 in 1934 and 1935, and to 105 in 1937. For capital goods the corresponding data on the base 1929 were 43, 64, 77 and 103 per cent. It was not, in effect, until the more rapid upswing of 1936-7 that output of capital goods increased to the 1929 level. The situation differed greatly by countries. In some, including both Canada and the United States, the previous upswing had left a considerably expanded stock of new capital, with the result that in the recovery substantial excess capacity prevailed, and investment was largely restricted to replacement. Investment lagged in the gold bloc countries also; over-valued currencies in these countries struck at export competitiveness, led to large outflows of capital, and exerted deflationary pressures throughout most of the upswing.

Another factor which slowed the recovery was the severity of the preceding slump. The extent of liquidation was so great, and the world trading and financial community so severely disrupted, that the effects were bound to linger throughout the upswing. The excessive nature of such downswing developments as the collapse in prices of primary products and increase in primary stocks, and the large degree of excess capacity, as well as the continuing high levels of debt, led to a cautious approach to new investment for some time to come.

The importance of the United States in world production and imports, noted earlier, meant that the slow and irregular nature of the recovery in that country contributed greatly to the incompleteness of world recovery. The recovery in the United States, compared to recoveries elsewhere, was rapid relative to 1932-3 but slow relative to 1929. Moreover, it was an exceedingly irregular recovery and culminated in a sharp recession in 1937-8.[2] The low and fluctuating level of imports into the United States in the thirties delayed world recovery, was partly responsible for the attempts to achieve more self-sufficiency elsewhere, and in turn led to discrimination against United States exports.[3]

The disintegration of the world trading and financial community also retarded the upswing. As already noted, world trade in various types of products lagged behind world production of such products in the upswing, and foreign investment was reduced to a trickle. The contrast in international economic policy in the twenties and thirties was extreme. In the earlier period most countries had directed their efforts to achieving stability in the foreign value of their currency, convertibility, and a fair degree of stability in tariffs. In the thirties restrictions multiplied as countries retaliated against others, attempted to protect domestic industry from foreign competition, and strove to meet problems in their international payments situation. Not only did tariffs move up sharply in the downswing, but ex-

2 For a diagrammatic representation of the fluctuating recovery of industrial production in North America, contrasted with the more steady improvement in Europe, see League of Nations, *World Production and Prices, 1935-36*, p. 30.

3 See Department of Commerce, *United States in the World Economy*, particularly the Summary and Recommendations. Note also Table 18 on p. 187 of that publication, which compares imports by the United States and by all other countries from 1929 to 1938.

change controls, flexible currencies, discriminatory trade agreements, and other devices as well grew in importance as countries undertook to direct trade more closely and to insulate domestic economies from outside pressures. Trade tended to be concentrated more and more in economic blocs.[4]

Attempts to halt this trend were unsuccessful at first. The most ambitious attempt to stimulate foreign trade and investment and make a co-ordinated effort at recovery was the World Economic Conference of June 1933. The desire of the participating countries to pursue separate recovery policies was too great for the conference to achieve a general stabilization of currencies. Several countries had left the gold standard earlier, but a wave of them followed the United Kingdom in late 1931 to a fluctuating currency. Another group, led by France, attempted to protect the old gold parities after the World Economic Conference failed. These gold bloc countries generally found themselves somewhat in the position of the United Kingdom after 1925, in that deflationary measures had to be undertaken in order to offset the relatively high prices resulting from overvalued currencies. France lost large sums of gold to the United Kingdom and especially to the United States. Recovery in the gold bloc was exceedingly slow, which in turn tended to exercise a retarding influence on world recovery. The United States wrote down the gold content of her currency and stabilized it in terms of gold in January 1934. Thus three major types of exchange rate policies were followed.

With world recovery under way, attempts to clear away impediments to trade were more successful. Stability of currencies became more general after the United States dollar was stabilized. When France and the other major members of the gold bloc devalued in 1936, a tripartite agreement with the United States and United Kingdom was signed to ensure currency stability between them. Foreign trade was slowly liberalized, particularly after the United States reciprocal trade agreements act of 1934.

The more rapid recovery in the United States and other countries after mid-1935 expedited the recovery of world trade and prices. The terms of trade between primary and manufactured products in world trade improved in favour of the former as the upswing progressed, and stocks of primary commodities

---

4 This tendency is clearly revealed by a table on p. 34 of League of Nations, *Review of World Trade, 1938*, which shows the percentage share of "Empire Trade" in the trade of certain countries from 1929 to 1938.

were reduced. On the whole, however, recovery in trade and foreign investment was incomplete. Average prices of world trade commodities showed a very moderate recovery in the upswing. In contrast with the twenties, the net movement of long-term capital was to creditors; long-term capital outflows were small in the thirties and were exceeded by repayments. Reversal of the outflows of long-term capital from the United States, and a large volume of short-term inflows into the United States because of monetary and political instability in Europe, led to the depletion of the gold stocks of a number of overseas countries.

The Nature of the Recovery in Canada

There were some spectacular recoveries in Canada after 1933 if percentage changes are considered. Investment in new machinery and equipment, for example, rose from $84 million in 1933 to $281 million in 1937. The increase of $101 million in 1937 was almost the same as that in 1929, but the latter had taken place on a base two and a half times larger than that of 1936, with a population 10 per cent less than that of 1937. Rather than compare percentage changes from 1933, we shall consider to what extent the recovery was able to attain the previous 1929 peak or the 1926 level.

In commenting on the downswing it was emphasized that the most severe collapse occurred in domestic investment. Similarly, the most significant failure to attain the previous peak during the upswing was in domestic investment in durable assets. Business investment in durable assets, that is, excluding residential construction, was particularly low. By comparison, the recoveries in other sectors were much better. By 1937, government expenditures had virtually reached the 1929 level, consumer expenditure was at the levels of 1926 and 1927, and exports of goods and services were fairly close to every year in the late twenties except 1928. Merchandise exports were still well below the levels of the late twenties, but if gold is included 1937 is comparable to 1927 and 1929. Imports, on the other hand, were well below the levels of the late twenties. The recoveries of the major components of GNE were much stronger in terms of constant dollars, indicating the lack of a full recovery in prices; the implicit price index of GNE in 1937 and 1939 was about 13 per cent below the 1929 level. The exception, however, was business investment in durable assets, which showed about the same extent of recovery in constant dollars as in current dollars (both as a percentage of 1929).

To evaluate these recoveries properly, however, account must be taken of increases in population. In 1926 and 1929 the population of Canada was 9,451 thousand and 10,029 thousand respectively; in 1937 and 1939, it was 11,045 thousand and 11,267 thousand respectively. The civilian labour force grew from 4,105 thousand in 1931 to 4,476 and 4,598 thousand in 1937 and 1939 respectively. Viewed in the perspective of the increases in population and labour force, the recovery is much weaker.

Thus the recovery generally was incomplete, and particularly that of durable business investment. Even if one uses 1926 for comparative purposes rather than the peak of the boom in 1929, exports and imports of goods and services and investment in durable assets had still not fully recovered by 1937. If constant dollar series are considered, however, all components of expenditure except investment in durable assets had exceeded the 1926 level by 1937.[5]

Tables 11 and 26 indicate that some of the components of GNE had regained their former weight in GNE by 1937. Consumer and government expenditures played a relatively greater role for much of the recovery than they did in the late twenties. Exports of goods and services recovered steadily, as a percentage of GNE, to a figure generally higher than that of the late twenties. Merchandise exports recovered to their 1926-9 proportion only if gold is included. Imports rose more slowly to something less than their former weight. Finally, investment had a much smaller share in GNE throughout the upswing.

A good part of the increase in GNE and its components during the upswing was achieved in the last year of the period. Relative to the levels of the late twenties, in other words, the recovery was very incomplete until as late as 1937. Fully 36 per cent of the increase in GNE during the four-year period from 1934 to 1937 inclusive occurred in the last year. For consumer expenditure, the proportion was the same; for government expenditure, 50 per cent; investment in durable assets, 44 per cent; exports of goods and services, 21 per cent; and imports of goods and services, 39 per cent.[6]

[5] Inventory investment is subject to various definitions and is not considered in this paragraph.
[6] It should be added that government expenditure fell in 1936, and export increases slowed down considerably in 1937.

Let us turn to the mechanism of recovery after 1933. With rising export sales, inventory ratios would begin to fall. Prices had begun to rise, moreover. Thus the incentive to inventory disinvestment, which was so marked in the non-agricultural sector earlier, would be weakened. In fact, inventory disinvestment in this sector slowed down in 1933 and gave way to a small net investment in the next year. Although there was no significant inventory investment in the non-agricultural sector until 1936, at least the increases in sales could be transmitted to production.[7] The increases in output would raise employment and incomes and lead directly to some replacement expenditures in the industries concerned. Respending of these incomes would spread the effects throughout the economy, with the further effects on income depending on the size and continuity of the original stimulus and the extent to which increased incomes went to savings (including debt repayment), taxes and imports. These multiplier effects would induce at least some replacement of plant and equipment, particularly in view of the fact that costs were still low but rising. Investment, in turn, would affect incomes and expenditures. Thus the recovery would spread cumulatively under the impact of these spending and respending streams, and also with any independent increases in other types of expenditures.

A brief statistical outline of the course of the upswing to 1937 will help put the subsequent analysis in perspective. In 1934, the first year of general recovery in the annual GNE series, GNE rose by almost 14 per cent from the depressed 1933 level. A rise of almost 12 per cent in terms of constant dollars indicates that increases in volume played the major role in this year. The one significant exception was a large increase in prices of exports and imports. Exports of goods and services rose by $192 million, imports by $120 million, and a surplus appeared on current international account for the first time since 1926. The size of the increase in exports is apparent if one considers that consumer expenditure rose by $190 million, yet this item is several times the size of exports. Another highly important change was an increase in the value and volume of inventories. This was the first increase in volume appearing in the annual data since 1930.

The significant changes in absolute terms in 1934 were the increases in exports and imports and the appearance of a current surplus, the reversal of inventory disinvestment, and the

7 See Tables 21-22.

Table 26

CHANGES IN GROSS NATIONAL EXPENDITURE, 1929-39(a)

Component	1937 and 1939 as a percentage of 1929				Components as a percentage of current dollar totals		
	Current dollars		Constant dollars(b)				
	1937	1939	1937	1939	1929	1937	1939
Consumer expenditure	86.0	88.9	101.7	103.7	71.2	70.5	68.4
Government expenditure	98.4	107.8	105.9	118.0	11.1	12.5	12.9
Gross domestic investment							
Including inventories	53.3	67.3	51.7	72.8	22.6	13.8	16.4
Excluding inventories	48.6	45.5	50.8	48.1	21.6	12.1	10.6
Residential construction	71.3	74.9	79.0	84.1	4.0	3.3	3.2
Non-residential construction	39.1	34.2	41.5	37.4	7.9	3.5	2.9
Machinery and equipment	47.1	42.5	47.5	43.0	9.7	5.2	4.4
Exports of goods and services	97.5	88.9	112.8	113.7	26.5	29.7	25.4
Merchandise only excluding gold	88.4	76.9	102.9	113.0	19.1	19.4	15.9
Imports of goods and services	72.4	68.3	84.7	84.3	31.5	26.3	23.3
Merchandise only	61.0	56.1	75.2	75.4	20.6	14.5	12.5
Gross National Expenditure	86.8	92.6	97.5	106.1	100.0(c)	100.0(c)	100.0(c)

SOURCES: *National Accounts* or derived therefrom. Volume of foreign trade derived from D.B.S., *Export and Import Price Indexes, 1926-1948.*

(a) Data for 1933 are in Table 11 above.
(b) 1935-9 dollars.
(c) Does not add to 100 per cent exactly because of rounding and residual error.

rise in consumer expenditures. Government revenues and expenditures rose together, so that the deficit for all governments was not greatly changed. The percentage increase of investment in durable assets, though larger than that of any other major component of GNE, was primarily a reflection of the exceptionally low levels to which investment had fallen. Investment in durable assets continued to register larger percentage increases than other components of GNE in almost every year up to and including 1937. Yet, significantly, it was not until as late as 1937 that investment in durable assets exceeded capital charges relating to these assets. In other words, a very large part of the investment taking place in these years must have been for replacement, in contrast to the situation in the late twenties.

The initial increase in activity was rapid, both after the first quarter of 1933 and from 1933 to 1934. An initial spurt of activity is not surprising, given the dramatic stimulus from the United States in 1933, purchases in expectation of price recovery, and the desire to satisfy urgent replacement needs. Thereafter, however, the strength of the upswing might be expected to slow down. Excess capacity would weaken the accelerator effect of rising output. Much of the enlarged income might find its way to debt repayment rather than directly to new expenditures. Businessmen would hesitate to undertake substantial commitments for new investment until the extent of the upswing was apparent. The desire to restore lower inventory ratios might well lead to production being kept in pace with sales, that is, might lead to only a moderate inventory build-up. Thus, the pace of an upswing which follows a major decline could tend to be slower after an initial spurt. It was not, in fact, until 1937 that the 1934 rate of expansion in GNE was matched.[8]

In both 1935 and 1936 GNE rose by about 8 per cent. The volume increase in 1935 was the same, but in 1936 fell to less than 5 per cent. The implicit price index for GNE rose very little in 1934 and 1935; the increase of 3 per cent in 1936 raised it to an index level of only 98.5, compared with 93.7 at its lowest point in 1933 and 115.3 in 1929 (on the base 1935-9).

[8] The annual data hide significant variations within the year, particularly in 1937. Strong exogenous factors, if erratic, could change the above pattern. It is interesting to note that in the United States (taking major and minor cycles together) the rate of expansion of cyclical upswings typically slows down after the initial stage. See Mitchell, *What Happens during Business Cycles*, pp. 296-302.

The over-all price recovery was clearly very slow. Exports of goods and services rose steadily, and particularly sharply in 1936 with large wheat exports swelling the total. With imports rising but lagging behind exports, the current account surplus was steadily increased. In both 1935 and 1936 the increase in disposable income was almost wholly absorbed by consumer expenditure. Agricultural inventories fell in 1936 as the heavy stocks of grain which had accumulated were sharply reduced. Government spending on goods and services had risen once more in 1935 but levelled out in 1936, the only major component of GNE (apart from inventories) which did not increase fairly sharply in 1936. With rising revenues and a levelling of total expenditures, the deficits of both federal and other governments were sharply reduced in 1936. The decrease in inventories and levelling off of government spending explain why GNE did not rise faster in 1936 in spite of some very large increases in other types of expenditure.

The more rapid increases from mid-1936 to 1937 were associated with several factors. Industrial production in the United States was not much higher in 1934 than in 1933, but rose more rapidly in 1935 and 1936. Industrial production in the United Kingdom rose steadily and strongly from 1934 to 1937 inclusive. Exports, to both the United Kingdom and the United States, rose especially sharply in 1936. It is true that a large part of the export increase represented a drawing down of the heavy wheat stocks in Canada.[9] Nevertheless, the faster recovery in these years must be associated in part with the favourable expectations created by the elimination of the wheat carryovers as a result of short world crops, and by a rapid rise in wheat prices. The trade treaty with the United States went into effect on January 1, 1936, and exports of a number of products were favourably affected. In particular, export prices began to rise more rapidly in 1936 and especially in 1937, and the terms of trade were improving after 1934. Rising prices eased the burden of rigid costs such as interest and freight rates. Consumers' purchases of durables and producers' invest-

---

9 In effect, this part of increased exports was offset by induced disinvestment. Further, the proceeds on this would be used to repay debt incurred in carrying the wheat stocks rather than to raise farm cash income. See A. F. W. Plumptre, "The Distribution of Outlay and the 'Multiplier' in the British Dominions," *CJEPS*, p. 370. Exports of wheat and flour declined by $55 million in 1937 because of crop failure, after rising $81 million in 1936; but in 1937 such exports were well over the 1931-5 values. See also the next sentence in the text and Table 40.

ment both speeded up in 1937, as with more rapidly rising incomes the postponed demands for replacement began to be satisfied more fully.

The year 1937 would probably have led to a new phase of the upswing, with a more rapid revival throughout the economy. This much would certainly be indicated by the changes in that year. GNE rose by 14 per cent in value and 10 per cent in volume. The 9 per cent rise in consumption (6 per cent in volume) was the largest percentage increase of the upswing, and the absolute increase of $320 million exceeded that of any year in the late twenties by a wide margin. The increase in disposable income was large enough to finance the above increase in consumption and still allow personal saving to double to a level of $164 million; this level was only about half that of the late twenties, but the absolute increase in 1937 was far in excess of that for any year since 1926.[10] Government spending on goods and services rose by $71 million, in contrast to the stability of 1936; since total revenues and expenditures rose about the same amount, the deficit for all governments remained at the low level of the previous year. Investment in durable assets rose 38 per cent; the absolute increase was larger than the increases of 1935 and 1936 combined. Investment was beginning to get under way once more, but not so much in construction as in machinery and equipment. The ratio of the volume of non-residential construction to that of machinery and equipment in 1937 was, at 67 per cent, about the same as in 1926 and 1927, but considerably below the 80 per cent of 1928 and 1929. Evidently there was still some hesitation in undertaking larger construction projects. Inventories rose sharply in 1937, except in the agricultural sector where the large stocks accumulated in earlier years were once more drawn down.

The slower increase in exports of goods and services in 1937 was a less favourable development; although the increase in value was 11 per cent, volume rose by only 2 per cent. Wheat stocks had already fallen to low levels at the end of the previous crop year. With another very low crop, exports of wheat fell and offset much of the increase in other exports. Imports of goods and services rose 19 per cent in value and

10 From one point of view such a rapid increase would be regarded as an increased diversion from spending and therefore, as a retarding factor in recovery, unless offset elsewhere. The only point suggested here is that the more rapid increase in personal saving may indicate the emergence of a new phase in recovery, in contrast to negative or very low saving earlier.

10 per cent in volume, reflecting the sharper increases in consumption and investment associated with the more rapid tempo of the upswing. The current account surplus fell from its 1936 level, but was still quite high at $182 million.

In the third quarter of 1937 the indexes of physical volume of production and of industrial production remained virtually stable at the level of the second quarter. They rose slightly in the fourth quarter, then fell sharply in the first quarter of 1938 as the effects of the downswing in the United States and other factors were felt.[11]

The above section has given a brief review of the upswing. It is now time to look more fully at certain specific developments, and to explain why the recovery was so incomplete. Eventually, one must turn to an examination of industries in order to trace more specifically the effects of retarding influences and their relation to the period before the upswing.

It was noted earlier that large deficits developed in the current account as the investment boom of the twenties reached its peak, imports increased rapidly, and wheat and flour exports fell in 1929. The deficit on merchandise trade lasted only two years, 1929 and 1930. From 1931 to 1936 the trade surplus grew almost steadily, first as imports fell more rapidly (and over a longer period) than exports, and later as exports rose more rapidly than imports in absolute terms. After 1929, furthermore, non-monetary gold available for export grew steadily through 1937. At first net payments for invisibles were relatively rigid (basically because net payments of interest and dividends were relatively rigid), but after 1932 these were reduced also. Thus there were current account surpluses from 1934 to 1937 inclusive. The counterpart to these surpluses appeared primarily in repatriation of debt and outflows of direct investment funds. Retirements by governments and corporations rose steadily after 1932, while new issues (mainly by governments) were relatively stable. Direct investment flows were outward after 1931.[12]

[11] The 1937-8 recession is not directly relevant to the major themes of our analysis. For differing interpretations of this recession, see Marcus, *Canada and the International Business Cycle*, CHAP. VI; Edward J. Chambers, "The 1937-8 Recession in Canada," *CJEPS*; and Marcus' "Comment" in the May 1956 issue of *CJEPS*.

[12] A separation of the direct investment flows into Canadian and foreign capital is not available. The bulk of such flows were presumably foreign capital. See D.B.S., *Canadian Balance of International Payments* (1939), pp. 144-51.

Similar capital flows occur in more highly industrialized countries also, and within the domestic economy. As funds accumulate in the upswing, but holders hesitate to make fresh commitments in terms of physical assets, such funds are used to retire debt. This use of funds would be particularly tempting when the extent of debt had been greatly increased by the previous upswing, and where governments and corporations had had unfortunate experiences in trying to meet large fixed cost liabilities with optional payment features. Subsidiaries and branches of foreign companies in Canada would not only increase their income transfers as earnings rose, but might also transfer any surplus balances abroad if the outlets for such funds in Canada were limited or parent companies required the funds, or if unsuccessful operations were being liquidated. The difference between the Canadian upswing and those in some other countries lay in the fact that much of this drive for liquidity and clearing up of debt expressed itself in net outflows of capital. If such funds had been retained on balance in the Canadian economy, it probably cannot be assumed in the circumstances of the upswing that they would necessarily have found their way into physical investment. The need or desire to retire debt, wherever held, would be a retarding force in the recovery. Net withdrawals of funds from Canada could slow up the easing of monetary conditions, however, and the policy of retiring government debt abroad and re-funding in Canada was probably deflationary on balance.[13]

The slow increase in prices was a serious limitation on recovery. The wholesale price index (base year 1926) reached a low of 66.7 in 1932. By 1936 it was only 74.6; over half of the change from 1932 had occurred in the annual index for 1934. Prices of consumers' goods held up better than those of producers' goods in the downswing, although most of this differential had been wiped out by 1936. But the components of the index of consumers' goods reacted quite differently. Prices of manufacturers' materials fell from 95.9 in 1929 to 57.5 in 1933, and recovered to only 67.9 in 1936. This series, in effect, conformed closely to the composite index. But prices of building and construction materials were much more rigid, as shown in Table 12, and prices of producers' equipment even more so.[14]

[13] This point is examined further on p. 96.
[14] The index of prices of producers' goods includes manufacturers' materials, building and construction materials, and producers' equipment. The last of these, on the base 1926, was 94.6, 86.0, 90.0, and 93.8 for 1929, 1933, 1936, and 1937 respectively.

Those items which entered most directly into investment costs, in other words, were extremely rigid throughout the period. It was noted earlier that the fall in farm prices was sharper than that in prices of commodities and services used by farmers. Some of this differential in prices had been removed by 1936 because of the faster rise in farm prices. The terms of trade had also improved by 1936, though both export and import prices were very low.

The slowness of the recovery in prices to 1936 can be traced to the very slow recovery in both export and import prices, large world stocks, and the large degree of unemployment and excess capacity. Some part of the price maladjustments of the downswing had been corrected by 1936. In 1936-7 the recovery in prices was greatly speeded up, reflecting more rapid recovery abroad for a time and decreased international stocks of many raw materials and foodstuffs. The wholesale price index and export and import indexes jumped sharply, the terms of trade improved rapidly, farm prices rose more rapidly than costs. An unfavourable feature from the point of view of investment was the sharp rise in the prices of producers' goods. In 1937 prices of building and construction materials rose by 11 per cent, and those of manufacturers' materials by over 20 per cent. Wage rates, which had risen by only 5 per cent from 1933 to 1936, increased rapidly by over 7 per cent in 1937; the increase in the metal trades was 10 per cent, that in building only 3 per cent. While some of the more rapid of these increases were unfavourable in terms of their effects on investment and output, they were mitigated by lower overhead costs per unit as output rose, higher inventory profits as prices rose, and increased consumer purchases.

In line with our comments earlier on business men's reactions to an upswing, the volume of non-agricultural inventories rose in 1934 and 1935. These increases were exceedingly small, however, when considered in relation to increases in business sales, GNE, and other indicators.[15] It would appear that, in the face of increasing sales volume, business inventories were raised somewhat, but output was kept very close to sales volume for a few years. (What is likely to have happened, of course, is that some industries still with large inventories reduced them in response to increased sales, while others increased them.) By 1936 and 1937, however, the generally cautious attitude to inventory accumulation was changing. The

[15] See Tables 21 and 22, and note that, in constant dollars, GNE rose $436, $322, $208, and $463 million in 1934-7 respectively.

rise in prices now speeded up. The increase in the volume of non-agricultural inventories in 1937 was larger than that of 1928. In response partly to the very large stocks still remaining after the downswing, therefore, it was several years before this sector of investment grew strongly. In manufacturing the ratio of stocks to output was permitted to fall back to approximately that prevailing in 1929. Meanwhile, however, the rising price level was slowly adding to corporation profits because of the effect of rising prices on stocks on hand.

In the upswing the distribution of income by types partially reverted to that prevailing in 1929. In 1936-7 wages and salaries were 62-64 per cent of net national income, investment income 19-20 per cent, net income of farmers 6-7 per cent, and that of unincorporated business 11 per cent.[16] As compared to 1929, the first and second of these groups had gained while the third and fourth were below their 1929 proportions. It is difficult to analyse the effects of such changes on consumer expenditures without additional and more refined data. The rapid increase in the second of these shares in the upswing might tend to slow the recovery if one can assume that the marginal propensity to consume from this type of income was less than for the others.[17] Indeed, a very large proportion of investment income does not directly enter personal disposable income, and it was this portion (especially undistributed corporation profits) which accounted for the greater part of the increase in investment income after 1933. Thus about one-quarter of the increase in net national income from 1933 to 1937 did not directly affect personal disposable income. Furthermore, while transfer payments rose in the upswing, augmenting personal income, the increase in personal direct taxes offset this gain completely.

The actual behaviour of consumer expenditures and personal saving can be measured broadly.[18] The average propensity to save was markedly lower in the upswing than in the late twenties, reflecting the very low levels of income in the thirties. Personal saving in 1926-9 was 6.4-8.7 per cent of personal disposable income in current dollars (both excluding the change in farm inventories). In 1934 it was 0.6 per cent; as incomes rose, however, this percentage rose steadily reaching 4.1 in

[16] For the proportions in 1929 and 1933, see p. 52.
[17] This section is designed to cover consumer expenditures only. Effects on investment are neglected here.
[18] Somewhat different methods were used to estimate consumer expenditures before and after 1930 in the *National Accounts*. See p. 106 of that publication. See also Table 14 for data on disposable income and consumption.

1937. The marginal propensity to consume appears to have risen in 1935 and 1936, but not in 1937.[19] Thus it appears that while consumers tended to save a somewhat larger proportion of income as income rose, they also spent a rising proportion of additional income for a time. This would suggest an upward shift in the consumption function at the same time that income was rising.[20]

The pattern of change in types of expenditures in 1933-7 was as expected: expenditures on consumer durables doubled as postponed demands were satisfied; the largest group, non-durables (many of which are nevertheless postponable), increased by one-third; and the services group rose by only one-sixth. By 1937 durables were 8.3 per cent of total consumer expenditures, as compared to 8.8 per cent in 1929, but they had been well below the former figure in the earlier years of the upswing.

Government Policies in the Upswing

In the Ottawa Agreements of 1932 Canada increased preference margins by lowering her preference tariff and raising the intermediate and general tariffs.[21] Special taxes and exchange dumping duties were to be modified. The Ottawa Agreements opened some outlets for primary products in the United Kingdom. Since Canada was wedded to a heavily protectionist policy, the increased preferences were generally given by lowering duties on imports from the United Kingdom when Canadian output of these products was small, but otherwise by raising duties against imports from other countries. In 1937 a new agreement with the United Kingdom was negotiated, renewing the concessions of 1932 and effecting some further reductions. In 1932 and later, treaties were negotiated with

[19] See Table 32. The import content of such expenditures cannot be delineated at present. The estimates referred to, moreover, do not refer to the actual nature of the short-term relationship between changes in income and in consumption. They represent, rather, a historical relationship involving the effects of changes in a number of variables on changes in consumption.

[20] This would be so for a linear function. Alternatively, the data could suggest a curvilinear function, concave upward.

[21] For tariff policy in the upswing, see Parkinson, *Memorandum*, CHAPS. VII and IX; McDiarmid, *Commercial Policy in the Canadian Economy*, CHAPS. XII and XIV; and *Rowell-Sirois Report*, Appendix III, CHAP. VII. The effects of protectionist policies were evaluated briefly on pp. 92-5.

other Commonwealth countries and some other countries.

The 1932 agreements retained protection for manufacturers in Canada, while tending to increase the share of the United Kingdom and other Commonwealth countries in Canadian trade at the expense of other countries, and the United States in particular.[22] But increased preferences and heavy protection were, at best, only a partial answer to Canada's problems. The United States was Canada's largest export market from 1926 to 1932, and her second largest market from 1933 to 1937. She was the largest external source of supply throughout the period. And Canada was the largest export market for the United States.

A number of circumstances led to a breach in the high protective tariffs of the two countries. Legislation permitting reciprocal trade agreements was passed in the United States. With recovery, some concessions could be made more easily. And it was increasingly obvious in Canada that most of the primary industries were recovering very slowly. A treaty with the United States was signed in late 1935 to take effect on January 1, 1936. The reductions of the high Smoot-Hawley duties on many primary products were of particular importance to Canada, although quotas were introduced on such exports. Canada reduced protection for a number of manufactured products. The procedures for dealing with dumping and valuation were modified. Although both accorded the other most-favoured-nation treatment, the Imperial preferences were not changed and, indeed, limited the extent to which concessions were possible. It is difficult to separate the effects of the treaty from the effects of faster recovery and the drought in the United States, but it is at least suggestive that those Canadian imports and exports on which duties were reduced increased faster in 1936 than did those on which no concessions were made.[23] In November 1938, agreements were signed between Canada and the United States and the United States and the United Kingdom. The bilateral treaties made it possible for Canada to receive concessions by reducing some Imperial preferences.

In considering monetary policy in the downswing, the dil-

---

[22] The larger proportion of trade with the United Kingdom in the thirties reflects also the composition of trade. The capital goods in Canadian imports from the United States, for example, would show a slow recovery, relative to 1929, because of the low level of investment in Canada. The greater stability of income in the United Kingdom would also contribute to this result.

[23] McDiarmid, *Commercial Policy in the Canadian Economy*, p. 338. See also Parkinson, *Memorandum*, CHAP. IX, Table 14.

emma facing the government with respect to exchange rate policy was noted. Without developed institutions of monetary control, apprehensive of the consequences when much of the debt was held abroad, and unwilling to take action which might damage the national credit, the government decided not to act. With the appreciation of sterling in 1933, the political pressure for depreciation was lessened.

More use was made of monetary policy in the upswing than was done earlier.[24] In late 1932 the government had persuaded the banks to take $35 million of Treasury bills, to use them to obtain advances of currency under the Finance Act, and not to pay off these advances for two years.[25] Commercial loans continued to fall in 1933, but security holdings rose and deposits were finally stabilized. With the appreciation of the Canadian dollar to parity with the United States dollar in late 1933, and the easy money policies of the United States and the United Kingdom, the Canadian government could now pursue easy money policies in step with other countries and without as much fear of deterioration of the foreign exchange situation. In June 1934, legislation was passed to permit an increase of $53 million in the fiduciary note issue, and these proceeds were spent by the government for public works and other purposes. The resulting increase of bank reserves led to greater purchases of government bonds, rather than an increase in loans. In 1935 the Bank of Canada was formed to assume the functions of a central bank. It continued the process of adding to commercial banks' reserves by its purchases of gold, foreign exchange, and securities.[26] Since commercial loans could not be made on a large enough scale – at least, until late 1936 – the banks turned further to government bonds. This process tended to lower bond yields. Thus the decrease in interest rates, which had been very slow in the early thirties, was speeded up, and the rising government debt was financed.

While the decline in bond yields, which began early in 1932, continued with some interruptions throughout the upswing, it would be an error to assume that all borrowers could take advantage of this. After the severe monetary deflation,

[24] See Parkinson, *Memorandum*, pp. 215-26; the second footnote below; and Table 13.

[25] It appears some of the banks used the advances to repay previous borrowings under the Act. Parkinson, *Memorandum*, p. 217.

[26] For the operations of the Bank of Canada see Canada, House of Commons, Standing Committee on Banking and Commerce, *Memoranda and Tables Respecting the Bank of Canada*, 1939 Session.

Table 27

EXPENDITURES ON RELIEF WORKS AND TOTAL RELIEF, 1930-7
(Millions of dollars)

Item	1930	1931	1932	1933	1934	1935	1936	1937
All governments								
Relief works	10	64	43	17	50	68	56	42
Total relief	18	97	95	98	159	173	159	165
Federal government								
Relief works	4	27	16	10	21	48	39	22
Total relief	4	38	37	36	61	79	81	89
All private and public invest-								
ment in durable assets	1,287	881	491	327	416	505	590	828

SOURCE: *P.P.I.*, Appendix C.

bankruptcies, and defaults of previous years, easy money was limited (especially at first) to "credit-worthy" borrowers as defined by banks and lending institutions. Nor did the lower rates and increased availability of funds lead necessarily to increased physical investment, given the pessimistic expectations regarding the profitability of investment. Lower interest rates more typically meant re-funding of debt.

Unemployment relief in Canada was basically the responsibility of municipalities, although both federal and provincial governments contributed to the cost.[27] In 1932 the programme of relief works was gradually dropped in favour of direct relief as municipalities and provincial governments ran into financial problems, and as dissatisfaction with the work schemes grew. In 1934, however, the federal government initiated a new relief works programme of its own, gradually shifting the emphasis to ordinary public works rather than relief works. As recovery speeded up in 1936 and 1937, expenditures under this programme declined. The relief works programme as a whole was at times a large proportion of total private and public investment, but only because the latter was so low. Both its positive correlation with economic activity in 1931 to 1935 and its size suggest that the effects as a contra-cyclical policy were limited.

In 1935 a new programme of legislation was announced,[28] which included an employment exchange system, unemployment insurance, minimum wages and limitation of hours of labour, and limitation of unfair trade practices. The emphasis was on reform of certain practices and defects of the industrial system, rather than on a recovery programme as such. All but the last of these measures were declared *ultra vires* of the federal government; so was a marketing act for natural products. The Dominion Housing Act was passed in 1935, and other acts with respect to housing were passed later.[29]

An over-all view of some of the effects of government policies can be obtained by considering the contributions to and deductions from total expenditures made by all governments combined. Governments receive taxes and some other revenues and contribute expenditures on goods and services, transfer payments, and subsidies. Apart from the size of the government

[27] For an analysis of the relief programmes, see *P.P.I.*, Appendix C.

[28] See C. A. Curtis, "Dominion Legislation of 1935," *CJEPS*.

[29] See the section on housing, p. 131. For wheat policy and farm debt adjustment, see pp. 118-20.

surplus or deficit, the actual levels and composition of expenditures and receipts should be considered.

The relative stability of government expenditures on goods and services was noted earlier, although substantial declines occurred in 1932-3 just as the recovery was getting under way, and such expenditures levelled out in 1936 when the recovery speeded up. The net contribution of both federal and other governments, at least as shown by the deficits, was considerably enlarged from 1930 to 1935 inclusive relative to 1929. On the other hand, the deficits of 1933-5 were smaller than those earlier, and the combined deficits were fairly constant; the deficits were almost eliminated in 1936-7, well short of full employment; and the changes in the deficits of federal and other governments throughout most of the upswing were offsetting in nature.[30] If one considers the individual revenue and expenditure items, moreover, further modifications must be made to the expansionary influence of government expenditure. The emphasis on regressive taxation is evident in the size of indirect taxes, and the proportion of these in total revenue rose in the downswing. The effects of a rising burden of taxation on specific industries will be noted later. Relief expenditures, which rose sharply both in absolute terms and as a proportion of total expenditures, could be expected to raise the marginal propensity to consume. On the other hand, the interest portion of expenditures also rose; total interest payments by governments rose from $235 million in 1929 to $283 million in 1933 and, in spite of re-funding at lower rates, were still $273 million in 1937. The effects of interest payments on consumption would likely be less than those of most other types of expenditures, and an important proportion of such interest was paid abroad.[31]

The way in which deficits were financed would also determine their expansionary effects. The increase in net public debts of governments was financed mainly in the home market. At

[30] As noted on p. 58, the deficits cannot be regarded as the result of deliberate anti-cyclical policy. It should be noted that fairly constant deficits, as in 1933-5, can be accompanied by a positive effect from over-all government budgets. Increased revenues and expenditures with constant deficits, as in 1934 and 1935, would tend to activate savings—subject to any changes in the composition of revenues and expenditures, or in the financing of deficits, which had the opposite effect.

[31] In 1938 interest paid abroad was $139 million. The issues accounting for this were Dominions, 31; provincials, 23; municipals, 16; steam railways, 48; other corporations, 21. D.B.S., *Canadian Balance of International Payments 1926 to 1948*, p. 132.

Table 28

GOVERNMENT REVENUE AND EXPENDITURE, 1929-37(a)

(Millions of dollars)

Item	1929	1930	1931	1932	1933	1934	1935	1936	1937
Expenditure									
Goods and services	682	767	738	643	526	568	603	600	671
Transfer payments	236	257	291	326	355	396	397	400	410
Subsidies	5	7	18	9	8	8	23	14	10
Total	923	1,031	1,047	978	889	972	1,023	1,014	1,091
Federal	323	342	331	303	303	316	357	345	346
Other	600	689	716	675	586	656	666	669	745
Revenue									
Direct taxes—persons	68	71	63	64	69	64	80	95	112
Direct taxes—corporations	48	40	33	32	37	52	65	83	101
Indirect taxes	686	600	575	546	545	585	608	674	714
Other	130	98	65	59	64	81	98	128	131
Total	932	809	736	701	715	782	851	980	1,058
Federal	396	271	227	211	245	294	310	399	460
Other	536	538	509	490	470	488	541	581	598
Deficit(+) or surplus(−)	−9	222	311	277	174	190	172	34	33
Federal	−56	96	160	154	114	93	121	37	−9
Other	47	126	151	123	60	97	51	−3	42

SOURCE: *National Accounts*, pp. 68-9.

(a) In order to show net revenues and expenditures of the three levels of government combined, transfers between governments were excluded. Federal government transfers to other governments were 17, 25, 56, 62, 51, 71, 74, 91 and 105 millions of dollars for the years shown. To secure the federal and other governments balances, as shown, these figures must be added to federal expenditures and other governments' revenues. The over-all deficit or surplus is not affected.

the same time there was a considerable repatriation of debt held abroad, along with re-funding in the home market. From 1933 to 1937 inclusive new issues sold abroad were $558 million, but retirements were $1,031 million.[32] Both governments and corporations re-funded foreign-held debt in the Canadian market. Re-funding gave lower interest rates, while re-funding in Canada would eliminate optional payment features. As a result of these factors, interest payments to non-residents fell from a peak of $180 million in 1931 to $142 million in 1937.[33]

The effects of the federal government's re-funding policies, however, were probably deflationary. If more of the re-funding had been financed abroad rather than in Canada, the decline in interest rates would have been accelerated, all other things being constant.[34] In one sense, of course, the re-funding and repayment of debt was a general feature of the upswing, reflecting the desire to clear the decks of debt, to secure lower rates, to get rid of optional payment debt, and the lack of alternative outlets for funds. The current account surpluses supplied a medium for debt repatriation without depreciating the exchange rate below "parity." The surpluses were also available, however, as a buffer if the government decided to embark on a more active programme of internal recovery or to secure export outlets by further tariff cuts. The problems posed by an open economy in carrying out an independent monetary policy in a downswing were noted earlier. The same problems would have to be kept in mind with respect to the upswing, with two important differences. First, the United States and others by this time had embarked on wider reflationary policies, and Canada would be in step with them. Secondly, with current surpluses there was some leeway in Canada for a more independent policy than was actually followed.[35]

32 *Ibid.*, p. 163.
33 *Ibid.*, p. 177.
34 Refinancing abroad in the presence of current surpluses would likely have appreciated the Canadian dollar, except in the context of a strong recovery programme.
35 It is also interesting to note the concentration of maturities of total government debt. See Bank of Canada, *Statistical Summary, 1950 Supplement*, pp. 18 and 19. These statistics indicate that, particularly after 1932, there was a very rapid increase in the amount of Government of Canada direct and guaranteed funded debt outstanding which had less than two years to run to maturity. The natural concentration of new issues in previous periods of prosperity, along with the lack of dispersion of maturity dates, meant very large refinancing operations had to be undertaken in a short period of time in the upswing.

In summary, the limitations of protective tariffs as recovery measures became obvious fairly soon, and first by preferences and later by broader treaties attempts were made to widen export outlets. Monetary policy as an instrument of control was hampered until 1935 by a rigid monetary system in which the government could not increase bank cash except by changing the law. While not embarking on a large programme of internal recovery, a number of measures were undertaken. The reform legislation clashed with the division of powers between governments, but relief works were used (rather erratically) and a modest housing programme was begun late in the upswing.

CHAPTER SIX

Exports and Domestic Investment in the Recovery

Before considering exports in the recovery, certain aspects of the downswing should be noted.[1] The downswing took the value of exports to the inter-war low of $39.0 million in the fourth quarter of 1932 – one quarter before the low in over-all economic activity.[2] Export values, moreover, had tended to level out through much of 1932. The country composition of exports changed greatly in this process. The decrease in 1929, reflecting lower exports of wheat, was to Western Europe and the United Kingdom. In 1930 and 1931 there was a drop in exports to each of the country groups being considered.[3] By 1932 the decrease had slowed down, and exports to the United Kingdom actually rose. In 1933 exports rose to all the country or area groups except the Other Foreign group, with exports to the United Kingdom showing the largest absolute and relative increase. Because of decreasing exports to Western Europe, exports to the Other Foreign group of countries did not reach their lowest point until 1935.

The largest percentage and absolute fall from peak to trough appears in the Other Foreign group, reflecting the enormous drop in wheat exports in the downswing. There were special factors affecting gold exports; gold available for export rose in 1930 and continued to rise steadily and rapidly throughout the thirties. If it is excluded, the absolute fall in exports to the United States is greater than in any other area. This in itself is not surprising since exports to the United States in 1929 were 44 per cent of total exports; but the percentage fall of 69 per cent from 1929 to 1932 (excluding gold) was more than the decline in any country group except Other Foreign. This

---

[1] Some portions of the sections on exports are from A. E. Safarian, "Foreign Trade and the Level of Economic Activity in Canada in the 1930's," *CJEPS*. See also pp. 77-9.

[2] See Table 52.

[3] The United Kingdom, Other Commonwealth, United States, and Other Foreign. The more important trading areas in the last of these are referred to as Western Europe, Central and South America, and the Far East. Non-monetary gold available for export is included with the United States and with total commodity exports in the following discussion, unless otherwise noted.

compares with a drop of 52 per cent for the United Kingdom from 1928 to the low point in 1931.

Table 29

ABSOLUTE AND RELATIVE CHANGES IN EXPORTS BY AREAS, 1928-37

Country or area		Millions of dollars	Percentage change		Millions of dollars	Percentage change
United States						
Including gold	1929-32	− 317	− 57	1932-7	+ 297	+ 124
Excluding gold	1929-32	− 350	− 69	1932-7	+ 222	+ 131
United Kingdom	1928-31	− 149	− 52	1931-7	+ 246	+ 177
Other Commonwealth	1929-32	− 66	− 63	1932-7	+ 69	+ 177
Other Foreign	1928-33	− 324	− 72	1933-7	+ 34	+ 28
Total, including gold	1928-32	− 816	− 59	1932-7	+ 621	+ 110

SOURCES: D.B.S., *Canadian Balance of International Payments, 1926 to 1948*, except for Other Commonwealth which was estimated from Bank of Canada, *Statistical Summary, 1946 Supplement*, p. 118. Data are adjusted for balance of payments purposes.

The composition of exports by commodity indicates quite clearly the major role of agricultural and vegetable products in the period under review. In 1926-9 such exports were 45 per cent of all exports (excluding gold); if animals and products are added, the two groups together were almost 60 per cent of all exports. Of the fall in (unadjusted) exports of $849 million from 1928 to 1932, $447 million was in agricultural exports, wheat and flour alone representing $352 million. Animals and products accounted for a further $107 million of the decrease, and wood products for $155 million.

From the above discussion a number of salient points emerge. One is that the drop in exports was heavily concentrated in a few products – wheat, animals, wood products (especially newsprint), and to a lesser degree non-ferrous metals. This, of course, was partly a reflection of the heavy concentration of Canadian exports in these products. Another point is the role played by Other Foreign countries, and particularly Western Europe, in the collapse of wheat exports. Finally, the fact that the turning points in exports to the United States and the United Kingdom occurred at different times was related earlier to differences in the timing of recovery in those two countries, to Imperial preferences, and to the situation in wheat, which affects exports to the United Kingdom greatly.

The Recovery in Exports and Imports

After five years of recovery, merchandise exports in 1937 were 8 per cent or $100 million below the average of 1926-9; if gold is excluded, however, 1937 exports were 17 per cent or $211 million below the 1926-9 average.[4] The recovery was incomplete, but did come close to the levels of the late twenties if gold is included. Exports to the United States and to the Other Commonwealth group of countries had approximately attained their 1928-9 levels by 1937; if gold is excluded from the United States total, exports to the United States were still about one-fifth below the 1928-9 levels. The considerable increase in exports to the United Kingdom between 1928 and 1937 offset about one-third of the approximately $300 million decline in exports to Other Foreign countries between these years. The most significant shortfall in exports in 1937, compared to the peaks in the late twenties, occurred in exports to Other Foreign countries – particularly wheat exports.

The great change in the composition of exports must be emphasized, for it had important effects on the impact of the export recovery. By 1937 the groups of exports which had recovered to approximately their 1928 levels were the relatively smaller ones of iron, textiles, non-metallic minerals, chemicals, and their products. Of the large groups, animals and products were still about 12 per cent below the 1926-8 levels, wood products and paper about 10 per cent below the 1928 level, and agricultural and vegetable products fully 57 per cent below 1928 and about 50 per cent below 1926 and 1927. The important increase, in relative and absolute terms, was in non-ferrous metals. This group exceeded the 1928 level by over 100 per cent in 1937, and had added $102 million to exports between the two years. Gold contributed a further increase of $105 million in this period, or about 250 per cent; furthermore, unlike the other non-ferrous metal exports, this increase had been persistent and rapid in every year since 1929.

4 If the comparisons are made with the peak for exports in 1928, the shortfall in 1937 was $195 million and $300 million respectively. Exports of all goods and services in 1937 were 5 per cent below the average for 1926-9.

Table 30

SELECTED MERCHANDISE EXPORTS AS A PERCENTAGE OF TOTAL
EXPORTS, INCLUDING NET NON-MONETARY GOLD, 1926-9 AND 1933-7

	Four years, 1926-9		Five years, 1933-7	
	Millions of dollars	Percentage of total	Millions of dollars	Percentage of total
Wheat and wheat flour	1,635	32	867	19
Newsprint, pulpwood, and wood-pulp	775	15	668	15
Non-ferrous metals and products	365	7	602	14
Net non-monetary gold	139	3	592	13
All exports	5,105		4,453	

SOURCE: *Bank of Canada, Statistical Summary, 1950 Supplement*, pp. 116-17.

All groups of exports to the United Kingdom in 1937, except for agricultural exports, were higher than for any year from 1926 to 1929. Some of the large groups were substantially greater in 1937 than in 1928; the phenomenal rise in total Canadian exports of base metals over the 1928 levels was due to exports to the United Kingdom. The agricultural and vegetable products group was substantially below the 1926-8 figures, but not enough to prevent a large increase in total exports to the United Kingdom. The largest group of exports to the United States, wood and products, was well below the 1928-9 levels in 1937, as was the large group of animals and products. Increased exports to the United Kingdom made up for a large part of the latter decrease, but only a small part of the former. Exports of non-ferrous metals to the United States had recovered to the 1928 levels, while agricultural and vegetable products recovered to and exceeded 1928 in 1936 and 1937, owing mainly to the drought in the American mid-west.

The better recovery of exports to the United Kingdom than to the United States was mainly due to the former country's more complete domestic recovery, in terms of the levels of the late twenties.[5] The United Kingdom's construction boom, in

5 See CHAP. VIII for the recovery in the United Kingdom and United States. See also Marcus, *Canada and the International Business Cycle*, pp. 124-5 and 135.

particular, contributed to the substantial increase in Canadian exports of base metals. The trend to greater concentration of Canada's exports in sales to the United Kingdom was also accentuated by Imperial preference, combined with high tariffs and other barriers in the United States and the Other Foreign group of countries.

The most striking feature of movements in export prices was that no group, except non-metallic minerals and products, reached or exceeded its 1926 price level in any year from 1927 to 1939. Price indexes for the three largest groups, which in 1937 comprised 86 per cent of total exports (excluding gold), were well below the 1926-9 levels all through the thirties.[6] Even with a sharp rise in prices in 1937, the price indexes for these three groups of exports were still 20 to 35 per cent below the 1926 levels, and 10 to 25 per cent below 1929 levels. The largest part of these three groups comprised agricultural products and raw materials, while products which involved only processing or partial manufacturing rather than a high degree of manufacturing made up much of the remainder. These are commodities for which price tends to fluctuate greatly, either because of inelasticity of supply (as in agriculture) or because of severe fluctuations in demand for the end products incorporating them (as in lumber and metals).[7] In contrast to these, export prices of iron and products and non-metallic minerals and products fluctuated in a range of only 20 per cent over the whole period, and miscellaneous products (including many consumer manufactures) and chemicals in a range of about 39 per cent. It was the three largest groups of exports which experienced the greatest price fluctuations.

A quite different picture emerges for the recovery in export volume. By 1937 most of the volume indexes were well over the 1926 level; the only important exception was the index of agricultural and animal products, which was 97 per cent of the 1926 level in 1936 but fell to 63 per cent in 1937. The volume of exports of non-ferrous metals and products by 1937 was three and a half times the 1926 level, even if gold is excluded. Wood and products exceeded the 1926 volume in 1935 and the 1929 peak in 1936 and 1937. Except for the important

---

6 The three groups are agricultural, vegetable, and animal products; wood and wood products; and non-ferrous metals and their products.

7 The picture is more complicated than this, as will appear from some industry studies.

TABLE 31

PRICE AND VOLUME INDEXES FOR EXPORTS AND IMPORTS, AND TERMS
OF TRADE, 1926-37 (1926 = 100)

| | Exports | | Imports | | Terms of trade |
	Price	Volume	Price	Volume	
1927	95.9	100.2	94.5	114.1	101.5
1928	92.9	114.3	92.9	130.5	100.0
1929	91.2	100.2	90.5	142.4	100.8
1930	77.2	88.7	81.7	122.4	94.5
1931	63.3	73.7	69.1	90.2	91.6
1932	57.7	67.3	67.2	66.9	85.9
1933	57.1	73.4	64.5	61.7	88.5
1934	61.3	84.0	69.4	73.3	88.3
1935	62.3	92.3	67.1	81.3	92.8
1936	66.1	112.5	68.3	92.3	96.8
1937	76.7	103.1	75.0	107.1	102.3

SOURCE: Derived from D.B.S., *Export and Import Price Indexes,
1926-1948.* Data exclude gold.

group of agricultural and animal products, whose volume was
low and relatively unchanged until 1936, the volume increases
were fairly regular throughout the recovery. This growth was
in direct contrast to the price increases, which were fairly slow
until 1937. Export prices fell 37 per cent from 1929 to 1932,
and rose 33 per cent to 1937. Volume also fell sharply by 33
per cent from 1929 to 1932; yet, in spite of crop failures,
volume increased by 54 per cent from 1932 to 1937 (and by
67 per cent to 1936, when grain exports were heavier).

In brief, the depression in exports affected both prices and
volume, but the recovery was greater in volume than in prices.
If one keeps in mind the large weight and slower recovery of
the agricultural and animal group and the exclusion of gold
in the volume and price indexes, the situation can be summarized by stating that the volume of exports in 1935-7 was
equivalent to that in 1926-9, but prices on the average were
30 per cent lower. Finally, the greater recovery in volume in
most groups suggests that the factors depressing the prices of
major exports were not just demand factors. These depressing
forces included maladjustments on the supply side going back
to the twenties, such as those in newsprint, as well as cyclical
fluctuations in demand and restrictions on trade.

Import volume fell much more sharply than export volume, declining by 47 per cent from 1929 to 1932 as compared with a decrease in export volume of 33 per cent; import volume continued to fall in 1933, furthermore, while export volume rose. In comparison with the peaks in the late twenties, export volume was 90 per cent of the 1928 peak by 1937, and import volume only 75 per cent of the 1929 peak.[8] If gold is taken into account, the relatively greater rise of exports is enhanced.

These differing changes in merchandise trade, along with the increase in gold, were the chief factors in the disappearance of the current deficits of the early thirties and the appearance of current surpluses after 1933. The incomplete recovery of domestic investment was the major factor in the failure of imports to revive greatly, relative to 1929. It is significant that the turning point in import volume did not come until 1934, when investment in durable assets rose; and that its largest percentage increase[9] was in 1937, when investment in machinery and equipment and non-agricultural inventories rose rapidly.

The second point with respect to imports is the greater stability in prices. The terms of trade fell drastically to 1932. They were moderately higher in the next two years, then improved steadily in the next three years. In 1930-6 Canada was paying from 4 per cent to 17 per cent more in exports in real terms for one unit of imports, as compared to 1926-9; and over the period 1930-6 the unweighted average amount paid for imports, in terms of export volume, was 10 per cent more than in 1926-9. Had there not been a slower recovery in import volume than in export volume, such a deterioration in the terms of trade could have eliminated much of the current surplus in the upswing.[10] It raised the real cost of imports in terms of exports, created special cost-price problems for some sections of the economy, and for the economy as a whole lowered the real gain from trade.

The Impact of the Recovery in Exports

The impact of exports can be looked at in a number of ways. First, there is the behaviour of exports at the lower turning

---

[8] It should be noted that the volume of wheat exports fell in 1937, after a sharp rise in 1936.

[9] Except for 1934, when it was rising from the low point of 1933.

[10] The differing price changes and relative recoveries in volume were partly related, of course.

point. Secondly, how can one measure the importance of exports from the point of view of their effects on income and employment? Since the important gains from specialization and trade to a country such as Canada have been widely recognized, the section below is concerned only with the shorter-run cyclical effects.

There is much evidence to suggest that exports were one of the major forces which led the recovery in 1933. This point has already been dealt with above.[11] The rise in exports in the first quarter of 1933 was not by itself large enough to spark a recovery. When this is combined, however, with the levelling out of exports in 1932, the favourable expectations fostered by the agreements at the Ottawa Conference, improving world conditions generally, and particularly the recovery programme in the United States, an important stimulus to production was to be expected.

The effects of exports on income can be measured in a number of ways. We shall use some aggregative measures first, then look at the effects by industries.

From 1929 to 1933 the fall in exports of merchandise alone (including gold) was 23 per cent of the fall in GNE; the increase in such exports contributed 32 per cent of the increase in GNE from 1933 to 1937. Since the peak of exports was in 1928 and the low in 1932, it is also useful to compare the change from 1928 to 1932. GNE fell by $2,553 million in the 1928-32 period; exports of goods and services fell by $969 million, while merchandise exports alone fell by $816 million.

The primary impact of exports as a whole is shown most simply by expressing their value as a percentage of GNE.[12] In the second half of the twenties, commodity exports were between 20 and 22 per cent of GNE, except in 1926 when they were 25 per cent. From 1930 to 1934 they were between 14 and 19 per cent, but recovered to between 20 and 23 per cent in 1935-7. The commodity export balance, which appeared in 1931, rose steadily until by 1936 (including gold) it was as high as 10 per cent of GNE. Private domestic investment in durable assets fell even more severely and recovered to only about half its previous weight, as a percentage of GNE. It was the relative stability of consumption and government expenditures which, particularly in the first half of the thirties, limited the

11 See CHAP. IV and Table 52 for the timing of various series in 1932-3.
12 See also p. 142 and Tables 11 and 26.

extent of over-all decline in the face of the collapse of exports and domestic investment.[13]

Another possible way to look at the contribution of exports is to measure the export balance as a percentage of GNE. The balance on merchandise account (including gold) was negative only in 1929 and 1930, and rose throughout the thirties until it was 10 per cent of GNE in 1936. If the non-merchandise transactions (on which there is customarily a deficit) are taken into account, there was a current account deficit until 1933, a rising current surplus from 1934 to 1936, and surpluses in 1937-9 as well. If one were to measure the impact of exports and current account receipts only from the surplus, the smaller role of imports in the thirties and a large and (for several years) growing current surplus would mean a higher total effect on the economy due to international transactions. The multiplier effects of a rising current surplus should, in other words, spur economic activity to higher levels, barring an increase in the marginal propensity to save domestic income.

A measure of the relative role of exports by its balance alone would be misleading, even though the use of the balance in other connections is useful. Imports are related to many factors besides the need to use them in manufacturing exports. On purely *a priori* grounds, and from the analysis to date, it seems plausible that imports are more directly related to invest-ment and consumer expenditure of certain types than to ex-ports. If one is concerned with the importance of exports relative to other variables, total exports must be used (adjusted for imports due directly to exports, and for multiplier-acceler-ator effects). Furthermore, there is the implication in some explanations of the multiplier, particularly those which dis-regard the stages of the business cycle, that a rising export surplus in itself will generate substantial increases in income.

[13] The percentages referred to in the previous footnote add up to more than 100 per cent in any year since each of the components mentioned includes an import content. To arrive at the net primary impact of exports, one should subtract imports used to manufacture exports, but estimates of these are not available. Another method would be to add imports of goods and services back to GNE and deduct indirect taxes (some of which do not affect export prices). Exports as a percentage of this total would be a better estimate of the primary impact of exports than that which is used, but a measure of the extent to which indirect taxes enter export prices is lacking. The percentages given above for the primary impact of exports are probably not too far from what would result if the methods just mentioned could be applied to this period.

One has to take into account, however, the level of exports and income at which the rising balance is attained. If the rising exports do not lead to significant multiplier-accelerator effects (and assuming autonomous investment is weak) a rising current account surplus will occur as imports lag – yet economic activity will remain relatively low. The experience of part of the thirties – large and growing export balances at relatively low levels of income – clearly suggests exports must also be considered separately from the balance, and in conjunction with the level of income. In Canadian economic history, at least, trade surpluses and prosperity typically have been inversely correlated, as a result of heavy imports of durable goods in periods of high exports and autonomous investment in conjunction with considerable induced effects on income.[14]

Although the results cannot be treated as conclusive, it is worth investigating briefly some of the techniques developed for the measurement of multiplier effects.[15] A linear correlation fitted to the years 1926-38, with exports as the independent variable and GNE as the dependent variable, yields a coefficient of regression of about 2.5.[16] Over this period, on the average, an increase in exports of $1 million was accompanied by an increase in GNE of $2.5 million, with a short lag. In this "gross" multiplier the assumption is implicit that exports were the only determinant of GNE in this period. That this assumption is not valid is at once apparent if a scatter diagram of exports and GNE is constructed and a regression line fitted by the least squares method. The increase in GNE in 1926-9 is in contrast with the relative stability of exports in this period, except for the increase in the latter in 1928; in the recovery to

14 See Malach, *International Cycles*, pp. 59-61 for a statement of the necessity of examining the absolute level of exports, and the place of induced investment in particular in the negative correlation of the current balance and the level of income.

15 Induced investment is considered in the next section of this chapter.

16 The regression equation of best fit in millions of dollars was $Y = 2,505 + 2.54 X$, with Y as GNE in year N, X as exports in year N minus nine months. The coefficient of correlation was 0.95. The rather long lag of nine months probably arises from the use of annual GNE data. Some short lag is warranted, as our earlier analysis suggested. Chang finds a lag of three months by inspection of a scatter diagram; see footnote 18 below. The data used for the simple correlations shown here are from D.B.S., *National Accounts, Income, and Expenditure, 1926-1947* (1948), and *Trade of Canada*.

1937, on the other hand, GNE tended to rise relatively more slowly than exports. Other forces were at work in these periods, particularly those determining the very great fluctuations in domestic investment.[17]

At this point, one might be tempted to use multiple correlation to show the net relation of both exports and investment. Such an estimate has been made by one writer, using national income as the dependent variable X_1, the value of exports including non-monetary gold as X_2, and domestic capital formation including government investment as X_3. The results were $X_1 = 1.452X_2 + 1.438X_3$ with $R = 0.956$. In other words, an increase of \$1 in either exports or home investment was accompanied, on the average, by an increase in Canadian income of about \$1.4 between 1926 and 1938. Using an estimated time lag of three months for the lag in income behind exports *plus* domestic investment, a multiplier of 1.5 was derived.[18]

This average may be useful for long-run considerations, but its limitations should be kept in mind. To use it for short-term analysis, in a period when such wide changes in income occurred, would require a great deal of faith in the constancy of marginal propensities to import and consume. The interrelation of the two independent variables of exports and investment, and the fact that they are included in the dependent variable of GNE, severely limits the meaningfulness of the coefficients of regression. There does not appear to be a fully satisfactory way in which to measure the net effect of two independent variables on a dependent variable, when the two independent variables are themselves related. Where the effect of one independent variable may be worked out partly through the variations in the other, it is precisely this aspect which is of interest in dynamic analysis.[19] One final point needs to be applied to all of the above correlations. For most of them, at

---

[17] Using the same technique, but with gross home investment in year N as the independent variable and GNE in year N as the dependent variable, the regression equation is $Y = 3,420 + 2.27 X$ and the coefficient of correlation is 0.98. As pointed out in the paragraphs which follow, however, part of the investment effect is induced by exports.

[18] Tse Chun Chang, *Cyclical Fluctuations in the Balance of Payments*, CHAP. V; also Chang, "A Note on Exports and National Income," *CJEPS*.

[19] It might also be noted that the "dependent" variable in this case is not entirely without effects on the "independent" variables.

least for data on GNE, observations are available on a uniform basis only since 1926. Thus, there are only twelve or thirteen observations to work with up to 1938, and this must seriously limit the reliability of the correlation "constants." If, as is necessary for some periods, independent movements in consumption and government spending were admitted, the independent variables would increase, and the problems associated with the use of a small number of years would be multiplied.

Another way to approach this problem of the multiplicative effects of exports and investment is to use one of the formulas for the instantaneous multiplier in an open economy.[20] One can use $(V + X - M)\dfrac{1}{1-c}$ or $(V + X)\dfrac{1}{1-c+g}$, the former being the Keynesian and the latter the earlier Clarkian multiplier.[21] Independent estimates of c and g would have to be made. The result, an average instantaneous multiplier over a long period, would again not be of much analytical use for the study of changes in short periods. The construction of a period multiplier would present very large statistical problems of its own. Both types of multipliers must assume constant marginal propensities to consume and import, or the laws of change must be known. In the period type of analysis there is the important task of determining the length of the time period. And in both there is the problem of distinguishing autonomous changes in imports and consumption (i.e., those changes in these variables which are not dependent on changes in income), which should be entered in the multiplicand instead of the multiplier. An autonomous fall in imports in favour of domestic goods would have the same effect on income as an autonom-

[20] There has been a great deal of controversy over this concept. The relevant issues are discussed in Haberler, *Prosperity and Depression*, pp. 455-73. Some of the points involved are further elaborated in articles by J. S. Polak and G. Haberler in the December 1947 issue of the *American Economic Review*. Colin Clark has attempted a statistical measure of the multiplier in, among other sources, *The National Income of Australia* by Clark and J. G. Crawford, CHAP. XI. Clark's multiplier for the United Kingdom, with criticisms by D. H. Robertson, Roy W. Jastram, and E. S. Shaw, appears in the *Economic Journal* for 1938 and 1939. For the multiplier in sequence analysis, see footnote 22 below.

[21] V is expenditure on investment goods, X is exports, M is imports, c and g are the marginal propensity to consume domestic goods and to import respectively. Haberler, pp. 463-5.

ous increase in exports, other things being equal, and should be placed with exports in the multiplicand.[22]

TABLE 32

CRUDE MARGINAL PROPENSITIES, 1927-37(a)
(Current and constant dollars)

	To make payments abroad from GNE		To consume from GNE(b)	To consume from disposable income(b)
	Constant	Current	Constant	Current(c)
1927	.37	.30	.78	1.59
1928	.43	.39	.54	.70
1929	18.71	2.24	1.44	1.45
1930	.62	.52	.41	.40
1931	.44	.49	.29	.95
1932	.59	.30	.57	.80
1933	.09	.34	.36	1.23
1934	.13	.25	.35	.66
1935	.19	.22	.53	.84
1936	.73	.47	.65	.88
1937	.27	.35	.44	.79

SOURCE: Derived from *National Accounts*.

(a) The reader should refer to footnote 19, CHAP. V, in considering the meaning of these estimates.

(b) The change in farm inventories has been omitted from income. See "The Concept of Disposable Income" by C. L. Barber, *CJEPS*, and the reply by S. A. Goldberg.

(c) Personal disposable income is not published in constant dollars.

[22] Fritz Machlup puts it as follows on p. 13 of his *International Trade and the National Income Multiplier:* "Foreign trade plays, thus, a double role in foreign-trade multiplier theory: once as multiplicand, and secondly, as one of the determinants of the multiplier. This double role of foreign trade, I believe, is likely to defeat every attempt at statistical verification of foreign-trade multiplier theory. For, unfortunately, the theoretically indispensable separation of the autonomous changes in foreign trade—constituting the multiplicand—from the induced changes in foreign trade—affecting the multiplier—would seem to be in most cases statistically impracticable."

We shall not, accordingly, go very far into the statistical measurement of the multiplier, but it is useful to consider some related magnitudes. Any correlation of imports with GNE indicates two distinct periods. The slope of the relationship in 1926-30 was much greater than that for the period 1932-8. Not only had the average propensity to make payments abroad fallen in the thirties, as was noted earlier, but the marginal propensity as well. The marginal propensity to make payments abroad, in constant dollars, was smaller than in the late twenties in every year of the upswing except 1936.[23] This would lead one to expect a larger multiplier in the upswing of the thirties than in the late twenties, other things being equal.[24] The other variable which multiplier analysis emphasizes is the marginal propensity to consume. The calculations in Table 32 indicate the marginal propensity to consumer GNE may have been smaller in the upswing than in the late twenties.[25] The year 1936 is again the only exception to the GNE comparison all through the upswing. On these grounds alone the multiplier should have been smaller in the upswing of the thirties, offsetting to a degree the increase in the multiplier from the decline in the marginal propensity to make payments abroad.

The decline in the marginal propensity to make payments abroad can be related primarily to the reduced weight of domestic investment in GNE in the thirties and the increase in import restrictions. A possible factor in the behaviour of the marginal propensity to consume will be noted shortly. But first it should be emphasized that it would be a mistake to insert the values in the table, or an average of them, into the formulae for the multiplier. Quite apart from the problems of interpreta-

23 In connection with Table 32, the estimates for 1929 show a special relationship. Current payments abroad and consumer expenditure continued to rise fairly strongly, while GNE and disposable income increased only moderately.

24 It is worth noting that, if the estimates in Table 32 had been made for merchandise imports alone in relation to GNE, the picture would have been different in certain periods. In the downswing, for example, the relative stability of interest and dividend payments abroad was in sharp contrast to the fall in merchandise imports. For statistical measurement of the marginal propensity to import, see Imre de Vegh, "Imports and Income in the United States and Canada," *Review of Economic Statistics*, p. 131; and Chang, *Cyclical Fluctuations in the Balance of Payments*, CHAP. II.

25 The picture is not clear for the marginal propensity to consume disposable income (in current dollars), particularly in view of the fact that two of the three estimates for the twenties are unusually high. See also footnote 23.

tion noted earlier, the marginal propensity to make payments abroad is partly included in the marginal propensity to consume, as measured above.

Nevertheless, it is worth asking whether any changes in the export multiplier can be inferred from the data and history of the period. It can be argued that the change in the composition of exports and a change in the determinants of investment were important factors limiting the stimulus from increasing exports in the thirties.

The various sectors of the economy recovered in quite different ways. Agriculture and some related industries, for example, remained depressed, but primary mining, non-ferrous metal manufactures, and related industries recovered more rapidly; it was not a balanced expansion in exports or in recovery generally. It has been suggested that, as a result of the changed composition of exports, the secondary income effects of rising exports were less than might otherwise have been expected.[26] This result would require the propensity to save, to import, or to make payments abroad to have been larger in mining and related industries than in agriculture and related industries.

With respect to dividend payments, although non-resident ownership of vegetable products industries was 43 per cent and of animal products industries 22 per cent in 1939, non-resident ownership of the important area of primary agriculture was negligible. In mining and related industries, non-resident ownership in 1939 was high; in mining and smelting companies, it was 40 per cent; in non-ferrous metal manufactures, 77 per cent; and in non-metallic mineral industries, 46 per cent.[27] The strong recovery in many of the mining and related industries, particularly in gold where capital investment by non-residents was high, led to heavy dividend payments abroad. In 1939, for example, dividend payments abroad of $56 million by mining and smelting companies, $24 million by non-metallic mineral companies, and $5 million by non-ferrous metal companies, together represented half of total dividend payments abroad.[28]

[26] The differing income effects of recovery in agriculture and in mining have been ably stated by A. F. W. Plumptre. See his article "Distribution of Outlay and the 'Multiplier' in the British Dominions," *CJEPS*, p. 369.

[27] D.B.S., *Canadian Balance of International Payments, 1926-1948*, p. 80.

[28] Data supplied by courtesy of the Balance of Payments Section, D.B.S.

TABLE 35

PRIVATE INVESTMENT IN DURABLE PHYSICAL ASSETS BY INDUSTRY, 1926-37(a)

(Millions of dollars)

	Agriculture	Primary mining (b)	Manufacturing	Steam railways and telegraphs	Central electric stations and gas works	Other utilities	Trade	Commercial services	Housing	Construction	Other (c)
Annual data											
1926	89	17	222	84	43	47	24	19	212	14	37
1929	121	46	374	188	76	80	68	44	247	33	52
1933	19	9	42	15	17	23	10	7	76	2	17
1936	53	31	83	38	20	35	19	22	139	7	22
1937	74	33	140	66	32	43	28	18	176	12	25
As a percentage of 1929											
1933	15.7	19.6	11.2	8.0	22.4	28.8	14.7	15.9	30.8	6.0	32.7
1937	61.2	71.7	37.4	35.1	42.1	53.8	41.2	40.9	72.5	36.5	48.1
Percentage of total investment in											
1926-9	10.9	2.7	28.5	11.8	5.4	5.7	4.0	3.2	21.6	2.1	4.2
1930-3	7.3	3.5	23.9	11.3	9.7	7.4	4.0	2.2	23.2	1.9	5.5
1934-7	11.3	5.9	18.9	8.2	5.2	7.2	4.4	3.4	29.3	1.2	4.6

SOURCE: *P.P.I.* and *National Accounts*.

(a) Excludes government investment, except by government business enterprises in the utilities.
(b) Primary mining, quarrying, and oil wells.
(c) Primary woods, fishing, trapping, private institutions, and finance and insurance.

TABLE 33

CAPITAL EMPLOYED AND EMPLOYEES IN SELECTED INDUSTRIES, 1937(a)

Item	Capital employed (millions of dollars)	Employees (thousands)
Primary mining	584.7	55
Manufacturing		
Food and beverage	559.0	108
Clothing (textile and fur)	143.1	76
Wood products	190.2	67
Paper products	622.8	45
Non-ferrous metal products	209.3	23
Non-metallic mineral products	131.3	15
Chemical products	163.7	22

SOURCE: Safarian, "Foreign Trade and the Level of Economic Activity," p. 343.

(a) Precisely comparable data for primary agriculture are not available, but data published in various issues of the *C.Y.B.* support the statement in the text about the labour-capital ratio in primary agriculture.

neither wholly autonomous nor wholly dependent on changes in current consumption and exports: in the thirties, however, it was particularly insensitive to such changes. The heavy capital outlays necessary to finance investment must be supported by the expectation of earnings, as determined by innovations affecting the industry over a period of time and the increase in sales. But the experience of the recent past and the conditions of the present also play a large role in the short-term determination of expectations. With a recent history of booming investment expenditures followed by excess capacity, heavy debts but reduced sales, relatively rigid costs, and other factors noted earlier, it is not surprising that business anticipations were low during the recovery. The low level of investment was not attributable solely to the existence of a large stock of capital, which limited the response to changes in sales: even in mining and related industries, where sales were strong, investment in plant and equipment remained surprisingly constant when it did recover, and often was quite small until 1937. A strong undercurrent of pessimism and extreme caution tended to slow the response of investment in the export industries and the other parts of the economy to rising exports and consumption and a rising export balance. Finally, a large part of investment, that in railways, utilities, and housing, is related more than other types of investment to very long-run prospects of growth, as well as to current and past sales and experience.

Domestic Investment in the Recovery

The first point which needs emphasis is the very heavy private investment in machinery and equipment, and non-residential construction, from 1926 to 1929.[30] Investment in residential construction rose more slowly. In constant dollars, investment in non-residential construction rose by 93 per cent between 1926 and 1929; in machinery and equipment, 71 per cent; and in residential construction, 9 per cent. The downswing was extremely violent; by 1933 investment in residential construction was only 39 per cent of the 1929 level, in non-residential construction 20 per cent, and machinery and equipment purchases were only 16 per cent (all in constant dollars). Although a number of increases occurred in 1933, they were small and were not in the major investment sectors. Furthermore, while total investment rose in 1934, there was no great stimulus from the most important investment groups of manufacturing and utilities.

The recovery to 1936 was very rapid in percentage terms but very slow if comparison is made with the peak of 1929 or with the year 1926. Investment in durable physical assets was so low, in relation to the heavy investment undertaken earlier, that replacement alone could account for most of it. Not only

[30] The data on domestic investment are from *P.P.I.* and the *National Accounts*. New investment in durable physical assets includes both new investment and replacement and major alterations. Allowance for depreciation, obsolescence, etc., is not made. Purchase of used assets and ordinary repair and maintenance are excluded. The *National Accounts* definitions of gross domestic investment include investment by government business enterprises; they exclude investment by government departments, government-operated institutions and government housing. The behaviour of investment by government business enterprises is much closer to that of private investment than to that of government departments and institutions. The latter are often dominated by non-profit motives; they are included in the government sector of the *National Accounts*. The estimates of investment in *P.P.I.* include detailed estimates of both private and government investment in durable assets. The base for the constant dollar series is 1935-9 throughout.

Table 34

ABSOLUTE CHANGE OVER PREVIOUS YEAR IN INVESTMENT
COMPONENTS, 1934-7(a)
(Millions of dollars)

Change in	Residential construction		Non-residential construction		New machinery and equipment	
	Current	Constant	Current	Constant	Current	Constant
1934	+ 22	+ 17	+ 13	+ 13	+ 32	+ 35
1935	+ 16	+ 18	+ 26	+ 26	+ 30	+ 29
1936	+ 25	+ 22	+ 34	+ 30	+ 34	+ 34
1937	+ 37	+ 26	+ 40	+ 27	+ 101	+ 86

(a) The actual current dollar series are shown in Table 49.

the small absolute increases but also the relatively stable nature of the annual increases suggest that replacement was the dominant factor for most of the upswing. It was not until 1937 that a sizable increase occurred in domestic investment, and even in that year all three groups of private investment in durable assets were well below the 1926 levels, in both current and constant dollars. The rise in 1937 was particularly sharp in machinery and equipment (and non-agricultural inventories) rather than in the general sphere of construction; investment in the latter involves both a need for larger capacity and confidence in prospects over a long period. The investment groups which rose fastest in 1937 were those in which relatively shorter-run prospects play a larger role; in other words, long-term expectations were still not optimistic.

By 1936 no group in the private sector shown in Table 35, except primary mining and commercial services, had equalled or exceeded its 1926 level of investment in durable assets. Investment in several of the largest industries in 1936 was still 50 per cent or less of the 1926 levels, while the smaller groups showed a better recovery. A substantial increase did occur in 1937, when the total investment in machinery and equipment and in non-residential construction rose from $330 million to $471 million, compared with a 1926 figure of $597 million and the 1929 high of $1,083 million.[31] In spite of the general

[31] In 1935-9 constant dollars, the data for these four years, in chronological order, were $565, 1014, 342 and 455 million.

TABLE 35

PRIVATE INVESTMENT IN DURABLE PHYSICAL ASSETS BY INDUSTRY, 1926-37(a)

(Millions of dollars)

	Agri-culture	Primary mining (b)	Manu-factur-ing	Steam rail-ways and tele-graphs	Central electric stations and gas works	Other utili-ties	Trade	Com-mer-cial serv-ices	Hous-ing	Con-struc-tion	Other (c)
Annual data											
1926	89	17	222	84	43	47	24	19	212	14	37
1929	121	46	374	188	76	80	68	44	247	33	52
1933	19	9	42	15	17	23	10	7	76	2	17
1936	53	31	83	38	20	35	19	22	139	7	22
1937	74	33	140	66	32	43	28	18	176	12	25
As a percentage of 1929											
1933	15.7	19.6	11.2	8.0	22.4	28.8	14.7	15.9	30.8	6.0	32.7
1937	61.2	71.7	37.4	35.1	42.1	53.8	41.2	40.9	72.5	36.5	48.1
Percentage of total invest-ment in											
1926-9	10.9	2.7	28.5	11.8	5.4	5.7	4.0	3.2	21.6	2.1	4.2
1930-3	7.3	3.5	23.9	11.3	9.7	7.4	4.0	2.2	23.2	1.9	5.5
1934-7	11.3	5.9	18.9	8.2	5.2	7.2	4.4	3.4	29.3	1.2	4.6

SOURCE: *P.P.I.* and *National Accounts.*

(a) Excludes government investment, except by government business enterprises in the utilities.

(b) Primary mining, quarrying, and oil wells.

(c) Primary woods, fishing, trapping, private institutions, and finance and insurance.

increase in 1937, only mining and trade exceeded the 1926 level.

As a percentage of 1929, the best recoveries in private investment by 1937 were in housing, primary mining, and agriculture. In the first and third of these, however, there was not as great an increase as in the other groups in the 1926-9 period.[32] Furthermore, investment in agriculture fell in 1929, or one year earlier than most other industries. It was precisely the remaining groups of investment by industry, which had the greatest increases in 1926-9, which generally showed the poorest recoveries by 1937 as a percentage of 1929. Such comparisons of single years may be misleading, especially since the major increases were in 1937, but if one looks at sub-periods the same picture appears. Agriculture, primary mining, and housing all absorbed a larger percentage of domestic investment in 1934-7 than in 1926-9, though in agriculture the change was slight. Some of the service industries and "other utilities" also increased their share in total private investment, but the large manufacturing and steam railways sectors accounted for a smaller proportion of investment than in the twenties, and electric stations barely regained their previous weight.

TABLE 36

SELECTED DATA ON EXPENDITURES BY GOVERNMENTS AND
GOVERNMENT AGENCIES, 1929-37
(Millions of dollars)

| | New investment | | Expenditure on other goods and services |
	Government-owned enterprises	Other government investment	
1929	153	188	494
1930	130	233	534
1933	21	88	438
1936	45	121	479
1937	66	181	490

SOURCES: *P.P.I.*, p. 148, and *National Accounts*, pp. 26 and 80. The last column was derived by deducting the second column from government expenditures as shown in the *National Accounts*. Some minor discrepancies with data shown earlier are involved.

[32] See Table 3.

In an earlier section, it was noted that investment by government departments, while fluctuating sharply, was more stable than private investment. It will be noted, however, that the relative stability of investment by government departments does not extend to investment by government-owned enterprises. The major factor in this sharp decrease and slow recovery was investment by government-owned railways. Investment by these in 1929, 1933, and 1937 accounted for $100, $8, and $35 million respectively of total investment by government-owned enterprises.[33]

It is not possible to measure directly the degree of pessimism as to the future resulting from the impact of the excesses of the previous boom, the severity of the downswing, and the slow recovery. But some of the effects of the fall in both actual and expected profitability of investment can be measured to a degree.

TABLE 37

PRIVATE INVESTMENT IN DURABLE
ASSETS MINUS CAPITAL CONSUMPTION CHARGES, 1926-39
(Millions of dollars)

Year	Amount	Year	Amount
1926	304	1933	− 213
1927	402	1934	− 149
1928	533	1935	− 88
1929	687	1936	− 20
1930	420	1937	119
1931	128	1938	65
1932	− 135	1939	38

Table 37 makes clear the large amount of net investment in the period 1926-30. From 1932 to 1936 inclusive, however, capital consumption charges actually exceeded new and replacement expenditures combined. This does not mean that no new investment occurred in this period, or that every industry was in this situation; an analysis by industry, if available, would likely show net investment appearing earlier in some industries

[33] Investment by privately owned railways was not much more stable, amounting to $88, $7, and $31 million in the same years.

in the thirties than in others. What the figures do suggest is that for much of the thirties the stock of capital goods was not maintained on balance. Even replacements were apparently kept to a minimum and postponed where possible. Net investment did not appear in the aggregate until 1937.[34]

Expenditures for repair and maintenance reached a low point before investment did in a number of industries (though not in the aggregate) and the decline in such expenditures was much more moderate than that for investment.[35] This can be attributed partly to the fact that such expenditures cannot be postponed indefinitely. Some deterioration in the quality of the stock undoubtedly occurred where funds for renovation were not available, or where production was concentrated in more efficient plants and the remainder not properly maintained. To postpone repair and maintenance for too long would lead to a higher cost of operation eventually and to very severe deterioration in the quality of capital stock. Given the uncertainties and excess capacity of the early thirties, when business men would hesitate to undertake new and replacement investment, repair and maintenance would play a larger role. This larger role was partly at the cost of less investment in durable assets, particularly replacement investment. In 1933 expenditures for repair and maintenance exceeded investment in durable assets, and throughout the thirties the ratio of expenditures for repair and maintenance to investment was substantially higher than that in the last half of the twenties. It could be objected that this higher ratio would simply be the result of cyclical fluctuations of repair and maintenance which were more moderate than those of investment. It is suggested, however, that the very existence of more moderate fluctuations arises partly from the fact that for a time such expenditures may act as a partial substitute for investment, particularly after a severe decline. Even in 1937, when investment in durable assets reached its highest level in the period 1932-9 inclusive, expenditures for repair and maintenance rose more quickly than they had (proportionately) in the late twenties, and also bore a much higher ratio to investment. The former fact alone might only indicate postponement of repair and maintenance

---

[34] See footnote 43, chapter II, for a comment on the inadequacy of depreciation charges as a measure of replacement or of capital consumption.

[35] Repair and maintenance expenditures on private and public investment were $498, 603, 353, 451 and 506 million in 1926, 1929, 1933, 1936, and 1937 respectively. *P.P.I.*, pp. 151-2.

in the earlier thirties; combined with the latter fact, it suggests a greater emphasis on such expenditures.[36]

Two factors which should affect the level of induced investment are non-wage income and current business sales.[37] The prospect of larger future sales and income is the prime consideration when induced investment is to be undertaken. Present and immediately preceding sales and income trends serve as one of the guides to future prospects. The impact of these factors on investment was much weaker and quite different in the thirties than it was in the late twenties.

A scatter diagram for 1926-39 indicated a close correlation, with a lag of one year, in private investment in durable assets behind the assumed independent variable of non-wage income.[38] Furthermore, two distinct periods appeared in the relationship; a freehand regression line for 1926 to 1930 was well above a line for the 1931-9 period, and the slope of the former line was much greater. The curve of best fit was concave upward, with 1926-30 in the upper right hand corner of the graph.[39] Put another way, an equivalent increase in non-wage income was accompanied by a greater increase in domestic investment in the period 1926-30 than later, and the amount of investment for a given amount of non-wage income was much higher in the period 1926-30. The latter point is particularly obvious in 1936 and 1937, when average non-wage income was about 70 per cent of the 1926-9 average while investment was only about 50 per cent.

The most variable part of investment income is corporation profits.[40] The tendency to maintain dividend payments to residents and non-residents, in the face of a sharp fall in corpora-

36 Put slightly differently, private and public investment in durable assets in 1937 was still about one-ninth below the 1926 figure, while repair and maintenance expenditures were slightly larger than in 1926.

37 Non-wage income includes investment income and net income of unincorporated businesses. If it were possible, it would be desirable to exclude taxes from this total. Net income of unincorporated business includes both labour income and investment income, but these cannot be separated.

38 The correlation was much better with a one-year lag than with no lag. Non-wage income reached its peak in 1928 and low in 1932, one year before investment in each case.

39 A line from 1934 to 1937 would have a very sharp slope, but this period fits neatly into the whole period from 1931 to 1939, and 1937 is quite out of line with the other years in the thirties.

40 See also pp. 87-8. The other highly variable part of non-wage income, namely the income of farm operators, is considered in the next chapter.

tion profits, led to negative undistributed profits in the down-swing. By 1936 corporation profits before taxes had exceeded the 1926-7 levels, and in 1937 were more than 10 per cent over the 1928-9 peaks. Almost 30 per cent of the increase in corporation profits and net income of non-farm unincorporated business from 1933 to 1937 can be attributed to increases in value of inventory stocks because of price increases. But it should be noted that close to 45 per cent of this latter effect occurred in the last year of this period, when price increases speeded up.

Undistributed corporation profits did not make nearly as good a recovery in terms of the 1926-30 levels. The reason is clear if some of the charges against corporation profits are considered. Corporation profits before taxes were not greatly different in 1927 and 1936, but corporation taxes had more than doubled in the interval. Moreover, while corporation profits after taxes were well below the 1926-9 total in 1934-7, dividend payments in the latter period exceeded those of the former.[41] Still, by 1937 profits after tax were at the previous peaks, and undistributed profits in that year were equal to the 1927 and 1929 levels, while investment in durable assets was only about half the previous levels.[42] Even if one assumes a lag of investment behind profits, the levels of the former, several years after the upswing began, were well below what one might expect from this alone. And in 1938, just as investment had begun to rise more rapidly, profits fell off once more in response to another downswing.

Conclusions drawn only from the consideration of one broad and heterogeneous factor must be guarded, of course. The following general statements seem to be warranted, however. The extent to which non-wage income helped determine the level

[41] Year-to-year comparisons cannot be made in this case, since decisions by subsidiaries to transfer accumulated earnings may greatly affect any particular annual figure. The excess in payments in the second period was due solely to dividends to non-residents; those to residents were lower in the second period. The reasons for the strong recovery of dividend to non-residents may reflect in part the transfer of accumulated earnings to parent companies in the face of decisions not to invest in physical assets. They also reflect, however, the large non-resident interest in mining and the substantial dividends from some of these mines.

[42] The correct comparison is between corporation profits and investment by corporations. It is unlikely that the statements in the text would be greatly changed if data on the latter were available.

Table 38

ANALYSIS OF CORPORATION PROFITS, 1929-37
(Millions of dollars)

Item	1929	1932	1933	1934	1935	1936	1937
Corporation profits before taxes	530	17	128	287	338	465	590
Deduct: incomes taxes	− 48	− 32	− 37	− 52	− 65	− 83	− 101
Corporation profits after taxes	482	15	91	235	273	382	489
Deduct: dividends paid to non-residents	− 158	− 130	− 98	− 104	− 120	− 161	− 166
Corporation profits retained in Canada	324	− 145	− 7	131	153	221	323
Deduct: dividends paid to Canadian persons(a)	− 108	− 25	− 68	− 82	− 82	− 78	− 100
Charitable contributions from corporations	− 5	− 2	− 2	− 2	− 3	− 4	− 5
Undistributed corporation profits(b)	211	− 172	− 77	47	68	139	218

SOURCE: *National Accounts*, pp. 76-7.
(a) $93 million in 1931.
(b) The peak was $263 million in 1928.

of investment, by serving as a guide to the possible profitability of investment, was quite different in the late twenties and the thirties. In the twenties, the response of investment to this (and other) forces was much more buoyant than in the thirties. Furthermore, heavier taxes and the relative maintenance of dividend payments to residents and non-residents drained off a very direct source of funds for investment.[43]

In considering the relationship of investment to sales, the proper concept is that of business sales.[44] Using business sales as the independent variable, scatter diagrams and freehand lines were drawn relating various components of domestic investment to business sales. All the relations showed a better fit over the whole period if there was no lag in investment. Once more a curve which was concave upward gave the best fit. In other words, a line fitted to 1926-9 always had a much greater slope than one fitted to 1933-7. An equivalent change in business sales was associated with a greater change in investment in the late twenties than in the thirties. Furthermore, the year 1937 showed larger sales than 1926, but investment in all cases was much smaller. When machinery and equipment or non-residential construction, or both together, were correlated with business sales, a line with a very small slope, or one which was in fact nearly horizontal to the X-axis, gave a good fit for the period 1932-6. In brief, investment was highly insensitive to increases in business sales until 1937.

Two related and important factors of the current or immediate preceding period which business men look to in making investment decisions were not making a very powerful impact

[43] The maintenance of dividends need not be considered as causally affecting the level of investment but simply as a reflection of lack of incentive to use funds for investment. But dividends may be maintained at the cost of current investment, for fear of losing public confidence and thus limiting future access to the market for funds. Note the excess of dividends over profits for several years.

[44] Business sales consist of sales to residents (persons and governments) plus sales to non-residents, both as defined on the revenue side of the Business Operating Account of the National Accounts. A good case can be made for including domestic investment in business sales for present purposes. This was done by a scatter diagram relating investment in durable assets to business sales, including sales to business on capital account in the latter. The statements in the text still apply, except that business sales in 1937 fall short of 1926.

on investment in the thirties.[45] Other factors affecting investment had become important as a result of developments in the twenties and in the downswing, developments whose effects were prolonged far into the upswing and limited the upswing. In part, these factors were reflected in the prevailing excess capacity (including large ratios of inventories to sales) which limited the working of the accelerator. In addition, they included such developments as the maladjustments in the previous upswing, and even longer-term considerations; the differing degree of price decline and the incomplete price recovery; the uneven export recovery, and outright crop failure late in the upswing; attempts to achieve liquid positions and retire debt; and a limited role for innovations.

Excess capacity can mean several things. The total rated capacity can be used as the standard, and the difference between rated capacity and actual output can be taken as excess capacity. A more realistic view, especially when investment is being rapidly increased, may be to take as the standard the operating ratio in a period of high employment, such as the late twenties; any decrease from this ratio would be excess capacity. One would probably still have to allow for those particular industries which were experiencing great difficulties in spite of general prosperity. In some industries such as mining, moreover, the definitional problems involved are also serious.

While comprehensive estimates of excess capacity do not exist, the extent of the problem can be seen if one considers the sharp increases in physical volume of investment from 1926 to 1929, and the completion of many projects in the downswing. On the other hand, between 1929 and 1933 consumption fell 17 per cent in constant dollars, exports of goods and services 25 per cent, and the decline in private and public investment itself decreased demand for products entering investment.[46] By 1937 these expenditures (except for investment) were at or

[45] It could be argued that if the net effects of non-wage income or business sales were considered, after allowing for other determinants of investment such as the stock of capital and the degree to which it was utilized, or the level of debts, or "anticipations" of the future, then the conclusions above would be modified. It is hazardous to apply multiple correlation analysis with several variables, however, when the number of observations is so small; for some variables, in fact, no meaningful set of observations is available. In any case, the full examination of the current and past background of the period and the major industries seems to us the more fruitful approach for present purposes.

[46] Part of these decreases represent lower imports rather than domestic purchases.

above their 1929 levels in constant dollars. Assuming very broadly that net additions to capacity in 1930 and 1931 were offset by net deterioration and deductions for several years, it was probably not until about 1937 that operating ratios were close to the 1929 levels. These are very rough and general estimates, of course, but they do suggest the extensive excess capacity which would help limit the response of investment to rising sales and income. At the same time, it would be a mistake to identify investment too closely or exclusively with operating ratios. An average firm operating at 80 per cent of capacity in both 1929 and 1937 would certainly not be inclined to undertake the same amount of investment in each period. The relative levels of prices, costs, debt, and other factors would be taken into account; the experience of the past decade would make firms cautious in undertaking new investment; and a great deal would also depend on just what innovations were available for exploitation, and how thoroughly they had been exploited earlier.

It is worth bringing together some data on the costs of investment to round out the aggregative picture of factors affecting investment decisions.[47] The costs of investment goods were generally much less flexible than most price series. The implicit price index for consumer expenditures in GNE was 79 per cent of the 1929 level in 1933 and 85 per cent in 1937. Export prices fell to 63 per cent of the 1929 level and recovered to 85 per cent in 1937. To take the most inflexible investment costs, prices for machinery and equipment fell only 10 per cent in the downswing, and interest rates on corporation bonds rose by over one-fifth. (The latter change reflects the sharp increase in interest rates after September 1931). Although in 1937 the two indexes used above to represent sales prices were still 15 per cent below 1929 levels, the price indexes for construction were only 5-10 per cent below, and machinery and equipment had recovered to the 1929 level. Interest costs had decreased steadily after 1933, although not all borrowers could secure the lower rates.

Some of the components of these cost series are available. The price index of imported machinery and equipment (excluding farm) fell to 88 per cent of the 1929 level in 1933. It remained fairly stable slightly below this level until 1937, when it rose to 92 per cent of the 1929 level. The price index of

TABLE 39

SELECTED INDEXES REFLECTING THE COST OF INVESTMENT, 1929-37
(1929 = 100)

	Residential construction	Non-residential construction	Machinery and equipment	Building and construction materials	Interest rates on corporation bonds	Wage rates in building trades
1929	100.0	100.0	100.0	100.0	100.0	100.0
1933	78.2	83.0	90.9	79.1	122.4	79.9
1934	82.1	83.9	90.1	83.3	99.2	78.4
1935	81.7	85.3	91.9	82.0	89.6	80.9
1936	84.1	87.4	92.8	86.2	77.6	81.3
1937	90.3	94.3	99.1	95.4	74.4	83.7

SOURCES: The first three series are the implicit price deflators for GNE, and the fourth is from D.B.S., *Prices and Price Indexes, 1913-1940.* Interest rates on corporation bonds are from Nixon, "Course of Interest Rates," p. 422 (that for 1937 is the first four months only). Wage rates in building trades are from *C.Y.B.*

imported farm implements and machinery was even more stable, falling only 8 per cent from 1929 to 1933 and rising to within 5 per cent of the 1929 level in 1936 and 1937.[48] Wholesale prices of building and construction materials exhibited more flexibility than these particular series, partly because of sharp fluctuations in export prices. Wage rates in the building trades fell by 20 per cent from 1929 to 1933, almost all of the decline coming after 1931. The various price series for imported machinery, building materials, and wage rates rose fairly slowly from 1933 to 1936. For certain groups in the economy, this meant that the price-cost disparities appearing in the downswing were being remedied. Thus export prices rose more rapidly than did these cost series in the upswing, and the same was true for farm sales prices. For many important sectors of the economy, however, the disparity of sales prices and these particular costs was only partly corrected in the upswing. In 1937, furthermore, while various indexes of sales prices rose

48 D.B.S., *Export and Import Price Indexes 1926-1948.*

more rapidly, those for investment costs (especially building and contruction materials) also rose rapidly.[49]

It can be objected that more important forces than the level of investment costs were at work retarding investment in the upswing. Although some of the analysis presented earlier would support this view, this need not mean that such cost rigidity was of no importance. Lower interest costs in some industries might have helped to lessen the impact of other factors unfavourable to investment, particularly after the upswing got under way; and some of these lower costs would not have affected personal income, since they accrued to the import sector. In 1937, in particular, when investment was beginning to revive more rapidly, some of the more substantial increases in the cost of investment goods on balance probably had unfavourable effects on investment.[50]

As was emphasized in the introductory chapter, the influence of current sales is more closely related to induced than to autonomous investment. Autonomous investment depends particularly on innovations, which raise the expected marginal profitability of investment. In the twenties a number of major innovations were present, particularly the rapid growth in the use of the automobile and the technological, market, and resource changes which gave such a great impetus to mining, newsprint, and related industries. This type of autonomous investment explains why total investment increased more rapidly than could be explained by sales or income alone.

Innovations, in the broad sense in which the term is used here, were not, of course, absent in the thirties; technological change continued in industry, new products or new uses appeared (as in textiles and metals), military demands began to be felt toward the end of the decade, and the outlook for particular products such as gold was greatly changed. But two points need to be emphasized concerning innovations. Many of the investment opportunities opened up by the innovations which came to fruition in the twenties had already been exploited, to a large degree, by the investment of the last half of the twenties and in the first year or so of the downswing. Some

[49] In 1937 wholesale prices for consumers' goods rose 6.4 per cent and the implicit price index for consumer expenditure rose 3.2 per cent; on the other hand, the implicit price indexes for non-residential construction and machinery and equipment rose 7.9 and 6.8 per cent. Export prices rose 16 per cent and farm prices 27 per cent, however.

[50] See p. 150.

of them, as pointed out earlier, had been exploited to the point where investment was levelling out, or even falling, before the cyclical fall in demand abroad began. In some important industries there was no extensive backlog of investment opportunities to expedite the recovery. Where such opportunities did exist, the events of the downswing would moderate or temporarily postpone their exploitation.[51] This leads to the second point, namely, that where innovations did occur in the downswing and upswing their over-all effects clearly were not strong enough to offset the existing deflationary forces to any marked extent. This was partly because no really major series of innovations occurred until World War II completely transformed the picture. One does not have to depend solely on the incomplete recovery of domestic investment in 1937 to support this view. As noted earlier, the types of investment which rose most rapidly in 1937 were those which tend to be geared to shorter-run prospects. The decline of domestic investment in 1938 (and again in 1939), when the components of domestic demand either levelled out or continued to rise on an annual basis, and when the fall in export demand was brief, again suggests autonomous investment could not have been playing a major role.[52] The weakness of innovation effects has also been suggested in terms of the tendency for changes in production by sectors of the economy from 1929 to 1937 to concentrate somewhat closer to the average, as compared to the greater divergency of the twenties.[53]

In part, of course, it is likely that some innovations will not be exploited on any large scale if the existing economic situation is badly depressed, even where the outlook for that particular product is favourable. The general pessimism engendered by recent experience may be such as to lead firms to

[51] This point and that in the previous sentence are not the same, although related to some extent. It is one thing for a country like Canada to experience a world depression and recovery with much of the existing investment opportunities exploited, another to do so with a large backlog, even though the developments of the downswing will affect the rate of exploitation of such investment opportunities.

[52] International political uncertainty was an additional depressing factor late in the thirties. See pp. 178-9 for further comments on the point discussed here, and contrast the behaviour of domestic investment in 1938 with that in 1911, p. 25. Chambers, in "The 1937-8 Recession," pp. 305-8, emphasizes the absence of growth elements as a significant factor in the 1937-8 recession.

[53] See Malach, *International Cycles*, pp. 45 and 94.

proceed cautiously even with favourable specific developments.[54] As a general phenomenon, however, this should affect the downswing phase rather than the upswing. Finally, the relatively limited effect of innovations on investment in the thirties may reflect the fact that such changes have their greatest impact after the initial developmental stages. It has been noted, however, that the major investment opportunities opened up by innovations at the more advanced stages of development had already been exploited to an important degree in the twenties.

Without substantial backlogs of investment opportunities in the thirties, and with the host of problems created by the severe downswing and projected into the upswing, the expectations of profit from new investment in the thirties were low. Even induced investment would react slowly to rising sales and income, given excess capacity and the other problems affecting investment in the upswing. Several years of relatively high sales and incomes would have been necessary before accumulated replacement demands and induced investment could rally strongly, and some time would have to elapse before any new industries and products could begin to make large contributions to investment. But, by contrast, the more rapid increase by 1937 was partly reversed by a further setback in economic activity.

[54] In this sense the distinction between induced and autonomous investment may become blurred at times.

CHAPTER SEVEN

Recovery in Selected Industries

In the preceding chapters the nature of the recovery has been examined primarily on an aggregative basis. It is necessary now to look more closely at the industries which were examined in the twenties in order to note more precisely the types of problems which limited their recoveries.

The Wheat Economy

No major industry suffered as much as agriculture in the downswing or recovered as slowly, judging by data on national income by industry. From its peak in 1928 to the low in 1933, national income fell by over 50 per cent. Income in agriculture in the same period fell by almost 80 per cent and accounted for well over a quarter of the drop in total income. By 1937 total national income was still $761 million short of the 1928 level, and the loss in agriculture alone represented $411 million of this shortfall. The reasons for this incomplete recovery lie basically in wheat.

The instability of wheat income is related to several factors. In part it is associated with a relatively inelastic world demand in any short period, combined with large harvest fluctuations. The individualistic nature of production (so that one farmer cannot affect price), the relatively constant overhead with variation in output, and the uncertainty of yields, all mean that acreage may be expanded rather than decreased in response to (and as an offset to) lower prices. With relatively fixed expenses, variation in net income can be even larger than that in gross income. The variation in farm purchasing power can be extremely severe since farm prices fluctuate more than prices in the imperfectly competitive markets in which farmers buy.[1] Sales in international markets, furthermore, mean that a low yield does not necessarily lead to a compensatory increase in price; quite apart from cyclical variation in demand, in-

[1] See the following articles in the *CJEPS:* F. W. Burton, "Wheat in Canadian History," p. 210; R. McQueen, "Economic Aspects of Federalism," p. 356; and G. L. Burton, "The Farmer and the Market."

creases in the crops available to competing exporters and in importing countries, or large carryovers, may offset the price effects of smaller crops in an exporting country. Thus yield, acreage, and price are all uncertain.

The actual decrease in exports and variation in income were due to both external and internal factors. World output from the crop year 1927-8 to the crop year 1933-4 inclusive was high, about 3.7 billion bushels per year. The carryover for all countries at the end of the season rose rapidly from 191 million bushels in 1926-7 to from 434-625 million bushels from 1928-9 to 1933-4 inclusive.[2] The large carryovers exerted a strongly depressing influence on price throughout the first half of the thirties. Yields were good in Europe in much of the thirties. Restrictions on imports of wheat were made much stronger in most European countries through the extension of bounties for home production, import quotas, and milling regulations. Finally, the depreciation of the currencies of Australia and especially of the Argentine, before September 1931, helped reduce the world price of wheat and also set Canada (whose currency was stable) at a competitive disadvantage. This disadvantage continued for a time after September as the British and Australian pounds and the peso depreciated more than the Canadian dollar.[3]

The factors within Canada which were responsible for the fall in exports and slow increase include the holdback of wheat in 1929-30, the stabilization measures up to 1935, and a succession of low yields. The average yield per seeded acre from the crop year 1922-3 to 1928-9 never fell below 17.8 bushels, except in 1924-5. This contrasts with the much lower yields throughout the thirties, as shown in Table 40. Larger seeded acreages partly offset the lower yields. Acreage was increased by almost one-fifth from 1927-8 to the peak in 1932-3, and remained at about 24-26 million in the rest of the thirties – compared to 21-23 million in 1922 to 1927.[4]

The wheat pools ran into difficulties in late 1929 and early

<hr>

[2] *Financial Post*, December 19, 1936.
[3] See Marcus, *Canada and the International Business Cycle*, pp. 97 and 103.
[4] D.B.S., *Handbook of Agricultural Statistics*, Part I, p. 1. J. B. Rutherford has estimated (on the basis of a projection of 1919-28 acreage, yields, and prices of five grains in Saskatchewan) that from 1929 to 1932 the loss of income was due to price changes and volume changes in the ratio of 60 per cent to 40 per cent, with about the reverse true in the next four years. See his article "Agricultural Income," *CJEPS*.

1930, when a policy of holding back supplies proved disastrous in the face of prices which fell below their initial prices to farmers. The provincial and finally Dominion governments stepped in, and the latter appointed a general manager to take over the pools' selling agency. From 1931 to 1935 wheat was purchased by the agency under a government guarantee of its borrowings from banks. The policy was to feed supplies gradually to the market and to purchase when necessary, in an attempt to prevent price breaks.[5] The carryover of wheat continued to rise, and in 1932-3 and 1933-4 the Canadian carryover was about a third of the world carryover. At the end of 1935 the Canadian Wheat Board took over responsibility for the wheat situation and proceeded to liquidate stocks. Short crops in many countries (including Canada), economic recovery, and a policy of moving stocks, combined to reduce the Canadian carryover to the levels of the early twenties for a time.

TABLE 40

SELECTED STATISTICS ON CANADIAN WHEAT, CROP YEARS 1926-7 TO 1937-8

(Millions of bushels except as noted)

Crop year(a)	Pro-duction	Average yield per seeded acre	Average farm price per bushel (dollars)	Exports as wheat and flour	Carry-over, end of crop year	Cash income (millions of dollars)
1926-7	407	17.8	1.09	293	56	401
1927-8	480	21.4	1.00	333	91	375
1928-9	567	23.5	.80	408	127	451
1929-30	302	12.0	1.05	186	127	334
1930-1	421	16.9	.49	259	139	165
1931-2	321	12.2	.38	207	136	95
1932-3	443	16.3	.35	264	218	120
1933-4	282	10.8	.49	195	203	118
1934-5	276	11.5	.61	166	214	142
1935-6	282	11.7	.61	254	127	146
1936-7	219	8.6	.94	210	37	146
1937-8	180	7.0	1.02	96	25	139

SOURCE: D.B.S., *Handbook of Agricultural Statistics,* Parts I and II.

(a) Beginning August 1.

5 *Financial Post,* April 7, 1934.

The stabilization policy was based on the view that since the over-all demand for wheat was inelastic, and competitors were ready to meet Canadian prices, lower prices would probably not be compensated by increased world sales or a greater Canadian share in these sales.[6] Canadian wheat prices at Liverpool, in fact, were often well over those of other exporters for comparable grades. The result of government policies, therefore, was to defer wheat sales to years when crop failures occurred. Other attempts to aid wheat sales were not particularly successful. The preference on wheat in the United Kingdom was not large enough to have significant effects, and the London Wheat Agreement was quickly invalidated.[7]

Wheat was the principle source of deflationary influences in agriculture, but by no means the only one. The market for cattle in the United States had been partly blocked in 1922 and was virtually closed in 1930, while the United Kingdom restrictions on cattle imports were not lifted until the 1932 Imperial Conference. There was some revival in exports to the United Kingdom, in spite of renewed restrictions, but it was not until 1935 and later that the more important United States market was again available. Expenditure on foods within Canada appears to have been much better maintained than the export of foodstuffs, however – largely reflecting the great role of wheat in exports of foodstuffs.[8]

Thus agriculture was subjected not only to a cyclical fall in demand, but also to special restrictions and short crops. A number of factors heightened the severity of the effects of fluctuations in sales. The fixed charges facing agriculture meant sharp fluctuations in net income. Farm cash income fell by about 60 per cent from 1928-9 to 1932-3, gross income fell by about half, but operating and depreciation charges fell by only about one-third. The interest component of these charges actualy rose throughout the downswing, and taxes and freight rates remained relatively rigid. In addition, the relatively rigid prices of manufactures purchased by farmers, owing to the imperfectly competitive markets for such products and the

[6] Marcus, *Canada and the International Business Cycle*, p. 144.
[7] For appraisals of wheat policy, see *ibid.*, pp. 143-6; V. C. Fowke, "Dominion Aids to Wheat Marketing, 1929-39," *CJEPS*; Parkinson, *Memorandum*, CHAP. VIII; and the *Financial Post* for October 6, 1934 and January 26, 1935.
[8] Including, of course foreign restrictions on food imports. The conclusion on domestic sales is based on partial data appearing for selected years in the *National Accounts*, p. 74, and from analysis of cash income from the sale of farm products.

increase in Canadian tariffs, struck at farm purchasing power. The decisions of the past heightened the impact of the depression. The wheat problem reflected in part the rapid increases in acreage and output, during and after the war, in Canada and elsewhere; by the end of the twenties, the world wheat situation was showing signs of over-expansion. The movement of wheat farming some decades earlier into southern areas which were more suitable for ranching exposed large areas to drought. Somewhat more land might have been used more wisely for ranching, other grains, and mixed farming to avoid the effects of extreme specialization. Such a movement did occur to some extent in the thirties.[9] The extreme specialization and lack of alternatives, however, meant whole areas were impoverished.

The large investments made by prairie governments in the twenties in highways, telephones, and other projects left a tremendous burden of debt. Relief increased this burden in the depression, as the delayed social costs of opening areas subject to drought, combined with the effects of the world cycle, put these governments in desperate financial straits. Private as well as public debt was a severe burden for the area. The burden of debt not only increased sharply with lower prices but absolutely as well, for a time, in order to meet operating losses and growing arrears of interest and taxes.[10] Debt continued to be a severe problem in the upswing; an important part of higher cash income had to be used for arrears of interest and taxes, for repayment of debt, or to cover operating costs without further increase in debt, rather than for replacement or additions to investment. Some part of the debt burden was eased by provincial and federal farm debt legislation and by private negotiation, but the process was slow and difficult and no very extensive downward readjustment was involved.

The results of continued agricultural depression were widespread. They appeared in the sharp fall and very incomplete recovery in agricultural income, in government and railway deficits, in unemployment in eastern manufacturing industries supplying the prairies, in actual or threatened default or repu-

---

9 G. E. Britnell, "Saskatchewan 1930-35," *CJEPS*, p. 145. The movement could not go very far, since much of the prairies was technologically better suited to wheat. See D. A. MacGibbon, "The Future of the Canadian Export Trade in Wheat," *Contributions to Canadian Economics.*

10 See Britnell, "Saskatchewan," p. 162.

diation of debt (which, in turn, further restricted the willingness of creditors to lend), in the failure to replace depreciated or obsolescent buildings and equipment, and the low level of new investment. Agricultural investment in the upswing retained the same weight in total investment as that in the late twenties. But its role in total investment in the twenties represented a declining proportion over time, at least for prairie farm investment, and the increase in durable investment in agriculture in the late twenties was relatively slow.[11] By 1933 such investment was only 14 per cent of the peak 1928 level and by 1937 only 53 per cent. The low levels of investment through 1936 suggest replacement rather than additions to capital stock.

As to specific alternatives in agricultural policy, it is worth noting that western agriculture bore the full brunt of both fluctuating export income and the rigid costs of the Canadian economy. Where some parts of an economy are exposed to sharp cyclical changes in prices and other parts largely avoid them, the short-run policy alternatives are difficult to suggest. Price stabilization in the exposed sector will only increase the problem in an open economy, since export volume will fall; subsidies designed to keep export prices low, while increasing the return to exporters, aggravate the cost problems of other sectors of the economy – and also invite retaliation from abroad. To attempt by *direct* means to lower the more rigid prices, such as interest and administered prices, may be equally difficult – and the attempt to do so may have unfortunate effects during a general decline.

It is likely, however, that a more effective use of monetary policy would have supplied an important alternative, by indirect means, as a buffer to ease the adjustment between the two sectors. Although not necessarily successful in starting an upswing, effective monetary policy can expedite an upswing once it has begun. Operations to lower interest rates, had they begun earlier and been undertaken more effectively, would have eased the burden greatly. Some depreciation in the exchange rate, after it came to parity in 1933, would have helped distribute the inevitable burdens of the depression more evenly by taking some of the continuing pressure off export sectors. On balance, this would probably have provided a net stimulus to general expansion, if contrasted with the effects of having one or more large sectors of the economy very severely de-

[11] See Tables 3, 4 and 35.

TABLE 41

SELECTED STATISTICS ON AGRICULTURE, 1926-37
(Millions of dollars)

	Cash income	Gross income (a)	Operating and depreciation charges	Taxes and interest (b)	Net income	Gross durable investment
1926	966	1,205	575	111	630	89
1927	945	1,246	602	111	644	109
1928	1,070	1,289	625	116	664	139
1929	938	1,054	621	119	433	121
1930	647	919	579	120	340	86
1931	476	628	490	121	138	36
1932	412	575	441	121	134	29
1933	423	542	425	120	117	19
1934	506	658	448	121	211	36
1935	536	701	458	120	242	41
1936	591	709	468	118	241	53
1937	642	807	490	113	317	74

SOURCES: D.B.S., *Handbook of Agricultural Statistics*, vol. II, pp. 14 and 56, and *P.P.I.*, p. 154.
(a) Includes cash income, income in kind, and value of inventory changes.
(b) Taxes and interest (which are included in operating charges) are those on owned land and buildings only.

pressed.[12] Such a policy, furthermore, would have had some of the protective aspects of the tariff, but because of its more temporary nature might not have led to as much longer-term rigidity and growth of less efficient industry.

[12] "Those opposed to any plan of Canadian currency depreciation on the ground that it would increase the external debt burden and injure the credit standing of the country are compelled to consider losses measured by the extent of the increase in public and private indebtedness, especially in Western Canada, accompanying the rigidities and burdens produced by tariff and sound money." Westcott, "Approach to Problems of Tariff Burdens," p. 217.

Newsprint

In an earlier section it was noted that Canada's largest manufacturing industry, the pulp and paper industry, was running into difficulties before the downswing began.[13] The downswing and slow recovery showed up primarily in the price of newsprint, which fell sharply and recovered very slowly.[14] Volume of output and exports fell more slowly and were almost at the 1929 peak as early as 1934; this reflected the strong longer-term upward demand for newsprint and the smaller fluctuations in volume of a product related to advertising and, therefore, largely to consumer purchases. But export values (and about 90 per cent of the newsprint was exported) were only somewhat over half the 1929 level by 1934 and 80 per cent of the 1929 value in 1937.

With production and export volume well in excess of the previous peaks after 1934, pricing in the industry needs to be explained, for in this lay much of the industry's problem. Some special difficulties, such as the growing use of radio and other media for advertising, reduced newspaper size and newsprint demand. At times the Scandinavian supplies were able to cut into Canada's vast share of the United States market to a limited degree, because of exchange rates more depreciated than the depreciated Canadian dollar of the early thirties. United States output, however, failed to recover from the downswing, reflecting the long-term tendency of foreign supplies to absorb the growth in United States demand.

The basic factors in the *débâcle* in the newsprint industry, however, were the doubling of capacity in 1925-30, with much unwise financing, and the monopsony buying power of some large purchasers. The latter, of course, was heightened by the former and by the downswing in demand, which led to large excess capacity and pressure from heavy overhead costs. In spite of the fact that three companies controlled half the large eastern output, and one exercised some price leadership functions, the bargaining strength of the producers weakened under the sharp pressure to win contracts and ease the burden of overhead costs. With most of the larger producers bankrupt or

[13] See Bladen, *Introduction to Political Economy*, CHAP. VI, for an able analysis of the newsprint industry's structure and problems; also see *Financial Post*, September 28, 1935; September 25, 1937; and September 24, 1938.

[14] See Table 42. If discounts, rebates, and similar disguised price cuts are taken into account, the low was closer to $30 rather than the $40 shown in the table.

TABLE 42

THE NEWSPRINT INDUSTRY IN CANADA, 1924-38

	Daily capacity (thousand tons)	Capacity of new machines installed (thousand tons)	Annual production (million tons)	Percentage of capacity utilized	Price per ton(a) ($)	Exports ($ million)	Investment in durable assets(b) ($ million)
1924	5.8	190	1.4	—	79	91	—
1925	6.4	175	1.5	—	77	99	—
1926	8.0	375	1.9	86	70	114	44
1927	9.9	433	2.1	73	70	123	47
1928	10.9	459	2.4	73	68	141	49
1929	11.9	277	2.7	75	62	149	26
1930	12.6	260	2.5	66	62	133	25
1931	12.6		2.2	63	57	107	13
1932	12.6		1.9	51	48	83	3
1933	12.6		2.0	55	41	69	1
1934	12.6		2.6	70	40	83	4
1935	12.7		2.8	73	40	88	5
1936	13.1		3.2	82	41	104	5
1937	14.0		3.7	94	43	126	11
1938	—		2.6	62	50	105	7

SOURCES: Bladen, *Introduction to Political Economy*, p. 159. The last two columns are from Canada, *Bank of Canada Statistical Summary*, 1950 Supplement, p. 117, and *P.P.I.*, p. 160. A dash indicates figures not available on same basis.

(a) Yearly averages of contract prices of large Canadian producers for newsprint delivered at New York.

(b) Investment data are for all of the pulp and paper industry, other data are for newsprint only.

in default on interest within a few years, the pricing situation deteriorated even more as competition for contracts increased.[15] The depreciation of the Canadian dollar with respect to the United States dollar after 1931 helped ease the downswing, since newsprint prices were in United States dollars.

15 By 1934 about 54 per cent of the capacity of the industry was in the hands of mortgagees. Bladen, *Introduction to Political Economy*, p. 186.

The improvement of the position of the industry began in mid-1933, when United States newspaper linage started to increase and purchasers raised stocks in the expectation of a price increase. Pooling of tonnage and pricing agreements were not successful in the downswing, but did lend some stability for short periods when recovery began. Prices rose very slowly. Attempts to raise prices in 1935 and 1936 were frustrated by the tactics of monopsony buyers; by the use of the lowest-price clause in contracts; and by the fact that individual mills, because of large excess capacity, hesitated to turn down contracts at the existing prices.[16]

A number of adjustments were made in the downswing and upswing to meet the problems of the industry; as shipments fell, production was confined to low-cost mills, and administrative and other costs were reduced; numerous reorganizations, writing down of capital, and transfers of fixed debt for equities were effected; the lowest-price clause in contracts was gradually withdrawn. In addition, unit overhead costs would fall with the strong recovery in output. By 1937 operating ratios were satisfactory, but prices were still well below 1929.

Extensive damage was done to the industry by over-expansion and over-financing,.by the pricing structure of the industry, and by the decline in United States demand in the downswing. The merger movement of the late twenties greatly increased the problems of several large producers, because of interest on funds used to acquire control of other companies and because of power and other commitments resulting from the mergers.[17] At the end of 1936 almost half of the rated capacity was still in receivership or operating under default conditions.

Turning to the effects on investment, it will be noted that gross domestic investment in pulp and paper was about $50

[16] Newsprint was sold on long-term contracts, but the price was subject to review every year or less and the buyer generally had the privilege of securing the lowest price charged by any mill with a capacity of 100,000 tons or more. For the influence of newspaper chains on prices, see the *Financial Post*, March 21, 1936.

[17] In referring to one large company, a writer in the *Financial Post* of May 30, 1936, remarked, "But two-thirds of the assets, represented in that figure (of $122 million) have been so far a millstone around the neck of the company. If the company had never taken over these water laden assets with their contingent obligations it would still in all probability be a solvent company even if the book value of the assets still remained at the $33 million shown back in 1925 and 1926."

million in 1927 and 1928, but fell sharply to half this level in 1929 and 1930. Again one finds some investment put in place after the general downswing began. From 1930 to 1935, however, daily capacity was virtually unchanged. Judging from the data in Table 42, even replacement was very low – probably partly because much of the stock was fairly recent, and partly because of the financial problems of the industry.[18] With operating ratios low until 1936-7, a poor recovery in price, and much of the industry bankrupt for a large part of the thirties, it is hardly surprising to find little investment activity. Not until late in the upswing was capacity enlarged once more.

Mining

By 1935 the mining industry as a whole had almost attained the 1929 level in value of production and had exceeded it in volume. Metallic minerals were the driving force of this recovery. The two most significant factors were the increase in the price of gold and the sharp rise in exports of base metals to the United Kingdom.[19]

The strongest stimulus came from gold. In the downswing the price of gold in foreign currency remained fixed, while costs fell sharply. The return in terms of Canadian dollars was greatly increased when the Canadian dollar depreciated in terms of the United States dollar. Output of gold rose sharply in the downswing. As a result of the events in the United States which led to the embargo on gold exports in April 1933, and the expectation of a higher official United States price for gold, the actual price rose sharply until February 1934, when the United States

---

[18] Some of the increase in the investment data shown in Table 42, moreover, reflects not enlarged newsprint capacity, but enlarged capacity for sulphite pulps to meet the rapidly growing industrial demand for cellulose. See the *Financial Post,* July 31 and September 25, 1937.

[19] Exports of non-ferrous metals and products rose from $118 million in 1929 to $195 million in 1937; in millions of dollars, the country distribution in these years was 15 and 101 for the United Kingdom, 64 and 45 for the United States, and 39 and 49 for other countries. The strong recovery of the United Kingdom relative to 1929 (and her building and electrification boom in particular), along with efficient Canadian production, were important factors in the great increase in base metal exports to the United Kingdom. See Marcus, *Canada and the International Business Cycle,* pp. 133-40.

devalued the dollar in terms of gold.[20] It remained at this high level (adjusted for fluctuations in the Canadian dollar) throughout the thirties. By 1937 the volume of gold production was more than double that of 1929, and its value was three and a half times greater. The higher fixed price and assured market for gold in the United States were of major importance to the mining industry and gave strong support to the balance of payments.

Nickel also served as a stimulus to recovery. The 1934 volume and value of output exceeded those of 1929, and by 1937 had more than doubled the 1929 figures. Canada exported 99 per cent of her output, but was in a strong position since this represented about 90 per cent of world output and almost all of it was produced by one company.[21] Since nickel was used in durables such as automobiles and machinery, volume fell sharply in the downswing, but it also rose sharply in the upswing. The price, however, was maintained — in fact, it was unchanged from the middle twenties throughout the depression and upswing. The basic factors in the strong recovery of nickel were the revival of industrial activity in the United Kingdom and the United States, the extensive research programme which widened the market for the metal, and the growing armaments budgets of the thirties.[22] Although facilities had been greatly extended in the late twenties, by late 1934 the company had once more embarked on an expansion programme.

Copper, lead, and zinc did not fare as well as gold and nickel. Their use as producers' materials and for construction meant a sharp decrease in volume of demand in the downswing. Copper was the most important of these three metals for Canada. The potential world supply of copper was greatly

[20] The official old and new prices were $20.67 and $35.00 per ounce. The Canadian dollar equivalents had been substantially higher than $20.67 since the depreciation in 1931.

[21] In 1934 Canadians held 21 per cent of the shares of the International Nickel Company of Canada, the United Kingdom held 33 per cent, and the United States 42 per cent. The Canadian company was legally the parent of the United States subsidiary, but the company was directed from a New York office. See Marshall, Southard and Taylor, *Canadian-American Industry*, CHAP. II.

[22] See the *Financial Post* of November 5, 1938. According to this report, about 20 per cent of nickel output went to the automobile industry; 15 per cent to railways, farm implements, and general machinery; 10 per cent to chromium plating; 9 per cent to monel metal uses; and the remainder into a variety of uses. The company's estimate of use in armaments was given as 10 per cent.

increased in the late twenties and thirties as other low-cost producers with large reserves came into extensive production in several countries. Stocks accumulated and, along with the rapidly expansible nature of supply and lower world demand (especially in the United States), kept prices low. The United States tariff of 4 cents per pound, introduced in mid-1932, virtually cut off this market for Canada for several years. With recovery, the United States market again took larger amounts of copper, but it was mainly the United Kingdom market which accounted for the increase in copper exports to new peak levels.

TABLE 43

SELECTED STATISTICS ON THE MINERAL INDUSTRIES, 1929-37
(Millions of dollars)

	All mineral industries			Metallic mineral industries		
	Capital em- ployed	Net value of pro- duction	Index of volume	Capital em- ployed	Net value of pro- duction	Index of volume
1929	867	315	100.0	427	163	100.0
1930	887	271	100.2	427	137	111.8
1931	842	238	90.4	391	132	108.8
1932	685	197	76.3	269	120	100.9
1933	800	222	80.1	407	150	112.9
1934	831	267	93.7	466	187	133.3
1935	778	303	101.4	437	217	145.3
		239(a)			174(a)	
1936	859	292	116.2	508	211	165.2
1937	957	373	134.5	585	277	189.8

SOURCE: *C.Y.B., 1939*, pp. 322 and 330-1.

(a) Net value had formerly been defined as gross value less freight and treatment charges for mines and value of ores for smelters. After 1934 the cost of fuels, electricity, and supplies consumed in production was also deducted. The figures for 1935 are available on both bases to facilitate comparisons.

The drop in production of copper, lead, and zinc did not reflect the full decrease in world demand as these metals are produced in Canada in conjunction with precious metals and nickel. Canada's major producers were thus able to benefit from the very favourable position of gold, and also to continue production of other metals at low cost. By 1937 export values of copper, lead, and zinc had exceeded their peaks of the late twenties. More rapid recovery in industry and construction in several countries, armaments demand or purchases for war reserves, and speculative purchases were responsible for decreases in stocks and increases in price.[23] In copper a world cartel (not including United States and Canadian producers) was partly effective in restraining output.

TABLE 44

PRODUCTION AND EXPORTS OF SELECTED METALS, 1926-37
(Values are millions of dollars)

	Gold		Nickel		Copper	
	Output (million fine oz.)	Value (a)	Output (million lbs.)	Export Value (b)	Output (million lbs.)	Export Value (b)
1926	1.8	36.3	66	12	133	15
1929	1.9	39.9	110	26	248	37
1930	2.1	43.5	104	21	303	31
1931	2.7	58.1	66	14	292	17
1932	3.0	71.5	30	7	248	16
1933	2.9	84.4	83	23	300	17
1934	3.0	102.5	129	29	365	23
1935	3.3	115.6	136	36	419	30
1936	3.7	131.3	170	45	421	37
1937	4.1	143.3	225	59	530	56

SOURCE: *C.Y.B., 1939,* CHAP. XII and Bank of Canada, *Statistical Summary, 1950 Supplement,* p. 117.
(a) Gold values are on basis 1 fine oz. = $20.67 up to 1931, and since then at world prices in Canadian funds.
(b) Includes products of these metals.

Metallic minerals (and related processing) show one of the few strong recoveries in Canada. They help explain to a very important degree why commodity exports (including gold) by 1937 had almost attained the 1929 level. Investment in primary mining alone rose from 3 per cent of all private investment in durable assets in 1926-9 to 6 per cent in 1934-7. But several qualifications are necessary to the emphasis laid on mining

[23] *Financial Post,* March 13, 1937.

and its effect on recovery. Production of the very important mineral coal did not recover nearly as well. The recovery of metallic minerals directly benefited certain areas only, to any important degree. Finally, in another section it has been suggested that the effects on employment and income of a strong recovery in mining were lessened by large "leakages" via payments abroad, and by the relatively small ratio of labour to capital in that industry.[24]

Utilities

The decrease in demand for power in 1931 and 1932 was relatively mild. Industrial use of power was most seriously affected, mainly because of falling newsprint output, and exports of power fell sharply. Domestic service and commercial lighting sales were much better maintained. A substantial part of the surplus generating capacity was diverted to electric boilers to raise steam; by 1934, close to 25 per cent of the output of central electric stations was marketed in this way.[25]

By 1933 a very strong expansion in the use of electrical power was under way. As early as 1934 output far exceeded the previous peak, and gross revenues were close to that peak. The contributory factors were the rapid expansion in mining and related metallurgical processes, recovery in newsprint volume beyond the earlier peaks, the widening use of power for domestic service as facilities were extended and the use of some electrical appliances continued to spread, sales for electric boiler purposes, and general industrial recovery. Direct exports of power did not play a very large role in the recovery; it was not until 1937 that exports exceeded their 1928 peak of 1.7 billion kilowatt hours.

In spite of this, however, it will be noted that gross domestic investment in central electric stations was almost stable at very low levels from 1933 to 1936 inclusive, and the increase in 1937 left investment well below the levels of the late twenties and early thirties. In part this reflects a lag in this type of investment, associated with the length of time required to complete large installations. With a general downswing under way and the sale of power declining, profit expectations were revised downwards, but investment could not be cut rapidly. Such a long and deep trough is evident in steam railways and

24 See pp. 175-77.
25 *Financial Post*, March 30, 1935.

other utilities as well, which also involve heavy capital outlays and favourable long-term prospects. The size and nature of investment by railways, power, and other utilities help explain the long and deep trough in total investment in the thirties as well as the maintenance of some types of investment in the first year or two of the downswing.[26]

Although gross revenues from the sale of power were not seriously affected, it should be noted that the industry had very heavy interest costs because of the large bond capitalization involved.[27] Much of the debt was held abroad and much of this was in optional payment bonds; when the exchange depreciated in the downswing, the costs of power companies were greatly raised.[28] Privately owned utilities were affected also by relatively rigid taxes. Thus net revenues are likely to have fallen much more than gross.

An important factor in the slow recovery of investment in central electric stations was the reduced ratio of output to maximum capacity.[29] Although output declined little and increased far beyond the previous peak level, the considerable increase in installations in the first few years of the thirties sharply reduced this ratio. It had been rising in the twenties, in spite of greatly enlarged capacity, and by 1927-9 it was about 50 per cent. It fell to 36 per cent in 1932-3, rose to 42, 45, and 47 per cent in the next three years, and attained the ratio of the late twenties only in 1937. Thus the large overhead costs of the industry exerted pressure throughout the upswing, in spite of a strong recovery in output and gross revenue.

The large long-term commitments necessary in this type of investment, the great additions to capacity in the twenties and early thirties, the continuing low operating ratios, and the pressure from heavy debts ensured that large new installations would not be undertaken until the longer-term outlook improved considerably. No new large projects were undertaken

26 Note the sharp increase in the weight of power investment in total investment during 1930-3, in Table 35.

27 Capital employed in central electric stations in 1929 was $1.1 billion, as compared to $4 billion in all (other) manufacturing industries together. Furthermore, capital employed increased to $1.4 billion in 1933 and $1.5 billion in 1937.

28 Non-resident ownership of power companies has been estimated at 25 per cent in 1939, excluding properties owned by provincial and municipal governments. D.B.S., *Canadian Balance of International Payments, 1926-1948*, p. 80.

29 See the various issues of D.B.S., *Central Electric Stations in Canada*.

TABLE 45

ELECTRIC POWER AND OTHER UTILITIES, 1926-37

	Total installed hydraulic turbine horse-power (billions)	Central electric stations			Gross domestic investment in other utilities(b) ($ millions)
		Revenue from power ($ millions)	Kilo-watt hours gen-erated (billions)	Gross domestic invest-ment(a) ($ millions)	
1926	4.5	89	12.1	43	47
1929	5.7	123	18.0	76	80
1930	6.1	126	18.1	91	71
1931	6.7	122	16.3	77	50
1932	7.0	121	16.1	42	29
1933	7.3	118	17.3	17	23
1934	7.5	124	21.2	19	25
1935	7.9	127	23.3	23	26
1936	7.9	136	25.4	20	25
1937	8.1	144	27.7	32	43

SOURCES: *C.Y.B., 1939*, pp. 362-64, and *P.P.I.*
(a) Includes gas-works.
(b) Excludes steam railways and telegraphs.

after 1931 until 1937, although some projects were completed and installations were enlarged.[30] Along with the physical aspects of investment, there were less tangible factors affecting the outlook for the industry.[31] The industry was subjected to harsh criticism, especially on its rate structure. The pressure for public ownership of the privately owned firms was increased. The publicly owned companies also received strong criticism. In the last half of the twenties, the giant Ontario Hydro, planning for the long-range needs of the province, had contracted for large amounts of power from Quebec producers. The burden of costs in such contracts in the downswing led it to repudiate them.[32] This atmosphere was not conducive to financing further investment in power, even if the companies had been interested in large undertakings.

[30] *Financial Post*, March 10, 1934 and May 27, 1937.
[31] *Ibid.*, March 30, 1935.
[32] A. Brady, "The Ontario Hydro-Electric Power Commission," *CJEPS*.

In earlier sections it was noted that the railway problem goes well back before the thirties. The heavy natural costs of Canadian railways, the multiplication of lines and determination of routes by governments, and the competitive investments of the twenties, all contributed to the heavy cost structure.

With the decline in net operating income after 1928, the CNR had substantial deficits throughout the following decade. The CPR was able to cover its (smaller) fixed charges, except in 1932, but was forced to cancel its dividends and reduce its surplus. Freight earnings of steam railways fell from $414 million in 1928 to $202 million in 1933, and recovered to only $270 million in 1937. Passenger revenue was even more seriously affected, in percentage terms, partly as motor competition cut more deeply into this high revenue traffic. But it was not solely the effects of depression on revenues which affected the financial position of the railways. Operating expenses rose as a ratio of revenues, particularly in the CNR; payrolls were especially sticky. Fixed charges increased absolutely.[33]

Gross domestic investment by railways from 1926 to 1929 had accounted for about 12 per cent of private investment in durable assets. This proportion held up well in 1930-3, reflecting the relatively large investment in 1930. But from 1934 to 1937 it fell to 8 per cent of total private investment, in contrast with non-railway utilities which regained or exceeded their former weight in total investment. Railway investment by 1937 had reached only 35 per cent of the 1929 level. From 1932 to 1935 inclusive no orders were placed for railway cars compared to a peak of over twelve thousand in 1929.[34]

33 The ratio of operating expense to revenues for the CNR rose from 82 per cent in 1928 to 96 per cent in 1933 and fell back to 91 per cent in 1937; the comparable percentages for the CPR were 75, 79 and 80. Fixed charges for the CNR in the same years were 46, 59 and 53 millions of dollars respectively; for the CPR, 17, 25 and 24 millions of dollars respectively. (Data for the CNR include United States lines.) See D.B.S., *Canadian National Railways, 1923-52,* and *Canadian Pacific Railway Company, 1923-52.* For gross domestic investment by steam railways, see Table 35.

34 *Financial Post,* November 6, 1937 and March 12, 1938. The extreme irregularity of car orders and the concentration in 1929 led to heavy over-expansion in the transportation equipment industry. According to these sources, one large company greatly enlarged plant to meet rush orders placed in the late twenties — orders which could have been met from existing plant if spread over a few years. The absence of orders later forced this company to close down for several years.

The long-run growth in railways had slowed down in certain directions in the twenties, as noted earlier, but substantial investment had been made to improve road and rolling stock. Thus, an ample and improved capital stock was available to meet requirements for some time.[35] In addition, the problem of sharply falling net revenues was met in part by letting maintenance and replacement go for a time.[36] From 1930 to 1937 mileage was almost unchanged, and rolling stock declined.

The railway system was so widely involved in the economic structure of the country that the effects of its problems cannot be easily disentangled. The effect on government fiscal and monetary policy was profound. At the end of March 1935, the net federal debt of Canada was $2.8 billion. Well over one billion dollars of this had been incurred by railway investments.[37] The federal government guaranteed most of the funded public debt of the CNR, extended loans and advances, and covered CNR deficits.[38] As Innis has aptly pointed out, the usual policy for dealing with this debt appeared to be to increase its extent in order to decrease its burden.[39] Encouragement by governments of rapid exploitation of resources, to an important degree with foreign capital guaranteed by the gov-

[35] "At the end of 1931 the company was within sight of the end of a construction program begun in 1919. No new construction has been approved for the current year other than to complete lines partially built." CPR report 1931, as quoted on p. 16 of the *Financial Post*, April 2, 1932. The president of the CPR stated that, to meet the competition of the CNR, "The Canadian Pacific Railway was compelled to anticipate expenditures by building branch lines and providing facilities in advance of necessities, and to extend services and buy equipment which traffic returns did not justify." Beatty, "Canadian Transportation Policy," p. 119. It was not, apparently, until 1951 that the value of durable investment by steam railways and telegraphs exceeded the 1929 level, even though the costs of capital goods about doubled in the meantime. See *P.P.I.*, pp. 79 and 170.

[36] John L. McDougall, "Report of the Duff Commission," *CJEPS*, p. 81.

[37] See *C.Y.B.*, 1939, p. 901: *Financial Post*, April 20, 1935; and D.B.S., *Canadian National Railways*, pp. 12-13. At the end of 1936 almost two-thirds of CNR bonds and debentures were held abroad; D.B.S., *Canadian Balance of International Payments* (1939), p. 25.

[38] This list does not include the very large amounts of unpaid interest on government loans to railways. The sums required to cover CNR deficits in the thirties were roughly three-quarters of what the federal government spent on relief. See *C.Y.B.*, 1939, pp. 879-80, and *C.Y.B.*, 1934-35, pp. 889-90.

[39] See his *Problems of Staple Production in Canada*, Parts II and IV, and his article in the *Financial Post*, July 9, 1932.

ernment, brought increased traffic for railways, increased imports, and revenue (via tariffs) to help finance the debt. This alternative was not easily available in the depressed world conditions of the thirties. Nor was the financial expedient of bankruptcy and writing down of the heavy debt possible; the CNR finances were so closely linked with government guarantees that, to both resident and non-resident creditors, it might have appeared as a form of national default. Finally, exchange depreciation would have raised the burden of that part of both government and private debt held abroad, in so far as the issues were payable in foreign currency. The need to finance railway debt limited the alternatives in fiscal policy, and the large amounts in multiple currencies put additional limitations on the alternatives in monetary policy. The government could not escape the effects of past railway policies and the higher tariff, as the relief payments, interest payments, and contributions to CNR deficits indicate.

The Duff Commission of 1931-2 rejected amalgamation of the two lines or unification for administrative purposes.[40] The companies were required to co-operate to reduce costs, but this led to few reductions in cost. Although debt held by the public could not be written down, debt owed by the CNR to the government was revised in 1937. Such a measure could not, of course, reduce the real cost to the economy involved in duplicated lines and other facilities.[41]

Automobiles

The growing use of the automobile in the twenties had given a strong impetus to investment in many industries. The durable nature of the product meant a sharp decrease in Canadian sales in the downswing as purchases were postponed. The very large sales of new cars in Canada in the last half of the twenties aided this postponement.[42] Moreover, the total registered stock of automobiles fell as older vehicles were scrapped and not

[40] For differing evaluations of the Duff Commission's findings see the articles by J. L. McDougall and W. T. Jackman in the *CJEPS*.
[41] The long-run nature of the problem can perhaps be assessed by the fact that from 1923 to 1952 inclusive the CNR covered its fixed charges only in 1926, 1928, 1941-5 inclusive, and 1952. Clearly, recovery alone was not enough to solve this problem.
[42] The difference between the increase in registrations and cars sold in Canada (given comparable series for these) would represent new rather than replacement sales, except in so far as vehicles were not scrapped but left idle and not registered.

replaced – or as vehicles were simply not registered and operated. The fall in income, the uncertainty of income, the capital investment involved in a car, and the possibility of postponement for many years, all were effective in cutting back sales. Car prices, in addition, were higher or inflexible, further helping to reduce demand.[43] Export sales, which were about 30 per cent of total sales in 1926-9, fell even more sharply than Canadian sales.

The Canadian automobile industry has always had a large degree of protection against imports. In mid-1931 this protection was greatly increased, which encouraged the industry to do more of its manufacturing in Canada – or at least more assembly. The number of factories increased in the years immediately afterwards,[44] but the low level of investment in the transportation equipment industry would suggest that the investment effects of these tariff changes could not have been large. For the time being, many firms must have taken over idle plant and equipment rather than embarked on new investment. Cars from the United Kingdom came in free of duty after 1932, but it was not until 1935-6 that duties were reduced on American cars.

The capacity of the industry had been increased to 400,000 by 1930, which was well in excess even of the very large 1928-9 output. By 1933, output was less than one-fifth of capacity; by 1934, at 44 per cent of capacity; by 1935, at 65 per cent, or probably still slightly below the 1929 operating ratio.[45] It will be noted that the increased output in 1932-3 was apparently due to exports rather than domestic sales. The export market revived somewhat better than the domestic market, in relative terms, and the proportion of exports to total sales rose to almost

43 McDiarmid, *Commercial Policy*, p. 359. According to his data (collected by the Canadian Tariff Commission), between 1930 and 1934 average list prices for three popular cars fell by 2.5-6.4 per cent in the United States, but rose by 1.1-6.9 per cent in Canada.

44 *Financial Post*, August 27, 1932. The 50 per cent Canadian content provision of the 1926 tariff, necessary to qualify for drawbacks of duty on imported materials or parts, also worked in this direction. This was raised in 1937 to 60 per cent, and then 65 per cent, for larger producers.

45 The difficulty of defining capacity for most industries suggests that changes in the ratios may be more significant than the actual ratio in any one year. These ratios are from the *Financial Post*, July 4, 1936. See also p. 131 above. It should be noted that capacity was sharply reduced between 1929 and 1935.

TABLE 46

SELECTED STATISTICS ON AUTOMOBILES, 1926-37(a)
(Numbers, to nearest thousand)

Year	Pro-duction	Imports	Exports	Apparent domestic consump-tion(b)	Registra-tions(c)
1926	205	29	75	159	736
1927	179	37	58	158	822
1928	242	47	80	210	921
1929	263	45	102	205	1,014
1930	153	23	45	131	1,055
1931	83	9	15	77	1,025
1932	61	1	13	49	945
1933	66	2	21	47	917
1934	117	3	44	76	952
1935	173	4	65	112	990
1936	162	10	56	116	1,042
1937	207	20	66	161	1,103

SOURCE: *C.Y.B., 1939*, p. 663.
(a) Passenger cars and trucks, except for registrations.
(b) Includes changes in inventories.
(c) Registrations are from various Year Books and represent passenger cars only.

35 per cent in 1934-7. Under Imperial preference, most Empire markets were available if the requirement for 50 per cent Empire content was met. By 1937 both exports and domestic sales were still well below the peak 1928-9 levels, though they had attained the 1926-7 levels. In 1936 and 1937 some of the larger companies undertook expansion of their plant and equipment as sales were higher and a heavy replacement demand was anticipated.[46]

Investment by the transportation equipment industry had risen sharply from $2 million in 1926 to $14 million in 1929.[47]

[46] *Financial Post*, July 4 and December 19, 1936.
[47] Including railway rolling stock and some smaller groups as well as the motor vehicle industry. As noted earlier, the railway rolling stock industry was severely depressed by the lack of railway car orders for several years in the upswing.

From 1930 to 1936 inclusive it attained $5 million only in 1930 and 1935, and generally was far below this level. Only in 1937 did investment revive sharply to $10 million, then doubled in 1938. The extreme variability of investment in industries producing motor vehicles and railway rolling stock is a good example of the effects on investment of large fluctuations in sales of durable goods – whether consumers' or producers' goods. The durable nature of the automobile and the relatively large capital investment involved for the purchaser meant that sales experienced sharp fluctuations in the thirties, even though some of the evidence presented earlier suggested its growth trend was strong.

The indirect effects of motor vehicles on investment continued to be great, however. Thus the engineering construction of provincial government departments, which had fallen from $61 million in 1930 to $23 million in 1933, rose rapidly to $50 million in 1935-6 and $100 million in 1937.[48] The bulk of these figures is capital expenditure on highways, and there were substantial expenditures for maintenance as well. The net funded debt of provinces by 1937 was $1.6 billion, of which $0.6 billion was chargeable to highways.[49]

Residential Construction

In considering residential construction in the late twenties, it was suggested that there was little backlog to take up the slack when other types of investment fell off, or to speed the general recovery. On the other hand, there did not appear to be deflationary factors in housing, as there were in the United States.

From 1929 to 1933 gross residential construction fell to 31 per cent of the 1929 level, and rose to 73 per cent of that level in 1937. In the thirties housing represented a larger proportion of total investment than it did in the late twenties. This would reflect the fact that the purely physical need arising from growth in population and family formation would set some minimum limit; it would also reflect the much slower rise from 1926 to 1929, as compared to business investment, and government aid to housing late in the upswing.

It is well to note that on the average a house will last for approximately 60-75 years.[50] This durability means that re-

---

[48] *P.P.I.*, p. 192.
[49] *C.Y.B., 1939*, p. 668. Total net funded debt of provinces in 1919 was only $0.3 billion.
[50] Firestone, *Residential Real Estate*, p. 427.

placement can be postponed easily; in 1932-4, for example, gross residential construction barely offset the over-all depreciation on the stock of housing. For the purchaser and the lender it also means a very large and long-term commitment, which both may hesitate to undertake with costs, legislation, and income uncertain.

As the downswing developed, conditions in the housing market deteriorated rapidly. On the demand side, income and family formation decreased sharply.[51] Vacancy rates rose, in spite of a marked fall in the number of dwellings constructed. Physical need continued to grow, of course, but the adjustments to changed incomes were apparent in declining completions, higher tenancy rates,[52] and extensive doubling up. Insurance, trust, and loan companies were increasingly unwilling to lend funds with real estate and rental values falling, a growing number of defaults of interest and principal, the increasing burden of property taxes, and legislation which adversely affected creditors.[53] Their funds were diverted increasingly to investment in government bonds, the yield on which rose after sterling left gold. The price of new residential real estate fell much less than many other types of prices and income, further restricting the demand for housing. Mortgage interest rates were extremely sticky in the downswing.[54]

Even when general recovery came, the rise in housing construction was hampered by these problems. The attempts by the government to lower interest rates by re-funding and by housing legislation did help to reduce mortgage rates slowly. Interest on first mortgages, which was about 6½ per cent at the bottom of the downswing, was at an average of about 5 per cent by early 1937 (though the rates were still 7-8 per cent on second mortgages).[55] But loan companies were willing to lend at such rates only to borrowers whose prospects were quite good, and in areas where the record of mortgage legislation and taxes was not severe. Seven of the nine provinces passed

---

[51] Net family formation fell from an annual average of 36,000 in 1921-30 inclusive to 28,000 in 1931-7 inclusive. It fell from 48,000 in 1929 to 19,000 in 1932, recovering to 39,000 in 1937.

[52] Firestone, *Residential Real Estate*, p. 274.

[53] *Financial Post,* May 14, 1932.

[54] For wage rates in the building trades and prices of materials, see Table 39. Mortgage rates are shown in Table 13.

[55] *Financial Post*, February 6, 1937. It is not possible to tell how much higher the effective rates would be with varying risk factors.

moratoria legislation between 1931 and 1933, and both federal and some provincial legislation for debt adjustment was put into effect.

TABLE 47

SELECTED DATA ON HOUSING, 1929-37

Year	Dwell-ings com-pleted (000)	Residential construction		Vacancy rate (b) (per cent)	Price of resi-dential real estate (1939 = 100)
		Gross	Net(a)		
		(millions of dollars)			
1929	65	247	140	4.7	112.2
1930	53	204	97	4.1	109.3
1931	48	168	66	4.7	101.6
1932	28	96	—	6.7	93.3
1933	22	76	− 17	6.7	89.1
1934	28	98	—	4.9	92.3
1935	33	114	16	3.7	91.7
1936	39	139	37	3.3	94.4
1937	49	175	64	2.7	101.3

SOURCES: Firestone, *Residential Real Estate*. For footnotes, see Table 7.

One of the most serious obstacles to housing investment was the heavy property tax. With property values falling much faster than assessments, and municipalities facing rising relief costs, the tax burden was greatly increased. The primary responsibility of municipalities for relief, and their limited taxing powers, combined to place great emphasis on the property tax and to act as a deterrent to investment.

The policies and attitudes of institutions which supplied the great bulk of mortgage funds in Canada were an important factor in the market.[56] Statements by these companies clearly indicate their strong opposition to legislation which aimed at easing the burden of debtors, and to possible monetary experi-

---

[56] The insurance, trust, and loan companies. The law generally prohibited commercial banks from entering this market.

ments and deficit financing.[57] These views help explain why mortgage money was tight throughout much of the thirties. Their lending on the very depressed prairies was particularly restricted.

It was indicated in an earlier section that farm debt adjustment did not lead to any large reduction in debt.[58] It was not until 1935 that Dominion legislation was passed to assist residential construction.[59] In 1937 an act was passed to permit federal guarantees for home improvement loans. The National Housing Act of 1938 broadened the provisions of the 1935 act.[60] New housing constructed with federal government assistance was about 4 per cent and 12 per cent of gross residential construction in 1936 and 1939 respectively, or about 8 per cent of the total for the period 1936-9.

The recovery in housing reflected various forces, including recovery in employment and incomes and the gradual pressure of population and family formation. Mortgage rates fell slowly as arrears were paid off and funds were made available more freely, as interest rates decreased generally, and as government lending on housing increased. Some pressure on housing demand may have occurred early in 1937, when costs rose rapidly. Prices of residential building materials and wage rates in the building trades had both been sticky in the downswing. The latter recovered slowly, but prices of building materials by 1937 were not far from the 1927-9 levels, while gross residential construction was still well below those levels.

[57] See, for example, the views of the Dominion Mortgage and Investment Association as reported in the *Financial Post* of June 25, 1932, and the annual reports of the loan companies in the *Financial Post*.
[58] W. T. Easterbrook, "Agricultural Debt Adjustment," *CJEPS*.
[59] Small amounts had been loaned for housing since 1927 under the Canadian Farm Loan Act.
[60] For the terms of these acts, see Firestone, *Residential Real Estate*, Appendix B.

CHAPTER EIGHT

International Comparisons of Recovery

The Canadian recovery by 1937, relative to 1929, lagged considerably behind those of a number of countries. Canadian industrial production in 1937, excluding construction and electric power from the index, was 112 per cent of the 1929 level. Eight of the twenty-two countries shown in Table 15 were lower, relative to 1929.[1] National income in Canada had recovered to 85 per cent of the 1929 level; for the countries shown in the table just referred to, only Austria, the Netherlands, and the United States show a greater discrepancy between the 1937 and 1929 levels. Not only was the downswing comparatively severe in Canada, but the recovery, while rapid when compared to the low level of 1932, was comparatively incomplete if considered with respect to 1929.

The outstanding characteristics of the experience of the United Kingdom was the relative mildness of the decline and the steadiness of the recovery after 1932.[2] By 1937 national income and industrial production exceeded the 1929 levels by 11 per cent and 24 per cent respectively. The most striking change, and the most important factor in the recovery, was the strong increase in residential construction.

The United Kingdom's exports in 1937 were still substantially below the 1929 levels, since much more than a cyclical problem plagued a number of her export industries. The industrialization of younger countries, and the competitive power of such countries as Germany and the United States in pro-

[1] Poland, the Netherlands, Austria, the United States, Italy, Belgium, Czechoslovakia and France, in that order. It was noted earlier that five of the countries shown in Table 15 had a more severe downswing, but indexes for Belgium and Italy were not far above that of Canada in 1932. While both here and in the downswing the comparisons can be refined, for example by using actual peaks and troughs, the conclusion would still hold that the Canadian downswing was exceptionally severe and the recovery relatively poor.

[2] For analyses of the recoveries in the United States and the United Kingdom, the reader is referred once more to the studies mentioned earlier, namely, Wilson, *Fluctuations in Income and Employment*, CHAP. XVIII; Schumpeter, *Business Cycles*, CHAP. XV; Lewis, *Economic Survey*, CHAPS. IV, V, and VIII; and Gordon, *Business Fluctuations*, CHAP. XIII.

ducers' goods especially, had tended to decrease the United Kingdom's share of world exports over a long period. The overvaluation of sterling after 1925 had further diminished her export competitiveness and increased import competition.[3] In the thirties the United Kingdom attempted to meet some of her problems by the depreciation of sterling, a moderate degree of protection, and a system of Imperial preferences. Although these measures may have been successful for a time, they were offset to an important degree by other factors. The depreciation of the United States dollar removed much of any net advantage which may have occurred in foreign trade from the depreciation of sterling. The preferences increased the share of Empire trade with the United Kingdom, but this was by no means a net gain because of retaliation against preferences, and because of the more severe competition in non-Empire countries from countries denied access to preferential markets.

Along with the striking recovery in residential construction,[4] there was also strong growth in a number of fairly new industries such as automobiles and electric power. By 1937-8, moreover, expenditure on armaments was beginning to be important. In 1936-7, however, the degree of unemployment was still some 10 per cent. It was noted earlier that there had been a large degree of unemployment even in the twenties. One important reason for the better showing of the United Kingdom was simply the more moderate increases in output in that country in the twenties. While the cyclical downswing was comparatively mild, and the recovery strong relative to 1929, a number of longer-term problems centred around her export industries were not satisfactorily solved.

Nevertheless, the strength of the recovery in the United Kingdom, relative to 1928-9, was highly important in the recovery of Canadian exports. By 1937 total Canadian exports to the United Kingdom exceeded by one-third the peak of 1928, while non-agricultural exports were two and a half times that level. By contrast, exports to the United States in 1937 were four-fifths of their 1929 peak, or virtually at their 1929 level if non-monetary gold is included here. Exports to all other

---

[3] As a percentage of 1913, the quantum of world trade in 1929 and 1937 was 133 and 128 respectively. The quantum of United Kingdom exports in the same years, as a percentage of 1913, was 87 and 72. The United Kingdom's share in world exports fell from 14 per cent in 1913 to 11 and 10 per cent in 1929 and 1937. See Lewis, *Economic Survey*, CHAP. V and especially p. 79.

[4] See Schumpeter, *Business Cycles*, p. 964, for some of the factors in the strong recovery of housing.

countries were still less than half of their 1928 peak.

In the United States, a broad and vigorous policy aimed at recovery was initiated early in 1933. It included measures to remove certain obstacles to recovery, and government expenditure to start and sustain recovery. The recovery was disappointing, however. The discrepancy between the 1937 and 1929 levels of expenditures on construction was particularly large.[5]

Over the short term, the recoveries in Canada and the United States were very similar. Thus the lower turning point, the spurt of activity in 1933 followed by stability toward the end of that year, the faster recovery after mid-1935, and the recession of 1937-8 – in all of these instances Canadian experience owed a good deal to changes in activity in the United States. The over-all recovery appears to have been almost identical in the two countries, judging by GNP and national income in 1937 compared to those of 1929.[6]

But the over-all similarity in the aggregates conceals considerable differences in several important sectors. GNE in 1937 was at precisely 87 per cent of the 1929 level for each country. Among the four major components, only consumer expenditures show a similar degree of recovery in the two countries. Both government and domestic investment expenditures were significantly higher in the United States than in Canada, as a percentage of the 1929 levels. It has already been noted that external transactions are far more important to Canada than to the United States. It was precisely in this sector, however, that the Canadian recovery was far better than that in the United States.

The absolute contribution of each component to the difference in GNE in 1937 and 1929 is shown in Table 48, in order

[5] The reasons for the slow recovery of investment in the United States are at the crux of the recovery problem in that country. While it would take us somewhat far afield to go into these in detail, three major explanations should be noted. One view, forcefully put by Schumpeter (pp. 1038-50) holds that the inducement to invest was severely curtailed by the fiscal, labour, and industrial policies of the federal government. A second view suggests secular stagnation as the result of a declining rate of population growth, fewer new territories, and a reduced investment effect from more recent technological changes. A third view points to the thorough exploitation of investment opportunities in a number of important industries in the twenties, along with the effect on investment expectations of a number of developments in the thirties. For a statement and evaluation of these views, see Gordon, *Business Fluctuations*, pp. 408-11.

[6] See Tables 16 and 18 for comparisons of recovery in Canada and the United States.

TABLE 48

COMPARISON OF THE RECOVERY IN GROSS NATIONAL EXPENDITURE, CANADA AND THE UNITED STATES, 1929 AND 1937

	1937 as a percentage of 1929		Absolute contribution to difference in GNE, 1929 and 1937	
	Canada	U.S.A.	Canada ($ millions)	U.S.A. ($ billions)
Consumer expenditures	86.0	85.2	− 616	− 11,640
Domestic investment	53.3	72.3	− 650	− 4,388
Residential construction	71.3	50	− 71	− 7,400
Non-residential construction	39.1	46	− 296	− 2,737
Machinery and equipment	47.1	84.6	− 316	− 994
Inventories (a)	154.1	147.8	+ 33	+ 747
Government expenditures	98.4	136.8	− 11	+ 3,118
Foreign investment	(b)	(b)	+ 495	− 709
Exports of goods and services	97.5(c)	62.8	− 41	− 2,658(d)
Imports of goods and services	72.4	71.1	+ 536	+ 1,841(d)
Gross National Expenditure	86.8	86.9	− 811	− 13,616

SOURCES: See note to Table 17.

(a) The Canadian data are changes in book values (except in agriculture) while the United States data measure the value of physical change. Using the latter concept for both countries, and excluding agriculture, the data for Canada in 1929 and 1937 are $144 million and $112 million respectively, and for the United States $1.8 billion in both years.

(b) When adjusted for purposes of the National Accounts, the current account balance for Canada was −$313 million and +$182 million in 1929 and 1937 respectively, while for the United States the corresponding figures were +$771 million and +$62 million.

(c) 90 per cent of the 1928 peak.

(d) Not adjusted for purposes of the National Accounts.

to give proper consideration to the relative size of each component in the two countries. This presentation underlines the extent to which the shortfall of Canadian domestic investment in 1937 determined the over-all difference between 1937 and 1929 levels of GNE.[7] What is also apparent is the somewhat different way in which a crucial question about the poor recoveries of the two economies should be phrased. As indicated above, one puzzling factor about the recovery in the United States is that, in spite of a sharp increase in federal government expenditures and several years of upswing, long-term investment recovered very slowly.[8] As stated in the introduction to this study, a very important question about the Canadian recovery is that, although exports recovered to the 1929 levels (and beyond in terms of volume), the recovery in durable business investment was very incomplete. While differently phrased, both questions centre to an important extent on investment of particular types.

The outstanding differences in recovery in the two countries can be summarized as follows. In the first place, the recovery in durable investment was poorer in Canada, except for housing. Total private and public investment in durable assets in the United States was 18.7 per cent and 14.5 per cent of GNE in 1929 and 1937 respectively; the comparable data for Canada are 24.6 per cent and 15.5 per cent.[9] Secondly, government expenditures in the United States increased far beyond both the 1929 level and the peak of 1931, while government expen-

[7] It is worth noting again that part of the shortfall of consumption and investment in 1937, relative to 1929, is reflected in the shortfall of imports between these years, and would not directly affect domestic output and employment. Even if this was assumed to be as high as $200 million for each of consumption and investment, our analysis would not be greatly changed. Any such figure is arbitrary, of course, and involves some difficult questions about induced and autonomous changes in imports. See also p. 103 above.

[8] While it did not stimulate long-term investment as much as one might have expected, such spending, combined with various other policies, did have other effects on recovery. For example, consumption was stimulated, the liquidity of the economy increased, and obstacles to recovery in a number of severely depressed industries and the banks were removed.

[9] Data for the United States derived from Kuznets, *National Product since 1869*, pp. 46 and 51. A different set of estimates, those of the U.S. Department of Commerce, show gross private investment in durable assets as 13.7 and 10.1 per cent of GNE in 1929 and 1937; in Canada, such private investment was 21.6 and 12.1 per cent of GNE in the same years. (Government business enterprises are included, however, in the Canadian data.)

ditures in Canada only approached the 1929 level by 1937 and remained considerably below the 1930 peak. Thirdly, recovery in current international receipts, while disappointing in a number of ways, was considerably better than that of the United States in aggregate.[10]

Turning to national income by industry, again one is struck by the close correspondence in aggregate recovery.[11] In several of the more important industries, however, the recoveries in the two countries were quite different. Particular attention should be drawn to agriculture. The more complete recovery of agricultural income in the United States takes on added importance when one considers that income originating in agriculture was fully 17.9 per cent of Canadian national income in 1926-8.[12] One very important factor sustaining agricultural income in the United States, which had no close parallel in Canada, was the programme of crop restriction and price support.[13] Mining recovered far better in Canada than in the United States, particularly because of the increased value of gold production, which in turn was related primarily to monetary developments abroad. The pattern of manufacturing recovery in the two countries was the result of somewhat different forces, reflecting the different types of industries involved.[14]

[10] Perhaps the differences can be brought out further by expressing the four major components of GNE as a percentage of the totals in 1929 and 1937, as follows:

	Canada		United States	
	1929	1937	1929	1937
Consumption	71.2	70.5	75.9	74.4
Domestic investment	22.6	13.8	15.2	12.7
Foreign investment	—5.1	3.4	0.7	0.1
Government	11.1	12.5	8.2	12.8

[11] See Table 18.

[12] See particularly footnote (a) in Table 18. The year 1929 is not a good basis for comparison because of the short crop.

[13] A similar programme in Canada would have had to cope with two serious problems: first, the necessity of having to sell the major part of the wheat crop in export markets, in competition with other exporters; secondly, the relatively greater effects on the non-agricultural sector, as compared to the United States. Canadian policy in this sphere was limited broadly to attempts to achieve more orderly marketing of wheat, in order to avoid selling at extremely low prices. The Natural Products Marketing Act of late 1934 attempted a broad control of agricultural marketing. It was declared *ultra vires* of the Dominion government in mid-1936.

[14] As noted earlier, Canadian manufacturing involves a large sector processing primary products. It also involves a smaller proportion of finished durables than in the United States. See pp. 104-6.

The smelting and refining of non-ferrous metals and the manufacture of newsprint represent much larger shares of Canadian
than of United States manufacturing output. The former industry had a very strong recovery in Canada; it was the ninth
largest manufacturing industry in 1929, and the largest after
1934. The factors in the poor recovery in the newsprint industry were noted in detail earlier. The recovery of industries
producing finished durable goods was incomplete in both countries, and appears to have been no better in Canada than in the
United States.[15] The stronger recovery of housing in Canada
than in the United States primarily accounted for the better
recovery of income originating in the finance, insurance, and
real estate group in Table 18, although neither country showed
a particularly strong recovery in this sphere. Finally, one should
note the rigidity and size of income paid to non-residents by
Canada; the total was at 87 per cent of the 1929 level in both
1933 and 1937, and, of course, was much more important in
Canada than in the United States.

It was noted at the beginning of this chapter that the Canadian economy suffered one of the worst downswings and most
incomplete recoveries, relative to 1929, judging by data on
industrial production and national income. A full explanation
of this would require more intensive study of the types of
fluctuations elsewhere than can be attempted here, but the
following comments, tentative and general as they are, may
throw some light on this problem.

The international downswing reflected both an industrial
downswing and a crisis in a number of primary products. Probably the most severe consequences, from the point of view of
international effects, were the extent of collapse in the United
States and the breakdown of the world trading and financial
mechanism. The Canadian economy in 1929 was peculiarly
susceptible to the type of international collapse which occurred.
Perhaps no other country had such close economic ties with
the United States. Both total and per capita exports were among
the highest in the world, and the concentration on exports of

---

[15] Income originating in manufactures of iron and steel, machinery,
and transportation equipment in the United States was by 1937
at 85 per cent of the 1929 level. Both net and gross value of
production for manufactures in the same industries in Canada
were by 1937 roughly 80 per cent of the 1929 value. The comparison should be regarded as very approximate because of
classification problems, and because different measures are used.

primary products was pronounced.[16] Not only was the period of rapid western expansion ending, at least in its extensive phase, but the opportunities in some of the newer industries were being saturated by an exceptionally high rate of investment. As a result of rapid development, difficult geography, and deliberate policy decisions, a large and rigid cost structure had developed.[17]

The fact that two of the most volatile components of income, namely primary exports and durable investment, both formed very large proportions of Canadian income, goes a long way towards explaining the severity of the collapse in Canada compared to many other countries – particularly if note is taken also of a large and rigid cost structure in an open economy. For example, not only exports, but domestic investment as well, contributed more to the total decline in GNE in Canada than in the United States. It is true that Canada did not experience the financial crisis which other countries experienced, but she could not escape the effects of such crises in her main trading partners, as events in late 1931 and early 1933 indicated.

The fact remains, however, that aggregate exports recovered to almost their previous levels (except for 1928), and that the country had been undergoing rapid development. Why, then, was the recovery incomplete compared to most other countries?

First, the conclusion about the comparatively poor behaviour of the Canadian economy was based on comparisons

[16] Canada was the fifth largest exporter and importer in 1928 and 1929. Per capita exports of domestic produce were $140 in 1928. Among the principal trading countries only New Zealand, at $183, exceeded Canada in per capita exports—all others were below $120. Reduced exports of wheat in 1929 lowered Canada's per capita exports, but she was still third in this respect and far ahead of all principal exporters except New Zealand and Denmark. See the C.Y.B., 1930, p. 480, and C.Y.B., 1931, p. 507. Footnote 111, CHAP. II, is also of interest here.

[17] It would be difficult to show convincingly that the various aspects of cost were a relatively greater burden in Canada than elsewhere. It should be noted, however, that rigid costs in an open economy create shifts of income both internally and (through competition and income payments) with respect to other countries. Net interest payments abroad appear to have been higher for Canada than for other countries, except for Australia and New Zealand. (See League of Nations, Course and Phases of the World Economic Depression, p. 36.) It would be difficult, moreover, to find a close parallel elsewhere to the over-all impact of the railway problem in Canada.

with 1929. Does the conclusion hold if we leave out the period of rapid investment in the second half of the twenties? Not many of the national income series shown in Table 15 go back to 1926 or earlier. It would appear, however, that comparisons with 1926 tend to close the discrepancy between the recovery in Canada's national income and those of a number of other countries.[18] It is also of interest to note that industrial production in the United States in 1937 was 3 per cent greater than in 1929 and 20 per cent greater than in 1926; the comparable increases for Canada were 12 per cent and 40 per cent.[19] Such comparisons, although subject to some criticism on statistical grounds, suggest that the Canadian recovery does not look quite so poor if the period of heavy investment in the late twenties is omitted.

It was suggested above that part of the reason for the incomplete recovery of the Canadian economy in the thirties, relative to that in many other countries, may have been the temporary saturation of investment opportunities in some lines of activity in the twenties. A large and relatively new stock of capital was available in Canada when the downswing began.

[18] See Table 15 for source, and for further data relating to the comparison below.

NATIONAL INCOME, 1937

	Percentage difference from 1929	Percentage difference from 1926	Effect of change in base
Canada	—-15	—3	12
Czechoslovakia	—11	18	29
France	2-22	20-44	18-22
Finland	39	57	18
Hungary	—13	—16	—3
Japan	39	45	6
Netherlands	—21	—13	8
Sweden	25	37	12
Union of South Africa	46	50	4
United Kingdom	11	18	7
United States (Kuznets' series)	—19	—14	5

[19] The revised index was used for the United States; the old index shows a decline of 8 percent from 1929 to 1937 and virtual stability from 1926 to 1937. Construction has been excluded from the Canadian index in order to bring it more in line with that for the United States. It should be noted that industrial production covers far less economic activity than national income; in particular, the former excludes agriculture, construction, and a number of services. The comparable increases for the United Kingdom were 24 per cent on the 1929 base, and 30 per cent on the base 1927.

Was it relatively larger and relatively newer, however, than that in many other countries? It is impossible to prove in any precise sense that this was the case, both because of the lack of data on capital stocks and "investment opportunities" and because the size of the capital stock will vary with a country's pattern of resources. Some points can be noted, however. The extremely strong rate of investment and general growth since 1900 and the very high proportion of investment in total output in the last half of the twenties, both relative to other countries, have been mentioned earlier. For example, the rate of increase in total domestic investment in the twenties was greater than that of Canada's dynamic neighbour, and several important sectors of domestic investment (but not housing) recovered less in Canada than in the United States in the thirties.[20]

Even when comparisons are made with 1926, however, the recovery in Canada was relatively incomplete. The investment boom of the last half of the twenties, in other words, cannot have been the only reason for the relatively poor recovery of the Canadian economy – although it was an important one. The other major set of factors centred on the role of exports in the economy, particularly the damage resulting from the collapse of exports in the face of rigid costs and the fact that the export recovery was not as complete as the aggregates alone might suggest.

In comparing the degree of recovery in Canada with that in many other countries, one other factor should be noted. In several of these other countries, strong government action was undertaken to expedite recovery. Central government action in Canada was undertaken slowly, except for tariff policy, and was often more limited in scope and more indirect than in a number of other countries. Any comparison with the strong recoveries in some totalitarian states must take into account the central control of economic decisions and the growing expenditures for armaments in those countries. In a number of other countries, such as the United States, extensive govern-

[20] See p. 65 and Corbett, "Immigration and Economic Development," p. 364. It might be objected that, if the relatively high rate of investment in Canada in the twenties reflected the relatively greater availability of investment opportunities, this state of affairs should have continued into the thirties and led to a stronger investment recovery. We have already attempted to show, however, that longer-term growth in some of the older industries had slowed, while investment opportunities in a number of relatively new industries had been rather fully exploited. Nothing quite like the backlog of housing investment in the United Kingdom was available in Canada to speed the upswing.

ment action was undertaken within the framework of a system of relatively free enterprise.[21]

Conclusions on the Upswing

The recovery in Canada was incomplete, particularly if account is taken of the growth in population and the labour force between 1929 and 1937. The following aspects of the upswing have been emphasized, both in aggregate terms and with reference to specific industries.

The recovery in world trade and finance was extremely slow. The volume of world trade lagged behind the recovery in world production, prices of world trade commodities showed little recovery in aggregate, many overseas countries lost gold to the United States, and varying (often antagonistic) recovery policies were followed. Recovery in the United States was slow and irregular. Canada was very severely affected by these factors, since her total and per capita foreign trade were among the highest in the world, primary products bulked large in this trade, and her economic ties with the United States were unusually close.

The upswing in Canada was incomplete because the effects of many of the developments of the previous boom and severe downswing lingered into the upswing. The prevailing excess capacity limited the effects of rising exports and consumption on induced investment. Because non-agricultural inventories had not been greatly reduced in the downswing, it was not until 1936-7 that strong increases occurred once more in this type of investment. The pressure from heavy debts, and the cautious approach to fixed commitments, meant that increases in funds

21 One must go on to note, however, that the animosity between business and government, which was a factor affecting investment decisions in the United States, was probably less extensive in Canada. This is a highly difficult matter to pin down, of course, and the following comments are only suggestive. Various groups in Canada, such as the agricultural group, certainly voiced strong opinions about particular government policies or the lack of them. But the general attitude of the manufacturing and financial communities in Canada toward the policies of central governments was probably less antagonistic than that prevailing in the United States after 1933. The high tariffs, orthodox monetary policies, and limited experimentation in the control of economic processes were well in line with the recovery policies which many members of these communities recommended, and were not fully offset by such developments as the investigation of price spreads and the establishment of a central bank.

were used to retire domestic and foreign indebtedness. The price recovery was slow, particularly because of the continuing large stocks of staples well into the upswing. The rigid costs which accentuated the downswing also limited the strength of the upswing.

، A somewhat broader attempt to alleviate the situation was made by the government in the upswing than in the downswing. But the government cannot be said to have embarked on a large internal recovery programme, some of its measures were undertaken late in the upswing, and reform legislation was hampered by the constitutional division of powers between governments.

The export recovery, although it attained something close to the 1929 level, was not balanced. The price recovery of staple exports was slow, and the largest sector of exports, namely agriculture, remained depressed. The major recovery in exports occurred in metals, where the multiplier is probably weaker than in agriculture. It was noted above, further, that the world trading mechanism was far from restored in the upswing. The incomplete recovery of durable investment was due to a complex of factors. The reaction of induced investment to increases in sales was necessarily slow for a time, given the excess capacity created by a reduced level of sales and the previous increases in the stock of capital. The lack of a strong recovery in autonomous investment was related particularly to the heavy previous exploitation of existing investment opportunities. The incentive for both types of investment was limited by the unfavourable environment created by the severity of the decline and perpetuated, to a significant extent, into the upswing.

The Canadian recovery was similar to that in the United States, both in the aggregate and in terms of short-run fluctuations. In part this similarity reflects the close trading and other ties Canada has with the United States. The similarity in the aggregate measures of activity, however, was also the result of quite different movements in the components, movements which cannot always be closely related with current economic developments in the United States. In particular, the Canadian recovery was worse than that in the United States in the relatively larger agricultural sector, in durable investment (except housing), and in government expenditures; but, mainly because of gold and exports to the United Kingdom, the Canadian recovery was much better in the relatively more important foreign sector.

CHAPTER NINE

Conclusion

This study has examined the nature of cyclical changes in Canada in the thirties, and particularly the reasons for the incomplete recovery of economic activity in the upswing. It was anticipated that, in a study of economic fluctuations, it would not be possible to prove in a definitive sense any particular hypothesis or set of hypotheses. By using a combination of theory, statistics, and history, however, it is possible to indicate the more reasonable hypotheses.

In the opening chapter it was noted that, in the analysis of this period, primary emphasis has usually been placed on external factors. It is quite clear that an open economy such as Canada will be greatly affected by sharp changes in the economic activity of its main trading partners. It will also be affected by the nature of the reaction of the domestic economy to external demand factors, and by internal determinants of economic activity – particularly the volatile element of domestic investment.

To be able to consider domestic investment, to some degree, as an autonomous variable, certain aspects of its relationship to external factors were explored in the introductory chapter. It was noted that the relationship of exports and investment over short periods was not necessarily close; that, even where a large part of domestic investment was financed from abroad, domestic entrepreneurs and governments made many of the decisions and took much of the risk; and that, in spite of large import leakages, the cumulative interplay of consumption and investment applies in Canada. Although the importance of changes in investment induced by current sales, especially the large and variable sector of current export sales, is not denied, it was suggested that the more important fluctuations in investment were determined by innovations – including those innovations related to external developments. Other determinants of the various types of investment must also be brought into play.

In brief, the analysis of economic fluctuations requires a broad frame of reference. This applies not only to the number of variables used in the analysis, but also to the time period covered. The nature of the downswing and recovery was determined to an important extent by the structure of the economy as it developed over a considerable period of time before the thirties.

These considerations suggest that the extent of fluctuations in Canada reflects both the nature of fluctuations in other countries and changes in the degree and pattern of development and adjustment within her own economy. If a downswing occurs in Canada's main foreign markets, the effect on Canada will depend to an important extent on such factors as the degree of industrial decline abroad, developments in the world market for primary products, the extent of damage to the world trading and financial mechanism, and the effects of these on the country's balance of payments. It will also depend on such factors as the underlying trend of expansion, the extent and manner in which existing investment opportunities have been exploited, the degree and distribution of cost rigidity, the size and nature of indebtedness (external and internal), the effects of government policies, the supply position of primary products, the strength of the banking system, and other more or less internal factors.

Similarly, the extent of the upswing will be determined to an important degree by the strength of the international recovery, particularly in its effects on Canadian exports. It will also depend on the underlying trend of expansion in Canada, the extent of saturation of investment opportunities in the preceding upswing, the degree of excess capacity, the severity of the preceding downswing, the extent to which internal cost and other adjustments were made in that downswing, the nature of the reaction of the economy to the stimulus of rising export and other sales, government reform and recovery policies, and some other factors. The degree of recovery in Canada was basically a function of the degree of recovery in exports and domestic investment. The degree of recovery in the latter, however, is not a function simply of the extent of recovery in the former, but of a variety of factors which can vary from period to period.

In line with this frame of reference, the reasons for the incomplete nature of the recovery were outlined earlier in a preliminary statement.[1] The major conclusions are brought together below.

In the first three decades of the century, two great surges of autonomous investment occurred, in response to such factors

[1] See pp. 14-17 for the major preliminary hypotheses.

as the availability of resources, technological change, the expectation of large demands at favourable prices, favourable cost trends, government encouragement, and the availability of capital, population, and technology from abroad. The long investment boom before the war centred around wheat and railways. In the analysis of the twenties particular emphasis was placed on investment in or occasioned by newsprint, mining, electric power, and the automobile, although some of the service and other industries had strong growth trends also. The rate of development in Canada before the war and in the last half of the twenties was exceeded by very few countries.

This long period of rapid development had two major consequences in the thirties. The structure of the economy which developed was such that it was highly susceptible to large fluctuations in income, but burdened with heavy rigid costs. The former were related particularly to the size of the export sector, the concentration on a few primary exports, and the uncertain yield of wheat. The extensive transportation facilities, the use of the tariff for developmental purposes, and the large foreign debt (much of it payable optionally in foreign currencies and guaranteed by the government) imparted a rigid burden of overhead, which was closely linked to government finance. These developments were dictated, to a large degree, by the nature and location of resources and the heavy capitalization required for effective exploitation. The volatility of income and rigidity of cost were also due to governmental decisions about the pattern and extent of railway development and the settlement of dry areas, and to over-enthusiastic exploitation of opportunities in such industries as newsprint.

The second major legacy of this rapid period of development was the extent of exploitation of investment opportunities.[2] The longer-term rate of growth was slowing down in some of the older industries, particularly because of the slower rate of western expansion. The impact on investment, as suggested by the acceleration principle applied to particular industries over long periods, was not fully felt for a time; high crop yields and technological change sustained investment in agriculture in the last half of the twenties, while competitive expansion and replacement gave a sharp boost to railway investment. In these and some other industries, however, the strong pre-war rates of growth were no longer available to expedite the recovery. At the same time the existing investment opportunities in

2 Or, to put it slightly differently, the size and recency of much of the capital stock relative to investment opportunity.

some of the new industries had been thoroughly exploited. In newsprint, over-expansion had occurred. In the automobile industry, the existing opportunities appear to have been temporarily saturated. In still other industries, such as housing, the stock of capital had increased to the point where there was probably no substantial backlog of investment opportunities. A great deal of unwise financing of industry developed, in addition, as a result of speculative excesses in connection with the stock boom and the merger movement. It was Canada's misfortune that the adjustments to such a period of heavy investment had to be made at a time of rapid deterioration in the international economy.[3]

The outstanding developments in the international downswing were the severity of the decline in the United States and the collapse of world trade and finance – particularly the collapse of primary prices, the growing restrictions on trade, and the financial crisis of 1931.[4] The Canadian economy – with its close ties to the United States, its large export sector heavily concentrated in primary products, and its international financial ties – was severely affected by the extent and nature of this downswing. The collapse of exports led to a cumulative downswing in both consumption and induced investment. The extent of deterioration in the international situation, and the comparative exhaustion of investment opportunities in some industries, led also to a sharp revision of long-term profit expectations. With the collapse of autonomous investment, the downswing accelerated greatly.

The extent of the general downswing and the unfavourable outlook for investment were accentuated by a number of other factors. The rigidity of many costs added to the uneven nature of the decline. The greatest rigidity was in interest rates, both those already incurred and market rates. The sterling crisis of 1931 raised market rates and, with the depreciation of the Canadian dollar with respect to the United States dollar, also raised the cost of optional pay debts previously incurred. Along with the very large burden of debt, rigidities included taxes, freight rates, the administered prices of manufactures, sticky

[3] There were other developments in the twenties which accentuated the downswing. The rapid spread in the use of the automobile, for example, increased the potential volatility of income.

[4] A number of weaknesses in the international situation had been apparent in the twenties, including the tendency to over-supply of several primary products, the accumulation of large and mobile short-term balances, and the decline in long-term capital flows after 1928.

wage rates, import prices relative to export prices, and the effects of tariff increases. Two effects of the uneven price declines were emphasized. Sales prices fell faster than investment costs, thus adding to the downward pressure on investment. Some important exporters of primary products bore a greater share of the downswing, with the result that their competitive power and their purchases of many rigidly priced manufactures were reduced. The downswing was also accentuated by the extent of monetary deflation. This deflation reflected not only the usual desire for liquidity in a period of rapidly falling prices, but also the speculative excesses and over-indebtedness of the previous period and the immediate effects of the international financial crisis of 1931.

During the downswing, a number of adjustments had taken place to put the economy in a better position to benefit from some stimulus to recovery. Some resistance to deflationary pressure occurred in mid-1932, partly as a result of such internal adjustments and partly because of signs of recovery abroad. This was short-lived, however, largely because of a further drop in construction in Canada and the renewed decline in the United States with the new banking crisis. The sharp recovery of Canadian prices and output after the first quarter of 1933 primarily reflected the reaction of the economy to external factors. The most important of these were the events in the United States early in 1933 – which at first affected Canada more by the expectation of price and sales increases than by increased exports – and increased exports to overseas countries, particularly the United Kingdom, both because of recovery and preferential trade agreements. Domestic investment contributed very little to the early stages of the recovery; in fact, the lag in completion of some major projects weakened the recovery in its initial stages. Neither fiscal nor monetary policy can be said to have contributed very much to the first phase of recovery. The smaller decline and earlier stability in the output of consumers' goods (relative to that of producers' goods) helped set some limits to the downswing, but did not provide a strong independent stimulus to revival.

With rising exports, falling interest rates, and continuing recovery abroad, an extensive recovery could get under way in Canada. Excess capacity would at first limit the effect of rising sales on induced investment, but the postponed replacement demands of business and consumers would be felt. Those longer-term investment opportunities which had not been exploited because of the severity of the decline would now be re-examined in the light of an improving economic situation. Both multiplier and (more slowly) accelerator effects should have taken the economy back to full employment.

Unfortunately, this did not occur until the war. The recovery in domestic investment was particularly disappointing. Three broad sets of factors, some of them involving developments during and before the downswing, account for the incomplete nature of the recovery.

First, the external factors in the recovery should be noted. The fall in world industrial demand, the collapse of primary prices, the growth of trade restrictions, and the financial crises abroad were together the most important set of factors in the Canadian downswing. The recovery in world trade and finance was incomplete and – of particular importance to Canada – the recovery in the United States was both very incomplete and irregular. In spite of this, however, the value of Canada's exports recovered to approximately the 1929 level, a surplus appeared in the current account and grew to a large proportion of total income, and the exchange rate was stable (and at par with the United States dollar) for most of the upswing. A closer look at the export recovery, however, suggested its effects on the economy were not as great as the aggregates might imply. The price recovery for staple exports was extremely slow, and the terms of trade did not regain their 1926-9 levels till 1937. The export recovery was not balanced, with little actual recovery in wheat. The major export recovery was in metals, where the multiplier was probably weaker than in agriculture.

Secondly, the many maladjustments which developed in the downswing (or earlier) were not fully or automatically cured in the upswing. Restrictions on trade were only slowly removed. The severe decline in agricultural income was not corrected because of continuing low prices, trade restrictions, rigid costs, and (later in the upswing) outright crop failure. With some areas strongly depressed, the momentum of recovery was slowed. Many of the uneven price-cost declines were not fully corrected after five years of recovery. Interest rates did not fall sharply, relative to 1929, until the upswing was well under way, and the lower rates were available at first only to prime borrowers. The effects of some of the financial abuses of the previous upswing, such as those in newsprint, lingered late into the upswing of the thirties. Because of the continuing large burden of debt and the experiences with it in the downswing, a strong desire for liquidity prevailed. Increased income was used, to an important degree, to repay such debt or to build up depleted balances. In an *ex post* and relative sense, the use of savings in the upswing was reflected by the current account surplus (involving particularly debt repatriation) and government deficits rather than by private fixed investment. The inability to reduce inventories greatly in the downswing led to a partial offset to the multiplier for much of the upswing, as inventories were worked back to about their previous ratio to output and sales. Even when the recovery speeded up in 1936 and 1937, well short of full employment, several offsetting factors came into play.[5] Investment costs rose rapidly. Part of the increase in exports was offset by inventory declines of wheat which, however, had favourable effects as well. Payments abroad rose more quickly, and in 1936 the government deficit fell as revenues increased more rapidly. Much of the recovery in income during the upswing was used, in effect, in ways made necessary by the downswing and by structural changes over a period of time.

The third broad set of factors limiting the upswing was the most important of all, namely the factors in the very incomplete recovery of domestic investment. The pessimistic expectations about future profitability were due primarily to two factors. The failure of autonomous investment to revive was clearly related to the extent of previous exploitation of investment opportunities. The cautious approach to both induced and autonomous investment was related also to developments in the downswing and upswing which weakened the incentive to invest.

Changes in sales and income, although important as a partial determinant of induced investment, cannot give a full explanation of the slow recovery of investment. Neither in the upswing of the twenties nor in much of that of the thirties was investment too closely related to such current variables.[6] Strong increases in investment involve surges of autonomous invest-

---

[5] Quite apart from the recession in the United States in 1937-8. In one sense, this recession can be regarded as a factor in the incompleteness of Canadian recovery relative to 1929. Our analysis, however, has concentrated on the reasons for the incomplete recovery of 1933-7, after an upswing of about four and a half years.

[6] This position is not inconsistent with the view that investment in the upswing of the thirties was primarily of the induced kind. For the early part of the upswing, excess capacity limited even induced investment; with the more rapid recovery in 1936-7, investment appears to have been mainly of the induced type. The crucial point is that autonomous investment did not play a significant role in any part of the upswing.

ment in reaction to major innovations, which have reached a stage where their effects are large. The weakening of such effects in the upswing of the thirties was related to several factors. Some longer-term rates of growth had slowed earlier, so that the potential buoyancy from these sectors was lessened in the upswing. The opportunities created by several major innovations, which came to fruition in the twenties, had already been largely exploited; so had some new investment opportunities in some of the older industries. Where additional investment might still be justified from the longer-term point of view, or because new opportunities appeared, the shock of the downswing (and various problems created by the downswing) would lead to a cautious attitude in exploiting such opportunities.[7]

In both induced and autonomous investment, a number of problems in the thirties limited the incentive to invest. Excess capacity is useful in explaining the lag of investment in the early stages of the upswing, particularly that of induced investment. In itself, however, it is not a sufficient explanation for the slow recovery of investment.[8] The reduced multiplier effects of the export recovery, and the crop failures, were noted earlier. Interest rates were eventually reduced (though lending policies were cautious), but the major effect of lower rates was larger re-funding operations. The heavy debts and speculative excesses of the twenties continued to plague many industries,[9] and strong efforts were made to build up depleted balances and repatriate, re-fund, or repay debt. The stock of business and consumers' capital deteriorated as replacement was postponed. Many of the distortions in price-cost relations were not fully corrected in the upswing, including the relation of a number of investment costs to sales prices.

7 As suggested on p. 193, this would be more generally true in the downswing than later. It should also be added that the major impact of new innovations would appear after their initial developmental stage.
8 The operating ratio of the newsprint industry, for example, attained its former peak, but investment remained seriously depressed. Just when excess capacity would cease to limit investment would depend on such factors as the age and condition of plant and equipment, the financial position of the industry, its experience in the downswing, and its prospects as determined by recent innovations.
9 Many financial commitments of the twenties were justifiable, of course, under the existing circumstances. One wonders, however, if even the optimism of that period could justify the extent of preferred share financing in Canada, optional pay debt, and financing of mergers.

The Canadian economy appears to have suffered one of the worst downswings and most incomplete recoveries of this period. A tentative explanation of this points to her close relations with the United States (which suffered very large swings in activity) and the importance of primary exports; to the size and behaviour of domestic investment; and to relatively limited anti-cyclical policies. The stronger recovery in the United Kingdom was, in part, a reflection of the slower upswing in that country in the twenties, and the (related) backlog of investment opportunities in housing and some other industries. The close similarity of aggregate fluctuations in Canada to those in the United States reflected, in part, the close economic ties with that country. The similarity in aggregate behaviour, however, conceals quite different recoveries in some sectors, differences which cannot be closely related to current developments in the United States. Some sectors of the Canadian economy recovered more strongly, partly because of a strong recovery in non-agricultural exports to the United Kingdom. But the relatively larger agricultural sector remained more depressed than that in the United States, the recovery in durable investment (except housing) was poorer, and direct government expenditure contributed more to recovery in the United States than to that in Canada.

While it has not been the major purpose of this study to analyse the nature and effects of government policy, a few observations on it are suggested by the findings. In terms of anti-cyclical policy, government policy in the downswing was largely restricted to using the tariff. Expenditures related to depression were generally directed, at first, towards relief rather than recovery. Recovery measures were slowly adopted in the upswing, in the fields of monetary policy, housing, and (most important) in tariff negotiation. Some reform measures were undertaken, but constitutional problems limited these. Apart from being slow to undertake direct anti-cyclical measures (except to the extent that tariff adjustments in the downswing can be so regarded), the government was not always noted for the consistency of its policies. The collapse of government investment just as the downswing was being reversed was a case in point, as were the unequal costs imposed by the tariffs of 1930-1.

The spheres of possible action lay in a number of directions. It was crucial to take steps to revive the greatly depressed export industries as rapidly as possible. In large part this revival was beyond internal control, depending on recovery abroad. It would also depend on internal policies, such as those which hindered or helped export competitiveness. The speed and extent to which other countries were willing to negotiate, and how far Canada would go in tariff reductions and modifications of preferences, were also of great importance. Measures to sustain and increase domestic investment, output, and employment would have to be designed to minimize adverse effects on exports or on the balance of payments, or the government would have to be willing to accept certain consequences because the effects of any alternative form of action (or no action at all) would be worse. There was more scope in the upswing for monetary and fiscal policies, given recovery abroad, the development of a current surplus and exchange parity, the creation of instruments of control, and the repatriation of part of the optional pay debt. A serious problem which was not approached comprehensively till the late thirties was that of allocation of responsibility and finances between governments. Lack of integrated action, in the field of taxation for example, had adverse effects in private investment. Along with the extent of recovery, and partly related to it, was the question of methods of modifying the unequal burdens involved in the downswing. Finally, the analysis suggests that if governments are to be successful in cyclical policy, much depends on what actions they take to guide or restrain activity long before the downswing.

It is not difficult to understand why policies were lacking or not always consistent. One should not minimize the porblems facing the policy-maker in an economy with important ties to other countries, and with a great diversity of interests between various areas. The actual reaction to the problems of the thirties was compounded partly of the view that policy was helpless in the face of external factors, and partly of the lack of experience of such a collapse, lack of institutions through which policy could be expressed, and problems of governmental allocation of powers and finances by the constitution. In the early years in particular, it also reflected the attitude that recovery would be automatic if interference was avoided and "natural" adjustments were allowed to operate. If, however, the above analysis is valid with respect to the continuing effects of private and public decisions in the past, the internal problems of recovery, and the nature of the reaction of the domestic economy to external recovery, then the external determinants of activity, important as they were, should not be unduly burdened with the responsibility for the slowness of the recovery.

Table 49

GROSS NATIONAL EXPENDITURE IN CURRENT DOLLARS, 1926-37

(Millions of dollars)

Item	1926	1927	1928	1929	1930	1931	1932	1933	1934	1935	1936	1937
Personal expenditure on consumer goods and services	3,687	3,919	4,194	4,393	4,204	3,646	3,108	2,887	3,077	3,243	3,457	3,777
Government expenditure												
Investment	108	138	160	188	233	188	129	88	110	127	121	181
Other goods and services	413	429	437	494	534	550	514	438	458	476	479	490
Gross domestic investment(a)												
New residential construction	212	217	236	247	204	168	96	76	98	114	139	176
New non-residential construction	240	299	411	486	381	264	121	79	92	118	150	190
New machinery and equipment	357	443	489	.597	469	261	145	84	116	146	180	281
Durable assets	809	949	1,136	1,330	1,054	693	362	239	306	378	469	647

Change in agricultural inventories(b)	-22	87	35	-95	-2	-52	21	-23	12	—	-153	-104
Change in business inventories	110	131	122	156	-152	-238	-237	-59	58	47	103	198
Exports of goods and services	1,650	1,618	1,773	1,632	1,286	967	804	826	1,018	1,143	1,428	1,591
Deduct: imports of goods and services	-1,522	-1,629	-1,808	-1,945	-1,625	-1,142	-901	-828	-948	-1,017	-1,183	-1,409
Residual error of estimate	61	5	56	13	14	-52	-33	-16	-57	-52	-20	-16
Gross National Expenditure at market prices	5,294	5,647	6,105	6,166	5,546	4,560	3,767	3,552	4,034	4,345	4,701	5,355
Gross National Expenditure — implicit price deflator	117.3	115.3	114.6	115.3	111.9	105.8	94.5	93.7	94.9	95.5	98.5	101.3

SOURCE: National Accounts, Table 2 and selected data from Tables 4, 26, and 41.

(a) Includes capital expenditures by private and government enterprises, private non-commercial institutions, and outlays on new residential construction by individuals. Other government investment is included in government expenditure.

(b) Data shown for agriculture are value of physical change, while data for business are change in book value.

TABLE 50

NATIONAL INCOME BY INDUSTRY, 1926-37
(Millions of dollars)

Item	1926	1927	1928	1929	1930	1931	1932	1933	1934	1935	1936	1937
Agriculture (a)	817	811	856	608	502	242	233	294	300	353	335	435
Forestry	67	69	74	79	61	37	27	31	41	46	57	81
Mining, quarrying, and oil wells	138	146	166	189	151	116	90	116	162	194	240	295
Manufacturing	914	997	1,101	1,175	968	753	549	559	694	771	894	1,089
Construction	201	208	242	290	241	196	107	69	76	95	113	147
Transportation, storage, and communication } Public utility operation	536	561	621	611	542	462	373	347	385	404	450	477
Wholesale and retail trade(b)	507	549	600	630	647	482	385	354	412	459	498	574
Finance, insurance, and real estate	390	424	463	474	462	414	347	317	312	322	366	364

Service(c)	503	528	571	610	586	496	384	321	339	362	378	417
Government(d)	320	340	358	384	412	417	400	370	387	388	392	409
Non-residents	−208	−216	−229	−261	−289	−282	−265	−226	−211	−206	−236	−226
Total	4,185	4,417	4,823	4,789	4,283	3,333	2,630	2,452	2,897	3,188	3,487	4,062

SOURCE: *National Accounts*, Table 20.

(a) Includes fishing and trapping, which varied from $7 million to $29 million in the period covered.

(b) Includes inventory valuation adjustment for grain held in commercial channels, other than the Canadian Co-operative Wheat Producers and the Canadian Wheat Board. This affects the movement from 1929 to 1930, while the adjustment for other years is relatively small. For 1929-31 the relevant adjustments were −4, 46 and 7 millions of dollars respectively.

(c) Includes income originating in the personal sector.

(d) Includes government non-business transactions only. Income from government business enterprises is included in the appropriate industrial group.

TABLE 51

BALANCE OF PAYMENTS BETWEEN CANADA AND OTHER COUNTRIES, 1926-37
(Millions of dollars)

	1926(a)	1927	1928	1929	1930	1931	1932	1933	1934	1935	1936	1937
Current account												
Exports	1,272	1,215	1,341	1,178	880	601	495	532	648	732	954	1,041
Imports	973	1,057	1,209	1,272	973	580	398	368	484	526	612	776
Balance on trade	+299	+158	+132	−94	−93	+21	+97	+164	+164	+206	+342	+265
Non-monetary gold	30	32	40	37	39	57	70	82	114	119	132	145
Balance on invisibles	−202	−200	−204	−254	−283	−252	−263	−248	−210	−200	−230	−230
Current account bal.	+127	−10	−32	−311	−337	−174	−96	−2	+68	+125	+244	+180
Capital account												
New issues of Canadian securities		301	207	297	400	200	104	134	111	117	106	90
Retirements of Canadian securities		160	200	150	110	202	105	166	169	256	270	170
Net new issues or retirements		+141	+7	+147	+290	−2	−1	−32	−58	−139	−164	−80
Net sales of outstanding securities(b)		+35	+21	+18	+37	+45	+85	+51	+9	−44	−62	−64
Direct investment		−171	−126	−2	+56	+10	−28	−59	−45	+51	+8	−5
Net change in external assets of banks		+16	+87	+88	—	+28	+38	+24	−19	—	+3	−13

Other capital movements(c)	−4	−6	+23	−10	+60	−1	+12	+49	+9	−29	−18
Net capital inflow (+) or outflow (−)	+17	−17	+274	+373	+141	+93	−4	−64	−123	−244	−180
Net monetary gold movement (outflow +)(d)	−7	+49	+37	−36	+33	+3	+6	−4	−2	—	—
Financing of current account balance	+10	+32	+311	+337	+174	+96	+2	−68	−125	−244	−180

SOURCE: D.B.S., *Canadian Balance of International Payments, 1926 to 1948*, pp. 154 and 163.
(a) Comparable data for capital account not available.
(b) Includes errors and omissions, 1927-32.
(c) Includes insurance transactions, miscellaneous capital movements and (after 1932) errors and omissions.
(d) Although this has been shown as the balancing item, the changes in external assets of banks shared in this special balancing role.

TABLE 52

Seasonally Adjusted Indexes of Economic Activity, by Quarters, 1932 and 1933 (1926 = 100)

	1932				1933			
	I	II	III	IV	I	II	III	IV
Physical volume of production(a)	83.7	78.9	77.8	74.6	67.8	76.1	88.2	86.6
Mining	96.8	96.4	85.1	91.2	99.6	108.6	109.9	120.1
Manufacturing	74.1	75.3	75.6	71.0	61.2	76.7	94.0	87.6
Distribution	95.5	94.4	90.4	87.3	84.3	86.2	90.5	89.9
Construction	77.1	29.3	36.0	29.9	22.8	19.4	30.7	40.5
Grain marketings(b)	113.4	123.6	123.2	125.2	122.1	114.7	107.2	95.6
Livestock marketings(b)	83.9	82.2	80.2	78.2	82.2	81.3	76.6	78.6
Import volume	73.2	68.1	63.9	66.0	51.1	51.9	65.1	72.3
Export volume	60.3	60.1	63.5	53.7	52.4	59.7	74.1	59.8
Export value, excluding gold(b)	40.8	39.7	37.7	36.9	38.3	40.2	43.4	46.8
Retail sales value, chain and department stores	76.4	73.4	69.2	67.0	65.5	66.3	67.3	67.0
Current loans	115.8	111.5	108.6	105.8	101.0	95.5	95.9	95.8
Employment in industry	95.4	89.7	83.2	82.6	82.1	79.5	82.9	88.7
Wholesale prices	69.2	67.6	66.8	64.6	63.9	66.5	69.6	68.6
Common stock prices(c)	64.1	47.7	57.2	53.2	50.3	65.8	83.3	75.1
Bond prices(c)	95.1	95.7	99.0	102.5	102.9	103.9	105.4	104.3

Sources: Various issues of D.B.S., *Monthly Review of Business Statistics*, except for the following; retail sales are from the *C.Y.B., 1937*, p. 622, while export values are from D.B.S., *Trade of Canada, 1941*, I.

(a) This index includes electric power in addition to the components shown.
(b) Series have been smoothed by a four-quarter moving average.
(c) Not adjusted for seasonal.

Revised Series for
Gross Domestic Investment

The National Accounts series used in this study are the historical series published in 1951. While this study was in press, a new publication appeared on these statistics. This publication by D.B.S., entitled *National Accounts, Income and Expenditure, 1926-1956*, incorporates a number of statistical revisions, and changes in concepts and terminology. Most of the changes which have been made in the National Accounts do not appear to affect directly the particular conclusions reached in this study, although these changes have improved the quality of a set of statistics which are widely used herein. The revision of the series on private domestic investment, however, calls for some comment, given the emphasis placed here on this particular series.

The data for gross domestic investment in durable assets (now called business fixed capital formation) have been revised downward sharply for the years 1926-32 inclusive. The revision is largely concentrated in expenditures for new machinery and equipment, and in the manufacturing sector of industry. In order that they may be compared with the data used in the present study, the revised figures are given below.

PRIVATE GROSS DOMESTIC INVESTMENT IN DURABLE ASSETS
(Millions of dollars)

	Total	Machinery and Equipment	Manufacturing
1926	702	261	129
1927	830	327	179
1928	1,007	374	215
1929	1,161	441	225
1930	926	351	163
1931	622	199	95
1932	319	108	47

The revision in this series does not affect the particular manufacturing industries which were given close attention in this study. Nor, in general, does it have much effect on the various comparisons made of the percentage increases from 1926 to 1929; for example, the striking contrast in the rate of growth in Canada and the United States in this period is still evident. The revision does change the proportion of GNE represented by domestic investment in the late twenties, and also affects the extent of decline and recovery in investment, relative to 1929. A few examples will show the effects on the conclusions reached in this study.

(1) Private and public investment in durable assets in 1929 is shown above as 24.6 per cent and 18.7 per cent for Canada and the United States respectively. The revised figure for Canada is 21.9 per cent.

(2) Private investment in durable assets is shown above as 18 and 49 per cent of the 1929 level in 1933 and 1937 respectively; the revised figures are 20 and 55 per cent. Expenditures for machinery and equipment are shown above as 14 and 47 per cent of the 1929 level in 1933 and 1937; the revised figures are 19 and 64 per cent. It was stated above that durable investment in manufacturing fell by 90 per cent in 1929-33, and recovered to only 37 per cent of the 1929 level in 1937; the revised figures indicate a decline of about 80 per cent, and a recovery to about 60 per cent of the 1929 level by 1937.

(3) It was suggested in this study that domestic investment made a particularly large contribution to the decline in Canada, and to the incomplete nature of the recovery, even by comparison with the severe experience in the United States. These views are modified but not changed by the revision noted here. It was estimated above, for example, that domestic investment (including inventories) contributed 47 per cent of the decline in GNE in Canada, compared with 30 per cent in the United States: the former figure would be revised to 41 per cent by the new series. In a similar sense, the gap between 1937 and 1929 levels of expenditure is still most striking in domestic investment, and relatively larger than in the United States. Even after some rough allowances are made of the import content of domestic investment, the Canadian experience with domestic investment still appears to have been somewhat worse than that in the United States.

Some other points are made in this study, less significant than those just considered, are also affected by the revision in the series on domestic investment. It might be noted that in some cases the effect is to strengthen, rather than modify, the conclusions given above. For example, the revised series show more clearly the less complete recovery of non-residential construction relative to that of expenditures for machinery and equipment, thus strengthening the view that short-term expectations dominated domestic investment in the thirties. In general, while some of the findings presented in this study are modified by the revised series on domestic investment, the major conclusions are not changed by it. In particular, the emphasis given to the relatively sharp fall and incomplete recovery of domestic investment is still warranted.

Note on the Author

A. E. Safarian took his B.A. in political economy at the University of Toronto and his Ph.D. in economics at the University of California, Berkeley. From 1950 to 1955, he served as statistician with the Dominion Bureau of Statistics, engaged in the compilation and analysis of data on Canada's international transactions. He was appointed Associate Professor of Economics at the University of Saskatchewan in 1956, and from 1962 to 1966 served as Professor and Head of the Department of Economics and Political Science at that university. He has been Professor of Economics at the University of Toronto since 1966.

In addition to *The Canadian Economy in the Great Depression*, Professor Safarian is the author of *Foreign Ownership of Canadian Industry* (Toronto, 1966), and *The Performance of Foreign-Owned Firms in Canada* (Montreal, 1969), and is the co-author of *The Canadian Balance of International Payments, 1946-1952* (Ottawa, 1953), and *Foreign Ownership and the Structure of Canadian Industry* (Ottawa, 1968). He assisted with the preparation of the study, *Canada-United States Economic Relations*, for the Royal Commission on Canada's Economic Prospects (1957), and has served on a wide range of academic and professional bodies.

Bibliography

Books

ABRAMOVITZ, MOZES. *Inventories and Business Cycles*. New York: National Bureau of Economic Research, Inc., 1950.

BLADEN, V. W. *An Introduction to Political Economy*. Toronto: University of Toronto Press, 1941.

BUCKLEY, KENNETH. *Capital Formation in Canada, 1896-1930*. Canadian Studies in Economics, no. 2. Toronto: University of Toronto Press, 1955.

BUCKLEY, KENNETH. "Capital Formation in Canada," *Problems of Capital Formation*. New York: National Bureau of Economic Research, Inc., 1957, pp. 91-145.

CHANG, TSE CHUN. *Cyclical Fluctuations in the Balance of Payments*. Cambridge: Cambridge University Press, 1951.

CLARK, COLIN, and CRAWFORD, J. G. *The National Income of Australia*. Sydney and London: Angus and Robertson Limited, 1938.

FIRESTONE, O. J. *Residential Real Estate in Canada*. Toronto: University of Toronto Press, 1951.

GORDON, ROBERT AARON. *Business Fluctuations*. New York: Harper and Brothers, 1952.

GORDON, R. A. "Cyclical Experience in the Interwar Period: The Investment Boom of the 'Twenties," *Conference on Business Cycles*. New York: National Bureau of Economic Research, Inc., 1951, pp. 163-210.

HABERLER, GOTTFRIED. *Prosperity and Depression*. Lake Success: United Nations, 1946.

HANSEN, ALVIN H. *Business Cycles and National Income*. New York: W. W. Norton and Company, Inc., 1951.

INNIS, H. A. *Problems of Staple Production in Canada*. Toronto: Ryerson Press, 1933.

INNIS, H. A. *Settlement and the Mining Frontier*. Vol. IX of *Canadian Frontiers of Settlement*. Toronto: The Macmillan Company of Canada Ltd., 1936.

INNIS, H. A., and PLUMPTRE, A. F. W. (eds.) *The Canadian Economy and Its Problems*. Toronto: Canadian Institute of International Affairs, 1934.

KUZNETS, SIMON. *National Product since 1869*. New York: National Bureau of Economic Research, Inc., 1946.

LEWIS, W. ARTHUR. *Economic Survey, 1919-1939*. London: Allen and Unwin, 1949.

MCDIARMID, O. J. *Commercial Policy in the Canadian Economy.* Cambridge: Harvard University Press, 1946.

MACHLUP, FRITZ. *International Trade and the National Income Multiplier.* Homewood, Ill.: Richard D. Irwin, Inc., 1943.

MALACH, VERNON W. *International Cycles and Canada's Balance of Payments, 1921-33.* Canadian Studies in Economics, no. 1. Toronto: University of Toronto Press, 1954.

MARCUS, EDWARD. *Canada and the International Business Cycle, 1927-1939.* New York: Bookman Associates, 1954.

MARSHALL, HERBERT; SOUTHARD, FRANK, A., Jr., and TAYLOR, KENNETH W. *Canadian-American Industry: A Study in International Investment.* New Haven: Yale University Press, 1936.

MITCHELL, WESLEY C. *Business Cycles: The Problem and Its Setting.* New York: National Bureau of Economic Research, Inc., 1927.

MITCHELL, WESLEY C. *What Happens during Business Cycles: A Progress Report.* New York: National Bureau of Economic Research, Inc., 1951.

SCHUMPETER, JOSEPH A. *Business Cycles*, II. First edition. New York: McGraw-Hill, 1939.

TAYLOR, K. W. *Statistics of Foreign Trade.* Vol. II *of Statistical Contributions to Canadian Economic History.* Toronto: The Macmillan Company of Canada Ltd., 1931.

U.S. Department of Commerce. *The United States in the World Economy.* Washington, D.C., 1943.

VINER, JACOB. *Canada's Balance of International Indebtedness, 1900-1913.* Cambridge: Harvard University Press, 1924.

WILSON, THOMAS. *Fluctuations in Income and Employment.* Third edition. London: Pitman Publishing Corporation, 1948.

Government of Canada, Ottawa

Dominion Bureau of Statistics Publications

The Canada Year Book, 1921-1939.

Canada's International Investment Position, 1926-1954. 1956.

The Canadian Balance of International Payments: A Study of Methods and Results. 1939.

The Canadian Balance of International Payments, 1926 to 1948. 1949.

Canadian Labour Force Estimates, 1931-1950. Reference Paper no. 23. n.d.

Canadian National Railways, 1923-1952. 1953.

The Canadian Pacific Railway Company, 1923-1952. 1953.

Census of Manufactures. Various issues in the thirties.

Central Electric Stations in Canada. Successive issues in the twenties and thirties.

Export and Import Price Indexes, 1926-1948. Reference Paper no. 5. 1949.

Government Transactions related to the National Accounts, 1926-1951. Reference Paper no. 39. 1952.
Handbook of Agricultural Statistics. Reference Paper no. 25. Part I, May 1951; Part II, February 1952.
Monthly Bulletin of Agricultural Statistics. September 1936.
Monthly Review of Business Statistics. Various issues, but particularly that for February 1944, and successive issues in 1932-3.
Monthly Review of Business Statistics. Supplements: *Economic Tendencies in Canada during the Post-War Period.* January 1938; *Recent Economic Tendencies in Canada, 1919-1934.* June 1935; *Twelve Years of the Economic Statistics of Canada, by Months and Years 1919-1930.* November 1931.
National Accounts: Income and Expenditure, 1926-1950. 1951.
Price Index Numbers of Commodities and Services used by Farmers, 1913-1948. 1948.
Prices and Price Indexes, 1913-1936. 1938; and the issue for 1913-1940. 1942.
Trade of Canada. Especially vol. I, 1941.

Other Government Publications

Advisory Committee on Reconstruction. *The War and Postwar Cycle in Canada, 1914-1923.* By B. H. HIGGINS, 1945. (Mimeographed.) *Sequence of Economic Events in Canada, 1914-1923.* By ALICE W. TURNER, 1945. (Mimeographed.)
Bank of Canada. *Statistical Summary, 1950 Supplement.* 1950.
Department of Trade and Commerce. *Investment and Inflation with Special Reference to the Immediate Post-War Period.* 1949.
Department of Trade and Commerce. *Private and Public Investment in Canada, 1926-1951.* 1951.
House of Commons, Standing Committee on Banking and Commerce. *Memoranda and Tables respecting the Bank of Canada.* 1939 Sess.
Report of the Royal Commission on Banking and Currency in Canada. 1933.
Report of the Royal Commission on Dominion-Provincial Relations. Book One: *Canada: 1867-1939.* Appendix I: *Summary of Dominion and Provincial Public Finance Statistics.* Appendix III: *The Economic Background of Dominion-Provincial Relations,* by W. A. MACKINTOSH, 1940.
Report of the Royal Commission on Price Spreads. 1935.
Report of the Royal Commission to Enquire into Railways and Transportation in Canada, 1931-1932. 1932.

League of Nations, Geneva

The Course and Phases of the World Economic Depression. 1931.
Economic Fluctuations in the United States and the United Kingdom, 1918-1922. 1942.

International Currency Experience. 1944.
Various issues in the thirties of *Review of World Trade, Statistical Year-Book, World Economic Survey,* and *World Production and Prices.*

Periodicals

Papers and Proceedings of the Canadian Political Science Association

BEATTY, E. W. "The Canadian Transportation Policy," VI (1934), pp. 108-27.

DAVIDSON, G. B. "Recent Legislation affecting International Trade in Farm Products," V (1933), pp. 106-26.

MACLEAN, M. C. "The Correlation between Population Density and Population Increase in Canada," V (1933), pp. 209-14.

PLUMPTRE, A. F. W. "Currency Management in Canada," IV (1932), pp. 139-50.

SMAILS, R. G. H. "Corporation Finance and Company Law Reform," V (1933), pp. 151-60.

Canadian Journal of Economics and Political Science

BARBER, C. L. "The Concept of Disposable Income," XV (May 1949), pp. 227-9; "Reply" by SIMON A. GOLDBERG (November 1949), pp. 539-42.

BATES, STEWART. Review of Gottfried Haberler, *Prosperity and Depression,* III (November 1937), pp. 598-602.

BLADEN, V. W. "Tariff Policy and Employment in Depression," VI (February 1940), pp. 72-8.

BRADY, A. "The Ontario Hydro-Electric Power Commission," II (August 1936), pp. 331-53.

BRITNELL, G. E. "Saskatchewan 1930-35," II (May 1936), pp. 143-66.

BURTON, F. W. "Wheat in Canadian History," III (May 1937), pp. 210-17.

BURTON, G. L. "The Farmer and the Market," XV (November 1949), pp. 495-504.

BRYCE, R. B. "The Effects on Canada of Industrial Fluctuations in the United States," V (August 1939), pp. 373-86.

CHAMBERS, EDWARD J. "The 1937-8 Recession in Canada," XXI (August 1955), pp. 293-308; "Comment," by EDWARD MARCUS, XXII (May 1956), pp. 249-50.

CHANG, TSE CHUN. "A Note on Exports and National Income," XIII (May 1947), pp. 276-80.

CORBETT, D. C. "Immigration and Economic Development," XVII (August 1951), pp. 360-8.

CURTIS, C. A. "Dominion Legislation of 1935: An Economist's Review," I (August 1935), pp. 599-608.

EASTERBROOK, W. T. "Agricultural Debt Adjustment," II (August 1936), pp. 390-403.

ELLIOTT, G. A. "Review of F. A. Knox, *Dominion Monetary Policy, 1929-1934*, VII (February 1941), pp. 88-91.

FORSEY, E. A. "The Pulp and Paper Industry," I (August 1935), pp. 501-509.

FOWKE, V. C. "Dominion Aids to Wheat Marketing, 1929-1939," VI (August 1940), pp. 390-402.

GRIFFIN, H. L. "Public Policy in Relation to the Wheat Market," I (August 1935), pp. 482-99.

HACKETT, W. T. G. "Canada's Optional Payment Bonds," I (May 1935), pp. 161-70.

INNIS, H. A. "Unused Capacity as a Factor in Canadian Economic History," II (February 1936), pp. 1-15.

JACKMAN, W. T. "Professor McDougall on Railways: A Reply," I (May 1935), pp. 246-65.

MACGIBBON, D. A. "Inflation and Inflationism," I (August 1935), pp. 325-36.

McDOUGALL, JOHN L. "The Evidence Presented to the Duff Commission," II (May 1936), pp. 195-208.

McDOUGALL, JOHN L. "The Report of the Duff Commission," I (February 1935), pp. 77-98.

McQUEEN, R. "Economic Aspects of Federalism; A Prairie View," I (August 1935), pp. 352-67.

MEIER, C. G. "Economic Development and the Transfer Mechanism: Canada, 1895-1913," XIX (February 1953), pp. 1-19.

NIXON, STANLEY E. "The Course of Interest Rates, 1929-1937," III (August 1937), pp. 421-34.

PLUMPTRE, A. F. W. "The Distribution of Outlay and the 'Multiplier' in the British Dominions," V (August 1939), pp. 363-72.

PLUMPTRE, A. F. W. "The Nature of Political and Economic Development in the British Dominions," III (November 1937), pp. 489-507.

ROLLIT, J. B., McDOUGALL, J. L., and CURRIE, A. W. "Aspects of the Railway Problem," V (February 1939), pp. 40-52.

RUTHERFORD, J. B. "Agricultural Income," IV (August 1938), pp. 420-31.

SAFARIAN, A. E. "Foreign Trade and the Level of Economic Activity in Canada in the 1930's," XVIII (August 1952), pp. 336-44.

SUTTON, G. D. "Productivity in Canada," XIX (May 1953), pp. 185-201.

WESTCOTT, F. J. "An Approach to the Problems of Tariff Burdens on Western Canada," IV (May 1938), pp. 209-18.

WRIGHT, C. P. "Report of the Royal Grain Inquiry Commission, 1938," V (May 1939), pp. 229-32.

Other Periodicals

DE VEGH, IMRE. "Imports and Income in the United States and Canada," *Review of Economic Statistics*, XXIII (August 1941), pp. 130-46.

GORDON, ROBERT A. "Business Cycles in the Interwar Period: The 'Quantitative-Historical' Approach," *Papers and Proceedings of the American Economic Association*, XXXIX (1949), pp. 47-60.

GORDON, ROBERT A. "Discussion on Business Cycle Theory," *Papers and Proceedings of the American Economic Association*, XLII (1952), pp. 100-104.

KEYFITZ, N. "The Growth of Canadian Population," *Population Studies*, IV (June 1950), pp. 47-61.

KNOX, A. D. "The Acceleration Principle and the Theory of Investment," *Economica*, New Series, XIX (August 1952), pp. 269-97.

MACGIBBON, D. A. "The Future of the Canadian Export Trade in Wheat," *Contributions to Canadian Economics*, V (1932), pp. 7-42.

SAFARIAN, A. E. and CARTY, E. B. "Foreign Financing of Canadian Investment in the Post-War Peroid," *Proceedings of the Business and Economic Statistics Section, American Statistical Association* (1954), pp. 72-79.

PREST, A. R. "National Income of the United Kingdom 1870-1946," *Economic Journal*, LVII (March 1948), pp. 31-62.

ULMER, M. J. "Autonomous and Induced Investment," *American Economic Review*, XLII (September 1952), pp. 587-89.

WILSON, T. "Some Reflections on the Business Cycle," *Review of Economics and Statistics*, XXXV (August 1953), pp. 244-50.

Other Sources

The Bank of Nova Scotia. *Monthly Review*. Toronto, 1932-3.

Board of Governors of the Federal Reserve System. *Federal Reserve Bulletin*. December 1953.

The Canadian Bank of Commerce. *Monthly Commercial Letter*. Toronto, 1932-3.

The Financial Post. Toronto, 1932-8.

PARKINSON, J. F. *Memorandum on the Bases of Canadian Commercial Policy, 1926-1938*. Submitted to the International Studies Conference, Twelfth Session, by the Canadian Institute of International Affairs. 1939. (Mimeographed.)

United Nations. *Statistics of National Income and Expenditure*. Statistical Papers, Series H, no. 1. Lake Success: United Nations, February 1952.

U.S. Department of Commerce. *National Income: A Supplement to the Survey of Current Business*. Washington, D.C., 1951.

Some Additional Publications on Economic Fluctuations in the 'Thirties

BARBER, CLARENCE L. *Inventories and Business Cycles with Special Reference to Canada.* University of Toronto Press, 1958.

BRECHER, I. *Monetary and Fiscal Thought and Policy in Canada, 1919-1939.* University of Toronto Press, 1957.

BRECHER, I. and REISMAN, S. S. *Canada-United States Economic Relations.* Royal Commission on Canada's Economic Prospects, Ottawa, 1957.

BROWN, T. M. *Canadian Economic Growth.* Staff Study for the Royal Commission on Health Services. Ottawa, 1965.

CHAMBERS, EDWARD J. 1) "Canadian Business Cycles Since 1919"; 2) "Canadian Business Cycles and Merchandise Exports." Both in *Canadian Journal of Economics and Political Science,* May and August, 1958, XXIV.

CHANDLER, LESTER V. *America's Greatest Depression, 1929-1941.* Harper and Row, 1970.

COURCHENE, THOMAS J. "An Analysis of the Canadian Money Supply: 1925-1934." *Journal of Political Economy,* June, 1969, LXXVII.

FRIEDMAN, MILTON and SCHWARTZ, ANNA J. *A Monetary History of the United States.* Princeton University Press, 1963.

GORDON, ROBERT A. and KLEIN, LAWRENCE R. (eds.). *Readings in Business Cycles.* Richard D. Irwin, 1965. Prepared for the American Economic Association.

HAY, K. A. J. "Early Twentieth Century Business Cycles in Canada." *Canadian Journal of Economics and Political Science.* August, 1965, XXXII.

HAY, K. A. J. "Money and Business Cycles in Post-Confederation Canada." *Journal of Political Economy,* June 1967, LXXV.

MACESICH, GEORGE. "The Quantity Theory and the Income Expenditure Theory in an Open Economy: Canada, 1926-1958." Comment by Clarence L. Barber and Reply by George Macesich. *Canadian Journal of Economics and Political Science,* August, 1964, XXX and August 1966, XXXII.

ROSENBLUTH, G. 1) "Changes in Canadian Sensitivity to United States Business Fluctuations"; 2) "Changing Structural Factors in Canada's Cyclical Sensitivity, 1903-54." Both in *Canadian Journal of Economics and Political Science.* Nov. 1957, XXIII and Feb. 1958, XXIV.

THOMPSON, R. W. *International Trade and Domestic Prosperity: Canada 1926-38.* University of Toronto Press, 1970.

URQUHART, M. C. and BUCKLEY, K. A. H. (eds.). *Historical Statistics of Canada.* Toronto: Macmillan Company of Canada Ltd., 1965.

WHITE, DEREK A. *Business Cycles in Canada.* Economic Council of Canada, Staff Study No. 17, Ottawa, 1967.

Index